THE PAPERCLIP
CONSPIRACY

Also by Tom Bower

Pledge Betrayed
Klaus Barbie

TOM BOWER
THE PAPERCLIP CONSPIRACY

The Hunt for the Nazi Scientists

LITTLE, BROWN AND COMPANY

Boston   Toronto

FIRST U.S. EDITION

This book was published in slightly different form
in Great Britain in 1987 by Michael Joseph Limited,
under the title *The Paperclip Conspiracy*.

Library of Congress Cataloging-in-Publication Data

Bower, Tom.
  The paperclip conspiracy.

  Bibliography: p. 294
  Includes index.
  1. World War, 1939–1945 — Technology. 2. Scientists —
Germany — Recruiting — History — 20th century. 3. War
criminals — Germany — History — 20th century. 4. Brain
drain — Germany — History — 20th century. 5. German
Americans — History — 20th century. I. Title.
D810.S2B69   1987   338.9'26   87-3257
ISBN 0-316-10399-3

FG

PRINTED IN THE UNITED STATES OF AMERICA

To Veronica

Contents

Glossary

A.I.1(g)	Air Intelligence, Technical (later A.I.2[g])
BIOS	British Intelligence Objectives Subcommittee
CAFT	Consolidated Advance Field Team
CIA	Central Intelligence Agency
CIOS	Combined Intelligence Objectives Subcommittee
CCS	Combined Chiefs of Staff
COS	Chief(s) of Staff
DGER	Direction Générale des Études et Recherches de Défense Nationale
DNI	Director of Naval Intelligence
FIAT	Field Intelligence Agency, Technical
G2	Army Intelligence
JCS	Joint Chiefs of Staff
JIC	Joint Intelligence (Sub-) Committee (of COS)
JIOA	Joint Intelligence Objectives Agency
MI5	Security Intelligence within Britain
NID	Naval Intelligence Division
OMGUS	Office of Military Government, United States
OSDR	Office of Scientific Development and Research
SA	Sturmabteilung (the Brown Shirts)
SHAEF	Supreme Headquarters Allied Expeditionary Force
SIS	Secret Intelligence Service
Sigint	Signals Intelligence
SS	Schutzstaffel (Himmler's elite guards, in black uniforms)
SWNCC	State-War-Navy Coordinating Committee

Note: Werner von Braun changed the spelling of his first name from Wernher at the end of the war; Helmuth Walter changed his surname from Walther; the later spellings have been used throughout.

Acknowledgments

SUSPECTING AND ALLEGING conspiracies are considerably easier than conclusively proving their existence. Similarly, it is more difficult to establish people's motives when the intense passion during which their decisions were made has not only evaporated but the circumstances have been either forgotten or, worse still, confused over the years. Fortunately in this drama, a sufficient quantity of government documents has been released and enough of the leading participants are still alive to establish precisely what actually occurred during the turbulent postwar years in Europe and America. The sources, however, are disparate, previously unexplored, and often unconnected, making the research intensely difficult. To have finally encompassed the saga within one volume inevitably depended upon the generosity of a great number of people whose patience, knowledge, and experience were very valuable.

First, I must thank Michael Howard, who initially suggested that I investigate the activities of the British army's T-forces in Occupied Germany, whose successful plunder on Britain's behalf, he felt, had been hitherto unrecognized by historians. The life of this book therefore started a long way from where it finally ended. Second, I must thank Charles Burnet, an enthusiastic researcher of aviation history, who generously helped me to understand the astonishing wartime achievements of Germany's aviation industry. Third, Charles Wheeler, the eminent television journalist, who during the war had served in the Royal Navy's elite 30 Assault Unit; over lunch in a desultory BBC canteen, he sparked my interest in the military's hunt for German scientists.

In the laborious trawl through government archives, my greatest help came from Wilbert Mahoney in the National Archives in Washington, but I am also indebted to John Taylor, Cathy Nicastro, Sally Marks, and especially the late John Mendelson. In London I am grateful to the staff of the Public Records Office, the Imperial War Museum, the Science Museum, the Tank Museum, Bovington, and the Wiener Library.

Thereafter, the field widened considerably, and literally hundreds of people helped me. Some will disagree with my conclusions, but I hope that none will deny the validity of my argument. Among those who helped me most and did not insist on anonymity were: Wilhelm Aalmans, I. G. Aylan, John Bagley, John Becklake and John Griffiths from the Science Museum, Robert Benford, Yves Béon, Bernard Blount, John Bray, Sir William Cook, Howard Cummings, Handel Davies, Karl Doetsch, Sir James Easton, Sir St. John Elstub, Rolf Engel, Roy Ewans, Sir Derek Ezra, Nicholas Faith, John Gimbel, T. J. Glanville, Dr. Joe Guilmartin, William Gunston, Richard Hallion, John Hubner, David Irving, R. V. Jones, Lord Kearton, B. C. Kervell (curator of RAE Farnborough Museum), Karl Kirch, Rudiger Kosin, Ulrich Luft, James McHaney, Ralph Maltby, the late Sir Bryan Matthews, Hector Morrison, Admiral A. Mumma, Hans Munzberg, David Nicholson, David Nutting, Frederick Ordway, Julian Perry-Robinson, S. John Peskett, Werner Pinske, Norman Polmar, Eli Rosenbaum, Walter Rozamus, Seymour Rubin, Arthur Rudolph, Henry Schade, Dr. Konrad Schaefer, Mitchell Sharpe, Daniel Simon (Berlin Document Center), Robert Staver, Hermann Treutler, Ian Turner, Harry Verity, H.D.B. Wood.

Special thanks are due to Patricia Eliades for her research; to Michael Kinsella and Bob Royer for their generous hospitality in Washington; and to my editor, Peter Leek, whose meticulous attention to detail and style in the final manuscript was of considerable help. I am also very grateful to my American editors, Perdita Burlingame and Deborah Jacobs, for all their care and help.

Finally, my incalculable gratitude to my faithful and long-suffering family — my parents, Nicholas, Oliver, and above all, to Veronica, whose patience, advice, and friendship were marvelous.

THE PAPERCLIP CONSPIRACY

Introduction

AS THE GIANT SATURN V ROCKET rose majestically through the morning sunlight from Cape Kennedy in July 1969, two groups of German scientists flushed with pride. Apollo 11's epic voyage, carrying astronaut Neil Armstrong toward the moon, was, they felt, their personal triumph. The first group, united and jubilant in the control center, was the famous World War II rocket team from Peenemünde, Germany, led by Werner von Braun. Inspired by the magnetic personality of the Prussian, von Braun's team had designed and produced the world's largest rocket, realizing their childhood dreams and ennobling them as national heroes in their adopted country.

The second group, scattered, relatively anonymous, but almost as important, was the team of aviation doctors. Led by seventy-one-year-old Dr. Hubertus "Strugi" Strughold, an arrogant but clever Westphalian who disliked flying, this pioneering medical team had by 1945 already carried out the basic research behind the delicate equipment that cocooned Armstrong and the other astronauts from the violent acceleration, the lack of oxygen, the unnatural temperature, the unusual noise, and the eerie weightlessness of outer space.

For both groups of elated Germans, the astronauts' confident messages to mission control confirmed the supremacy of German science. During the cataclysmic life span of the Third Reich, von Braun, Strughold, and twenty thousand German scientists had revolutionized the weapons of warfare. Twenty-five years later, the Americans were reaping the benefit of their former enemies' youthful genius. Understandably, however, neither von Braun nor Strughold willingly discussed the circumstances in which the scientific origins of their work had materialized. If pressed, both men would recite their abhorrence of Hitler's regime like automatons. Neither, however, would openly admit that his skills, which had suddenly thrust fame and fortune onto American astronauts, had been honed amid the calculated murder and brutal butchery of Nazi atrocities. Fortunately for both Germans, their involvement with those crimes had been smoothly and conspiratorially expunged after the war by sympathetic American army officers anxious to employ them in the United States.

Their recruitment after the war had followed interrogation by American officers. After selection, the chosen German scientists were identified simply with an ordinary paperclip on their personal file. Like so many other beneficiaries of the "Paperclip" conspiracy, they would eventually become respectable American citizens, their wartime activities notwithstanding, because senior military officers determined that, in the national interest, American immigration laws and a president's directive should be willfully ignored.

The fact that all the four Allies — the Americans, the British, the Russians, and the French — became involved in the frantic and at times ruthless competition for German scientists is particularly surprising when one realizes that the use of the Germans was simply not contemplated until as late as 1945. On the contrary, until the eve of peace, the notion of associating on equal terms with the men who had helped Hitler's regime perfect weapons to kill Allied citizens was totally unthinkable. Why did that sudden reversal coincide with the discovery of concentration camps and the exposure of the worst crimes of the Nazi regime? And how did those who orchestrated the hunt reconcile the fraught moral and practical issues? It remains a significant fact that at the very moment when thousands of determined Allied officers began the hunt for German scientists, only a tiny handful were charged to seek out the war criminals.

The answer to the riddle starts in the prewar years, when European engineering students learned German as a second language so that they could read the important scientific literature published by one of the world's industrial giants and its leading technical innovator. It was no coincidence that many of the scientists developing the American atomic bomb in Los Alamos had Teutonic names. Von Braun's rockets were the symbol of Germanic superiority. The substance was considerably broader — in engineering, chemical processes, and industrial design — but, before 1940, this was not appreciated by either the American or British military.

At the outbreak of war, complacent military chiefs and politicians in Washington and London misunderstood the nature of the conflict into which they had been cast. In Berlin, scientists and engineers were the welcome allies of politicans and military chiefs. But in London and Washington the government, the civil service, and the military chiefs largely ignored or even disdained the purveyors of technical innovation. Allied officers, startled by Hitler's momentous conquests, only gradually stumbled to the realization that their Achilles heel was the technical inferiority of many of their guns, planes, tanks, and submarines. On the eve of Hitler's final defeat, Allied scientists had narrowed the lead and occasionally overtaken their enemy, but in crucial areas Germany's superiority, even in the last year of the war, had actually increased. Acknowledgment of that reality bred a conviction — some would say a legend — of German scientific supremacy that was not far from the truth. Yet the complacent belief in Allied technical superiority, which had gripped so many in London and Washington until 1940, was automatically regenerated by the victory in 1945. Their reasoning was chanted with stunning naiveté; the Allied success had irrevocably proven the Allies' technical superiority: "We won the war, so we clearly possessed better weapons." Throughout the research and writing of this book, that sentiment has been often repeated. Unreasonably, it ignores the final imbalance between the encircling Allied juggernaut and the isolated Third Reich. The proof of German technical prowess is overwhelmingly established in the hundreds of reports written by Allied investigators who did not shy from describing the Germans' "astonishing achievement" and "superb invention." It is also established by the very survival of Germany during four years of total war despite the prediction during the first two years of war by British intelligence that the German economy and German industry faced imminent and total collapse. The blockade on essential minerals, chemicals, and petroleum products, it was argued, would cripple weapons production. But the very opposite happened, because German scientists developed an astonishing range of substitutes that not only humiliatingly neutralized the Allied blockade but heralded the dawn of a new scientific era. One absurd but nevertheless revealing example of German skills was the Allies' covert purchase in Switzerland during the war of large quantities of glass eyes manufactured in Germany for wounded Allied servicemen. German scientists had pioneered so many inventions that many Allied experts would complain that their plunder could do no more than scratch the surface.

Since 1945, the genesis of weapons by all four Allies has been dominated by the inheritance of Germany's wartime inventions. Indeed, the Korean War can be viewed, on the technical level, as a trial of strength between two different teams of Germans: those hired by America and those hired by the Soviet Union. The aerial dogfights between Soviet MiG-15s and American F-86 Sabres — both designed by German engineers — dispelled for many their doubts about the expediency of plundering Germany's scientific expertise.

As the war ended, Allied investigators, plunged into the hectic race to find their German competitors, were in turn shocked, excited, and then bewildered as they began to appreciate their own technical ignorance. For them, a haphazard series of interrogations conducted in the turmoil of a distraught and defeated nation was tantalizing and frustrating. The obvious solution was to transport the German experts to America and Britain, following the example of the French and Russians. The American haul, enthusiastically hailed as an Aladdin's cave, was worth alone, according to some American military estimates, "thousands of millions of dollars." But the moral cost was debatable. Although few would understand the full realities of power inside Hitler's Germany until the tons of captured documents and eyewitness accounts had been painstakingly sifted and analyzed, incriminating evidence that the Paperclip scientists had intimate connections with the leaders of Nazi society and those in charge of the concentration camps was available when they were selected and brought to the United States. The puzzle is why, when their own friends had died to liberate Europe from the Fascist scourge, the investigators deliberately ignored and concealed such crimes in the interests of plunder.

This book is not so much about the predicament of tormented officers and scientists grappling with a moral dilemma as about outright opportunism and Machiavellian deception and intrigue. Nevertheless, the question of whether the decisions taken were grossly immoral or courageously perceptive lies at the very heart of this previously unexplored conundrum. It is a saga of heroes becoming antiheroes and of outraged moralists suffering vilification. At the center stand the American and British military establishments, which earned their countries' unqualified gratitude for winning the war but in peacetime were unwilling to forsake their autocratic imperiousness. On the sidelines are politicians, govern-ment officials, and industrialists, all pursuing conflicting interests. Exhausted by war, elated by victory, apprehensive about the fu-ture, officers and government officials were often confused, torn between loyalty to their principles and determination to achieve their goals. Whatever their emotions, an infallible record of their actions remains in recently released government files. Recon-structing this final chapter of World War II has not been easy, but sufficient evidence exists to unravel the skein of events and the taut web of personal dramas and feuds that lies behind them, to judge the deeds and motives of the participants and apportion some measure of praise or blame. The unanswered question is still whether a hardheaded assessment of military advantage should have out-weighed the claims of just retribution. Forty years after the war, some of the protagonists will condemn a later generation for passing judgment on decisions taken in the unimaginable circum-stances of wartime and postwar Europe. To such critics, one can only reply that the record speaks for itself.

Seven years ago, I wrote *Pledge Betrayed*, a book that explored why the Allies not only failed to capture and punish many of the Nazi war criminals but restored seriously incriminated Nazis to influential positions of power in postwar Germany. This book, which is in many ways a sequel, investigates the dilemma that ambitious but inexperienced young officers confronted: Should the very ideals for which the war had been fought be betrayed for the temptation of future prizes?

Establishing exactly why the solemn wartime pledges of Roo-sevelt and Churchill to bring the war criminals to justice remained largely unfulfilled, whereas the recruitment of scientists — many of whom had readily embraced Nazism — was so successful poses another fascinating enigma. Why did the western Allies, having devoted considerable effort to recovering Germany's colossal war-time plunder, stashed away in banks and other hiding places all over Europe, abandon their quest, consoling themselves that the German scientists were, as Eisenhower claimed, "the only repa-rations we are likely to get"?

Legally, none of the four Allies had any difficulty in justifying their policy. While occupying most of continental Europe, German banks, industries, and individuals had without scruple plundered each nation of its mineral, economic, and artistic wealth — in total, worth tens of billions of dollars. The Allies were originally determined to recover some of that booty or its equivalent. Although their first plans were considered in London in 1940, five years later after millions of lives had been sacrificed and billions of dollars spent to destroy Hitler's regime, neither Churchill nor Roosevelt had approved the master plan known as the "Safehaven Program." All that existed were a few officials who, in true Sherlock Holmes fashion, planned to recover the German loot. Their problems were immense, and they were actively hindered by the military.

Even the most cynical and war-hardened GI or British infantry-man who had fought from the Normandy beaches to the death camps in Belsen and Dachau would not have believed that the old cliché "To the victor belong the spoils" would so abruptly and so flagrantly be turned on its head. Yet during the first five postwar years, America and Britain pumped more than $4 billion in aid into their defeated adversary and squeezed out minimal amounts in return. Eisenhower's historic acceptance of Germany's unconditional surrender was still a very recent memory when sages bitterly quipped that Germany might have lost the war but had obviously won the peace. Only one form of compensation remained — Eisenhower's contaminated "intellectual reparations." Safehaven failed and Paperclip succeeded because a handful of military officers willed it to be so and no one wielded the political strength to oppose them.

1

Imperial Delusion

NOTHING ILLUSTRATES the blinkered conservatism of the American and British military Chiefs of Staff between the two world wars more poignantly than their constricted vision of the deployment of tanks in future battle and their contemptuous lack of interest in the details of tank design. For officers and gentlemen oblivious of the technical revolution about to change the face of warfare, the thickness and metallurgical composition of armor, the reliability of gearboxes, the design of shells, and the competence of the industrial work force were all profoundly alien. Unlike government departments in Germany, the British War Office disdained any relationship with industry. Weapons research since 1918 had been exclusively conducted by Britain's Ordnance Board. In a noncommittal manner they had investigated and reported on the performance of German weapons used during the previous war, but their comments had been filed, unheeded by the army chiefs. Concomitantly, the chiefs never held an inquiry into the performance and failures of British weapons during that war. It was one of the misfortunes of the next generation that many of the weapons developments initiated during World War I had to be reinvented in World War II.

Tanks were first used by the British and French in the battles of the Somme and Cambrai during World War I and, despite limited numbers, spread terror among the entrenched German infantry. Yet after the war, in both Britain and America, tanks were treated as an interesting experiment rather than as harbingers of a revolution in military tactics. In both Washington and London, tanks remained the responsibility of cavalry generals loath even to contemplate the idea that their traditional skills had been relegated to mere historic interest. As late as 1936 the British cavalry training manual unambiguously explained the Army Council's stubborn position. Amusingly dividing the cavalry into "mechanised" and "horsed" sections, the manual explained: "Mounted drill (in armoured cars) is based on the same principles as that of Cavalry. The principles of training in field operations given in Cavalry training (horsed) are, in general, applicable to Armoured Car Regiments."

One year after the manual's publication, in August 1937, Hitler invited Sir Cyril Deverell, the chief of the Imperial General Staff, together with a large party of senior British military staff, to watch combined Luftwaffe and Wehrmacht exercises in Thuringen involving 150,000 highly disciplined troops and parachutists, more than 1,000 tanks and antitank vehicles, and seemingly endless waves of dive-bombers. They witnessed the massive maneuvers in the company of Hitler and Mussolini, but the display did not have the effect the dictators intended. Reflecting the corseted conservatism that permeated British military strategy, on his return Deverell proudly reported: "They look upon us as the authority on the use of tanks." It was an absurd statement, especially since Deverell had expressly forbidden Britain's leading tank expert, Percy Hobart, to teach student officers any tactics of tank warfare that offended against the sacrosanct cavalry and infantry manuals.[1] Any doubts Deverell might have felt were promptly laid to rest by reassurances that Hobart's new Matilda tank would match all the Germans' anticipated developments, although a succession of reports from British military attachés in Berlin had already stated the contrary.[2] Deverell was unshakably convinced that, since Britain had been victorious in 1918, there was nothing to be learned from her defeated adversaries; inbred imperial attitudes completely anesthetized him to the dramatic changes in military tactics that the German Chiefs of Staff were planning and implementing.

On Adolf Hitler's first anniversary as chancellor of the Third Reich, in January 1934, Colonel Andrew Thorne, the British military attaché in Berlin, graphically described in the annual review of developments in Germany that he sent the War Office in London the theatrical unveiling of fifteen years of secret planning.[3] Thorne had seized every opportunity to corner senior German officers and witness their new tactics and had perceptively recognized clues about "the size of mobile forces" and the "emphasis on mechanical traction." Although Thorne was still unable to put a name to it, he had identified the German General Staff's seismic master plan for future war and victory — the Blitzkrieg. In their bid to revolutionize warfare, the German military had conspired with scientists, engineers, and industrialists to produce weapons that would render all previous tactics obsolete.

Deverell and his staff at the War Office were puzzled by Thorne's report. Their thinking was still dominated by the memories of the trenches and mud of the Somme. After all, the lance had been withdrawn as a standard British battlefield weapon within living memory, and for them the horse was still the archetypal "fast moving vehicle" on the battlefield. The next war, they convinced themselves, would be fought in the colonies, not in Europe. Consequently, on the insistence of the commander in chief, India, the War Office had just postponed replacing the shrapnel shell with the more effective high-explosive shell, whose advantages no one was sufficiently qualified to explain.[4] Unprompted by a succession of masters of Ordnance, the British General Staff simply did not understand that diligent tinkering with chemicals could produce more effective shells.

The same critical lack of interest greeted Thorne's second, more substantial report, which asserted that "evidence of the Reichwehr [moving] toward mechanisation is strong" and that the German army would be battle-ready in 1939.[5] Ominously, while Foreign Office officials were clearly impressed by Thorne's wealth of information and authoritative analysis, his colleagues at the War Office remained skeptical.

Colonel Elliot Hotblack, Thorne's successor, suffered a similar shock when, soon after his arrival in Berlin in 1936, he realized how crucially future military successes would depend upon scientific innovation. "The British army," he wrote,

> still compares favourably with the German in training and tactical ideas, but would appear to be at a very great disadvantage in the matter of equipment since the German army . . . is apparently backed by an organisation which is prepared to make progressive use of any new developments. . . . An important factor in these rapid improvements is that comprehensively large quantities of experimental equipment are produced and, after experience has been gained, are rapidly replaced by improved material.[6]

Despite the emerging prospect of a new war in Europe, senior American and British officers still displayed a curious lack of interest in Germany's preparations for Blitzkrieg tactics. For the most part, military intelligence in both London and Washington was still rigidly restricted to reports on troop movements and strategic intentions, and nobody had seriously considered the possibility of using the intelligence agencies to gather technical details of the weaponry that a potential enemy would employ. As Captain Kenneth Strong of MI3 (a War Office intelligence section) discovered after arriving in Berlin in 1937 as a British military attaché, the architects of the new Panzer divisions had found the ideal compromise between weight, engine size, armor, and gun. Strong, who had just embarked upon a prestigious career in military intelligence, was startled by Germany's combined strategic battle plan of a rapid tank advance that depended upon the Luftwaffe's swift destruction of the enemy air force and its communication network. But to his chagrin, the War Office ignored his reports of superior German performance over British weapons.[7] Unlike his British and American counterparts, General Heinz Guderian, the German tank expert, had recognized that designing a tank was a complicated juggling act aimed at resolving glaring contradictions of speed, weight of armor, and size of gun. The ideal tank would be a fast-moving and well-protected vehicle bearing a powerful barrel; it also needed to be easily adapted to incorporate improvements and to match any technical advantages built into the enemy's tanks. But the design and construction of that ideal tank demanded a quality of intellectual agility that Strong knew was lacking among the traditionalists in London.

Deverell's dismissal as chief of the Imperial General Staff later that year removed a major obstacle, but the army still needed time to squeeze out of its technical and tactical straitjacket. After Strong's return to Britain he discovered that even as late as 1941 his dispatches describing German plans to improve tank armor were still dismissed as absurd by the War Office's technical branch. The same branch also ignored his eyewitness reports from Wehrmacht maneuvers that the Germans were using the 88-millimeter anti-aircraft gun as an unbeatable antitank weapon and had developed a single weapon, the MG 34, which could be used both as a heavy and light machine gun. Strong's only consolation was that the postwar attitude of the military establishment in Washington was, if anything, even more complacent and more conservative than that of the War Office.

In January 1919 Brigadier General William Westervelt led seven officers to Europe to report on the future artillery needs of the U.S. Army. His comprehensive report, the product of five months' exhaustive research, described the ideal needs of a future mechanized army. Yet the report was shelved. Although American technicians during World War I had successfully developed improved ammunition, delayed fuses, and bombs, twenty years later the U.S. General Staff seemed determined to equip its army with antiquated antitank guns and howitzers. The standard 75-millimeter howitzer was designed to be packed on a mule; the 37-millimeter antitank gun was reported in 1935 by the U.S. military attaché in Berlin to be already outclassed by equivalent German and Russian guns; and the heavy 240-millimeter howitzer was totally unsuitable for any prospective battle. As in Britain, the legacy of World War I was stifling.

General John Pershing, the hero of World War I, had insisted on his triumphant return from Europe that tanks should remain an infantry responsibility, deliberately forestalling the development of a separate tank strategy. To enshrine his decision, the National Defense Act passed in 1920 explicitly prohibited the re-creation of an independent Tank Corps. With the prospect of war so remote, Pershing's diktat remained uncontradicted among the traditionalist, technically uneducated U.S. Chiefs of Staff. Two years later, in granting very limited funds for tank development, the adjutant general laid down the basis for the grant: "The primary mission of the tank is to facilitate the uninterrupted advance of the rifleman in the attack."[8] Army appropriations for tank development averaged about sixty thousand dollars a year, just sufficient for one experimental model, and progress was barely at a snail's pace. Nine years later, when General Douglas MacArthur demanded a highly mechanized army, the tactical role of tanks in American strategy was unchanged. Confused by the lack of dialogue between designers and users, and influenced by the British, the American Ordnance Board had developed only vulnerable light tanks and had rejected outright the T-3 model, a pathfinder designed by America's tank pioneer, J. Walter Christie. An idiosyncratic and distrusted entrepreneur, Christie had not succumbed to the fatal error of designing the tank and its gun in isolation from one another. Unlike U.S. Ordnance, the Russians were interested and bought Christie's ideas, developing them to build the hugely successful T-34 tank. America's misfortune was compounded by the low caliber of their military attachés in Berlin.

Lieutenant Colonel Jacob Wuest, the attaché in 1933, possessed a markedly uninquiring personality, which apparently did not displease his superiors in Washington. Wuest's reports contained no original material but instead criticized articles by French and Belgian experts warning about Germany's rearmament. Hitler's violations of the Versailles Treaty's limitations on weapons were, according to Wuest, "not particularly alarming . . . so that she is not an immediate menace to her neighbors."[9] Over the next months, despite the general militarization enveloping the country, Wuest sent only superficial technical details to Washington after perfunctory and unproductive visits to showcase munitions factories.

Wuest's replacement, Major Truman Smith, continued his predecessor's ritual. For weeks during the spring of 1936, Smith hesitated over whether to visit a major German tank factory, preferring at the last moment to withdraw because of fear that the Germans would insist on a reciprocal visit. Smith's self-denial meant his reports were sparse and contradictory. In contrast, Captain René Studler, the U.S. military attaché in London, traveled throughout Europe, sending more than three hundred reports graphically describing the advanced technology of Germany's armaments industry. But Studler received little positive reaction from Washington, especially after Smith bitterly attacked the interloper. In 1937 Studler reported that Krupp, a leading German arms manufacturer, was developing a 47-millimeter or even 50-millimeter antitank gun to replace the standard 37-millimeter gun, but a contradictory endorsement written by Smith denying the possibility of a heavier gun undermined Studler's credibility. The result was summarized by the official history: "Real or seeming lack of interest in the Ordnance office in Washington tended to discourage the search for additional data . . . the testimony to a deep-seated complacency, inimical to ideas not originating within the upper echelons of the Ordnance Department, cannot be brushed aside."[10] As a result, throughout the war American troops were outgunned. "The Ordnance Department was by no means alone in its too frequent do-nothing attitude," admits the official history. "Every branch and service of the US Army, including the Air Corps, displayed it."[11]

In Britain the Royal Navy, basking in the memory of its past glories, shared the army's disdain for technical intelligence and its unwillingness to reassess tactics in the light of new developments, especially submarine warfare and the vulnerability of ships to air attack. The Admiralty was convinced that the Royal Navy had retained the advantages that it possessed during World War I. A series of seminars held by the Institution of Naval Architects in March 1921 had discussed a very limited postwar Admiralty investigation of German naval design and concluded that it was inferior to Britain's. "The proof of the pudding," Vice Admiral Sir Frederick Tudor told his colleagues, "is in the eating . . . their ships are mostly at the bottom of the sea; ours will, at any rate for one or two more years, continue to guard the safety of this nation." At the same meeting, the threat of submarine warfare was roundly dismissed by the Admiralty's investigator Sir Eustace d'Eyncourt, because three ships that had been torpedoed "got home safely to port."[12]

Thirteen years later little had changed. Part of the blame rested on the dismantling of the Admiralty's intelligence organization after 1918. The skeleton that remained, in the shape of the post of director of Naval Intelligence, was all but crushed by Foreign Office insistence that all future intelligence be channeled through Britain's overseas intelligence agency, the SIS, despite its notorious unreliability. This generated jealousy and unbridgeable interservice suspicion. The legendary power and influence enjoyed in Room 40 under Sir Reginald "Blinker" Hall disappeared, and the DNI was deliberately denied any prominence or resources by other sections of the naval staff. Naval Intelligence amounted to little more than haphazard monitoring of the movements of foreign navies on the basis of port sightings around the world. After 1935 its activities modestly expanded, following the appointment of Vice Admiral James Troup as the director of Naval Intelligence. Although Troup was condemned as "an absolute child about intelligence,"[13] he at least reestablished the Operational Intelligence Center, a framework for analyzing every source of naval intelligence. Section NID 7, however, which was responsible for technical intelligence, remained merely symbolic.

NID 7's director, Captain John Charley, notoriously distinguished himself by scornfully dismissing intelligence reports from British naval attachés in Germany that Admiral Erich Raeder's new fleet would far exceed the limitations set out in the Treaty of Versailles and that the *Bismarck* was substantially bigger than

officially conceded by the Germans. Charley breezily surmised that
Admiral Raeder would not deliberately lie. At the end of 1939
Charley would also ignore a British agent's report from Uruguay
that the *Admiral Graf Spee*'s guns were guided by radar, then a new
development. Charley filed and forgot the report,[14] but his status
in the Admiralty was in any case so low that he had no authority
to inquire within his own service whether any account was being
taken of German inventions.[15]

Hence Charley was not to blame when the Admiralty ignored
attachés' reports that Admiral Raeder's strategic intention in a
future war was to deploy a large fleet of submarines to enforce a
blockade against any potential enemy. Despite the chief of Naval
Staff's own warning that it would be "a dangerous illusion for us
to infer that we have a reliable measure of what she [Germany]
can do," the Admiralty Board comforted itself with the expectation
that any submarine menace would be swept aside by Asdic — a
new submarine-detecting device based on a quartz crystal picking
up underwater vibrations. "Progress in anti-submarine measures,"
reported the Naval Intelligence Division in 1936, "may have rendered submarine warfare less effective." Deluded about its technical superiority, the Admiralty assumed that any naval war would
be fought on the surface rather than beneath the waves, thus preventing any reassessment of its tactics for hunting down U-boats.
Asdic suffered from three major handicaps: It did not reveal the
depth of the submarine (which was vital for a successful depth-
charge detonation); it could not detect a submarine on the surface;
and it required highly trained operators. Eschewing new scientific
tests, the Admiralty relied on its 1914–18 strategy of deploying a
massive task force to comb the sea in the hope of finding its quarry.
Supremely confident, the Admiralty chiefs briefed a minister on
the eve of war to tell the House of Commons that "the submarine
menace has been mastered."[16] Six months later HMS *Courageous*,
a converted heavy cruiser, was ploughing the North Sea, with its
Asdic searching for U-boats, when it was struck by two German
torpedoes. More than five hundred seamen drowned, the first casualties of the Admiralty's conviction that it would be fighting the
same war, of heavy guns on enormous ships firing into the mist,
that Admiral John Jellicoe had won more than twenty years earlier.

Scientific development in the navy during the prewar years was
the responsibility of the Third Sea Lord, Rear Admiral Bruce Fraser.

Fraser both epitomized and was victim of the senior service's disdain for outsiders, especially technicians. Engineering was an unattractive career in a service where ambitious officers sought only to command a ship at sea. Directors of the research establishments changed with damaging regularity, frustrating long-term operational research. Without scientific assistance, Fraser's department ignored intelligence about a host of vital innovations and the intrinsic weaknesses of British designs. The atmosphere at the Admiralty Research Laboratory was pleasant and gentlemanly, but it was built on innumerable fallacies, none more perilous than the belief that "if a ship's gun shot at an aircraft, the aircraft would continue to fly in a straight line." With steadfast self-confidence, the naval planners invariably discussed any German threat on the unspoken but agreed premise that only naval guns could sink naval ships. Admiral Sir Dudley Pound was shocked when an irate air chief quipped that even if a bomb was to fall on a ship, the navy would nevertheless claim that the damage was caused by a mine. Bombing ships had been unquestionably disapproved of since 1925, when the Admiralty stipulated that naval aircraft would never carry bombs weighing more than one hundred pounds. The navy, Pound and his colleagues never ceased to boast, fought with ships, not with aircraft. Consequently, coastal command aircraft were not equipped with bomb sights, and depth charges were not adapted for use from aircraft.[17]

To protect the fleet from air attack, in the late 1920s the Admiralty had commissioned a "tachymetric system," which required naval gunners to aim at aircraft using guesswork rather than accurate scientific measurements. In 1936 Lord Chatfield, the minister responsible for defense coordination, wrote to Churchill that he was confident of the British merchant fleet's invulnerability, "because even one anti-aircraft gun in a merchant ship" would keep the aircraft at such a height that the chance of destruction was "very small."[18] Yet in the same year Admiral Sir John Fisher, the commander in chief of the Mediterranean fleet, complained that the navy had no defense against the new German dive-bombers. To resolve the dispute, a major exercise was held the following year, watched by an impressive collection of senior naval staff. A droning "Queen Bee" target flew a predictable course directly above the awesome guns of the home fleet. To the considerable discomfort of the onlookers, it serenely circled the armada for two and a half hours while the fleet unsuccessfully tried to shoot it down. After the fiasco, Chatfield admitted with characteristic British understatement that "our present system is very imperfect."

"A menace to the service," was how Charles Wright, the director of Scientific Research, described the Admiralty's disastrous anti-aircraft equipment.[19] Both the Americans and, more sinisterly, the Germans were known to have perfected a more reliable system, but the Admiralty had disdainfully rejected an offer of American cooperation two years earlier. In reply to Wright's criticisms, the navy's Ordnance Department vigorously defended its design, not least on the basis that British was always best. Yet the fault was fundamental; the gun designers had not even considered consulting scientists or technicians until their worthless system had been installed throughout the fleet. A full investigation was commissioned by the Committee of Imperial Defense.

The brilliant and mercurial scientist Henry Tizard was co-opted onto the "sub-committee on bombing and anti-aircraft gunfire experiments" in the knowledge that his presence alone would be a safeguard against any attempt at a political cover-up. The committee's report, in January 1939, was devastating: "Two hits on every aircraft carrier and one on every cruiser may be expected for every aircraft hit . . . destroyers are virtually defenceless from air attack. . . . It is difficult for us to avoid the conclusion that the protection of merchant shipping from air attack is at present unsolved."[20] Until then, many believed that the fleet could be partially protected by catapult-launched aircraft, a proposal that had been successfully urged by Admiral Sir Dudley Pound, soon to become Admiral of the Fleet. Yet neither Pound nor any other naval chief had considered that essential to the catapult's success was an effective autogyro, which had not been installed. For the generation of British sailors recruited to the service in the reign of Queen Victoria, the development of sophisticated technology was, quite simply, too puzzling.

Unlike the army and the navy, theoretically the Royal Air Force should not have been strangled by historic complacency. But neither the service chiefs nor the politicians realized that the advance of aviation technology would render Britain's traditional defense, the English Channel, largely ineffectual. The officials at the Air Ministry — condemned by Reggie Fletcher, an SIS section director, as "discards from Army and Navy" — were "gentlemen administrators" with little understanding of aviation technology.[21] Until

1935 favored manufacturers, cosseted by Air Ministry officials, earned huge profits from government contracts but remained stubbornly reluctant to reinvest in research and development. The American attitude was completely different. Asked to prepare a mock-up for Sir Arthur Harris, Lockheed complied without a murmur within twenty-four hours of his request. In Britain, Harris complained, it could not have been produced "in less than months."

Germany's dramatic announcement in 1935 of her intention to build a four-thousand-airplane Luftwaffe propelled those responsible in London to embark on a competition for superior numbers rather than technical superiority. Anxious British service staff and officials, still suffering the legacy of Stanley Baldwin's doom-laden prophecy three years earlier that "the bomber will always get through," began juggling a series of options for maximizing Britain's aircraft production, although, ironically, Baldwin's prediction reassured the RAF that British bombers would "always get through" too.

Alarmed by Hitler's bellicose announcement of conscription in March 1935 and his boast that the Luftwaffe had reached "parity" with the RAF, Neville Chamberlain commissioned Britain's rearmament without either adequate intelligence about the technical performance of the Luftwaffe's aircraft or accurate specifications for Britain's own fighters and bombers. The fragmented British aviation industry had no fewer than sixteen separate design teams producing planes that, with notable exceptions, were underpowered, undergunned, and underranged. Rashly, Chamberlain bowed to his officials' insistence on ordering Battle, Blenheim, and Whitley bombers, although all three types were known to be dangerously obsolescent. Sheer numbers were the only consideration. Meeting on May 10, 1935, the Ministerial Committee on Defense Requirements was presented with two wildly conflicting estimates of the Luftwaffe's potential size. While the Air Ministry suggested that the Germans had trained four thousand pilots, the SIS stated that it was exactly double that number.[22] Between 1934 and 1939 the RAF would produce twelve reports on the German air force, all of them substantially inaccurate.

In the absence of reliable intelligence, the Air Ministry assumed that the Germans, like the British, would need time to consolidate after building their first 1,500 aircraft. When the Germans reached their target in 1936 and unhesitatingly continued to expand, Air Ministry officials in London were perplexed.

Among the first to recognize the cost of Air Ministry attitudes was Air Chief Marshal Sir Edgar Ludlow-Hewitt, who was appointed commander in chief, Bomber Command, in September 1937. A rapid introductory tour of duty convinced him of the frightening absence of any professionalism and technical efficiency among the airmen who would soon be dispatched over Germany. "The present situation is most disquieting," he noted on his return to London.[23] The romantic notion of flying had blinded even the practitioners to the understanding that their success in battle depended upon the best aircraft, the best weapons, and the best instruments. To his horror, Ludlow-Hewitt discovered that the RAF proposed to fly without adequate navigational aids, safety devices, or guns and would attempt to deliver notoriously unreliable bombs using totally inaccurate bombsights. Even after he had spotlighted the "confusion and inefficiency" among his ranks, Ludlow-Hewitt remained a lone voice. According to the official history, "When war came in 1939 Bomber Command was not trained or equipped either to penetrate into enemy territory by day or to find its target areas, let alone its targets, by night."[24] In theory, the RAF should have been different from the other services. Every flight, even if not in combat, provided operational experience, and technically minded pilots should have been able to explain deficiencies and recommend improvements. Some did, but only a few men had the breadth of vision to recognize the Luftwaffe's true strength.

Roy Fedden, one of Britain's most brilliant aircraft engineers, was an intemperate maverick who, sadly, would become intensely disliked. After a visit to his substantial Bristol aircraft factory in 1936 by General Erhard Milch, the newly appointed state secretary at Hermann Goering's Air Ministry, and Ernst Udet, head of procurement for the Luftwaffe, Fedden was invited to visit Germany's new aircraft factories. The purpose of this reciprocity, an unusual breach of Germany's obsessive security, was to impress the British with the strength of German rearmament. Fedden, the Germans felt, would be an ideal witness — no one in London would doubt the report of such an undisputed authority. But, unknown to the German visitors, British Air Ministry officials were suspicious of Fedden and in 1934 had contemptuously rejected his proposals for fuel-injection engines.

At Milch's behest, Fedden was taken on a two-week tour of German aircraft factories, which convinced him that German technology and mass production techniques were beyond the imagination of anyone in Britain. His 110-page eyewitness account concluded that Britain would be in peril unless "fearless and drastic action" was taken to radically restructure her aircraft industry, since Germany's proposed aircraft production was 50 percent higher than Britain's.

The postulation of foreign superiority automatically prejudiced Sir Thomas Inskip, the new minister for Coordination of Defense, against Fedden's warnings. Convinced that Fedden was an alarmist and had been duped by the Germans, Inskip dismissed most of his proposals for restructuring Britain's aircraft industry as "too drastic" and politically unacceptable. *Inter alia*, Inskip emphatically rejected his recommendation that a controller of aircraft production (the post given to Lord Beaverbrook in 1940) should be appointed.[25] The minister's skepticism was not totally misplaced, since it was Fedden's "professional" projection of German aircraft production that induced the air chiefs to spectacularly overestimate the Luftwaffe's strength at the outbreak of war.[26]

However, since there was no British agency seeking technical intelligence, Fedden's correct observations regarding the superiority of the Luftwaffe's guns were ignored, and his silence about the impressive performance of the German planes was not noticed. Totally unable to appreciate the role of technical intelligence, the British military staff and the RAF did not even attempt to predict German tactical intentions by analyzing the enemy's weaponry. Fedden suggested that British aircraft should, like German aircraft, be armed with 20-millimeter Oerlikon or Hispano cannons — but Inskip rejected all his proposals. Nevertheless, at the very moment when Fedden's warnings were being dismissed, Sir Warren Fisher, the retiring Treasury chief, complained that "for some years we have had from the Air Ministry soothing-syrup and incompetence in equal measure";[27] and Lord Vansittart, who as under secretary for Foreign Affairs had consistently warned against the Nazi threat, vehemently protested at the "inferior intellects of service specialists." Yet neither could pinpoint precisely what information was needed.

Four years later, in February 1940, as the official history records, the shock of exposure to German aircraft dented the RAF's conviction of British technical superiority.[28] Today it seems incredible that the Spitfire, the Hurricane, and the Mosquito, Britain's three most successful war planes, were built as private or semiprivate ventures without Air Ministry support. Yet the Spitfire's success in the Battle of Britain concealed that even it was underarmed and underpowered — deficiencies that were not immediately apparent to technically unqualified "outsiders" — and improvements and improvisation invariably followed shattering defeats. It was only after the evacuation from Dunkirk that the RAF at last understood that fighters could be equipped with bombs; only toward the end of the Battle of Britain were Spitfires equipped with 20-millimeter guns; only after Rommel's rapid advances across the North African desert were RAF planes equipped with cannons; and only in 1941 were the more powerful Merlin engines installed. For seven years, from 1930 to 1937, Air Ministry officials doubted the wisdom of developing Frank Whittle's jet engine and withheld vital funds, while in Germany, Dr. Hans von Ohain received huge financial support from the aircraft manufacturer Heinkel and won the race to fly the world's first jet aircraft.[29] In retrospect, it can be seen that the RAF's very survival at the outset of the war was largely due to a memorandum addressed to H. E. Wimperis, director of scientific research at the Air Ministry, in June 1934, warning that "unless science evolved some new method of aiding our defence, we were likely to lose the next war if it started within ten years."[30]

The memorandum was written by Wimperis's personal assistant A. P. Rowe, who, following disastrous bombing trials over London in 1934, had called for the files on past air defense proposals. Fifty-three files landed on Rowe's desk, none of which promised any hint of protecting Britain effectively. With Wimperis's agreement, Rowe organized the Committee for the Scientific Survey of Air Defense, with Henry Tizard, who alone combined service experience with scientific expertise, as chairman. Tizard was without doubt a fortuitous choice, and he correctly sensed the precariousness of his appointment. The son of a naval captain, Tizard had been a lecturer at Oxford. During World War I he was rejected by the Royal Navy because of poor eyesight and joined the Royal Flying Corps, eventually becoming director of experimental flying at the Air Ministry. After the war ended, he joined the Department of Scientific and Industrial Research and then became rector of Imperial College. At the committee's first meeting, Tizard and the others discussed two scientific possibilities: the existence and wartime potential of "death rays," and Robert Watson-Watt's pioneering experiments with radar. As a result, they decided to commission further research, explicitly recognizing for the first time that "scientifically-trained research workers had a vital part to play not only in the weapons and gadgets of war, but also in the actual study of operations."[31]

Fears of unimpeded bombardment of London had simultaneously prompted a second initiative to the prime minister by another scientist, Frederick Lindemann, supported by his old friend Winston Churchill. While Tizard was politically unambitious and anxious to serve both science and his country unobtrusively, Lindemann was dogmatic, politically motivated, ambitious, and, above all, justifiably frustrated by the smug serenity that reigned among the military deities. In 1935, the roots were already established for the monumental clash between these two scientists that would continue throughout the war. Churchill insisted that Lindemann be appointed to Tizard's committee, since both Churchill and Lindemann were convinced that the group was defeatist and could become enmeshed within Whitehall's notorious machinations. From the very outset Lindemann needled Tizard, and eventually the conflict of personalities and political interests over a range of harebrained schemes — especially over Lindemann's proposed development and deployment of aerial mines — became so intense that the committee was acrimoniously dissolved at the end of July 1936.

A few weeks later the committee was reconstituted without Lindemann, and at Tizard's suggestion, Watson-Watt's infant radar apparatus was moved from the laboratories at Bawdsey to the RAF airfield at Biggin Hill. In total secrecy a small team of pilots and scientists plotted the interception of simulated bombing raids, using the primitive invention, and by the end of 1937 a defensive radar system was practically operational.

In 1930 Group Captain Frederick Winterbotham, a World War I scout pilot, had been appointed as the first chief of Air Intelligence in the SIS. During the prewar years Winterbotham's work had been unremarkable. Indeed, the SIS had made little progress in establishing an intelligence network for the air force since Chamberlain's announcement of rearmament in May 1935, when he urged the intelligence agencies to discover Germany's real intentions. Days later the Air Ministry submitted a two-line report stating that the Dornier work force had been moved from Altenrhein, Switzerland, to Friedrichshafen, Germany, to produce bombers. No technical details were provided, and none were requested. Besides Fedden's 1936 visit to Germany there were, before the outbreak of war, a few sporadic forays by private individuals to observe particular factories and the size of the labor force — but they discovered precious little, provoking the RAF's condemnation of SIS intelligence in July 1939 as "normally 80% inaccurate."

In early 1939 Watson-Watt, who by then had established a primitive but operating radar network along the south coast facing Europe, asked Winterbotham for information about German radar and aircraft developments, especially any German countermeasures that could neutralize the British invention. When he received Watson-Watt's request, Winterbotham, to his credit, realized that in order to assess whether the Germans possessed a credible radar network, a special intelligence operation was required, including an officer with scientific qualifications. Simultaneously, Tizard recognized that the Air Ministry needed a scientific officer to liaise with the Air Intelligence Branch "as a preliminary measure towards improving co-operation between scientists and the intelligence organisation." Their common candidate was R. V. Jones, a physics scholar, who would serve as Winterbotham's assistant and Britain's first scientific intelligence officer attached to the Air Ministry but with access to the intelligence of all three services. Such was the military's prejudice against scientists that Jones's appointment was not confirmed until a few days after the outbreak of war — but by then the opportunity to discover whether the Germans were also operating a radar network and the possibility of sabotaging it had passed. In the summer, a secret SIS/RAF covert intelligence team had been quickly assembled by the director of intelligence at the Air Ministry and dispatched to Germany. But when war was declared, the men were summarily recalled without achieving their objective.

Jones's appointment barely hastened the military's embrace of scientists. In 1934 the Committee of Imperial Defense had established a subcommittee to plan the recruitment of skilled labor for government service in the event of war. Believing that scientists and technicians would be needed in some capacity, they asked the three services whether they would cooperate in listing for universities the types of civilians they would require. Echoing the reaction of all three services, Admiral James Somerville replied that he "doubted whether the navy could employ them." The navy, unlike the army, "did not, even in time of war, engage men from outside."

Nothing changed during the last months of peace. Neither the army nor the navy followed the Air Ministry's example, and at the Air Ministry Jones's appointment remained unique. In June 1938 the War Office had appointed H. J. Gough as its scientific adviser, but Gough's brief was strictly limited to considering possible research programs, and he was expressly forbidden to investigate weapons use or development. Similarly, when the Admiralty organized a very limited call-up of scientists, they were used for research, not for intelligence work. And neither service was prepared to consider using scientists as executives or policy advisers.[32]

Early in July 1939, fearful that in the event of war the potential of science would be neglected, Sir William Bragg, president of the Royal Society, sent a memorandum to Lord Chatfield, head of defense coordination, voicing his concern that "secrecy, departmentalisation or merely lack of contact . . . [would leave service personnel] unaware of advances made in other departments or by scientific people in the world at large." Bragg suggested the appointment of a small nonexecutive liaison committee of scientists to act as a channel for information and advice. Bragg's proposal was rejected on the grounds that the services felt adequately informed about the possible contribution of science to any war effort. Disturbed and disappointed, five days before the outbreak of war Bragg wrote again to Chatfield. He pointed out that the services would need the help of civilian scientists, citing the recent development of radar as a civilian invention only fortuitously taken up by the RAF, and urged the "rapid application of scientific methods to practical problems arising in the course of war." For the second time Bragg was spurned by Chatfield, who claimed that "a wealth of scientific knowledge and experience is already at the disposal of the government" and that the proposed committee would be in "danger of overlapping with existing machinery." Chatfield was referring to the prime minister's recent agreement to the creation of a central register of seven thousand British scientists, listing their specialties. Ironically, the register had been set up as a result of an earlier letter from Bragg describing the scientists' "great anxiety to put their special knowledge and training at the service of the government in case of an emergency," since "under modern conditions, effectiveness depends to an extraordinary degree upon the skilful use of instruments which must be understood and kept in order, and upon the ordered assemblage and correct interpretation of observations."

Despite all Bragg's efforts, in September 1939 the army and navy still feared compromising their independence by going beyond the mere compilation of a list.

2

Harsh Lessons

ON NOVEMBER 21, 1939, Archie Boyle, director of intelligence at the Air Ministry, wrote to Major General Beaumont Nesbitt, his counterpart at the War Office: "It has been evident to me for some time that our arrangements for the study of scientific intelligence are inadequate." Investigations into the various reports about Germany's "secret weapon," he wrote, particularly demonstrated the difficulties. Boyle wanted support for Henry Tizard's proposal for a scientific intelligence agency serving all three services. Nesbitt was sympathetic, as were officials in the War Cabinet. "This is another example of the malaise which prevails in scientific matters in the service departments," wrote one of the prime minister's staff. "This is only one of the smaller and less important rooms in the very large scientific house which requires to be put in order. . . . [There] is, of course, no reason why this little room should not be tidied."[1] Formal approval was delegated to the directors of scientific research, who were due to meet on January 31, 1940.

Tizard was, however, convinced that interservice rivalries and dislikes would sabotage his proposal, and he turned to R. V. Jones for support. Since his appointment as scientific officer to the Air Ministry, Jones had been catapulted into the very heart of the British intelligence machine and had just completed two major investigations that embarrassingly exposed the military's ignorance about science. His first investigation followed a speech by Hitler at Danzig on September 19, 1939. According to the Foreign Office translation submitted to the prime minister, the Führer warned the British that Germany possessed a "secret weapon" against which there was no defense. In the hectic, early days of war, the Chamberlain government was plunged into panic. The threat of "death rays," long before dismissed by Tizard and Frederick Lindemann as a fantasy, now seemed to be confirmed. Chamberlain immediately demanded an explanation from his intelligence services, and unable to produce a satisfactory answer, they agreed that a scientifically trained intelligence officer should be granted carte blanche to read through files from SIS and Bletchley Park (the center for intercepts of German ciphers) to discover whether there were any clues as to the nature of Hitler's secret weapon. Although his appointment was still unofficial, Jones was the only qualified officer in the military's service. After a swift trawl, he confirmed that the Secret Intelligence Service was anxious to justify its earlier warnings that the Germans possessed "death ray machines" and discovered even more. SIS agents from London had in 1936 provided substantial finance for a Dutch inventor to develop a death ray machine for the British. No British scientists had been consulted. Only after the inventor repeatedly delayed the proving trials "for technical reasons" did British intelligence abandon the costly venture. As consolation, the SIS officer had reported that the machine was useful as a fruit preserver. This amusing episode highlighted the SIS's amateurish and unscientific approach, a fault confirmed when Jones, at the end of his search, returned to Hitler's original speech and unscientifically solved the problem. The SIS and the Foreign Office had misunderstood the context in which Hitler had used the word *Waffe* — weapon. The Führer had meant the Luftwaffe.

Soon after the Danzig crisis had passed, the SIS received from an unknown source in Norway a list of German scientific developments. The "Oslo report" had been mysteriously delivered through the British naval attaché's letter box after a prearranged signal transmitted during a BBC broadcast. Besides the seven pages of typewritten text, the package also included a glass tube containing a prototype of a proximity fuse for anti-aircraft shells. The anonymous informant warned the British that the Germans were also developing remote-controlled rocket-driven gliders at Peenemünde, remote-controlled rockets at Rechlin, an advanced radar system, and two new types of torpedo, one controlled by radio and the other with a magnetic fuse. The SIS was skeptical about the Oslo report, dismissing it as a plant. Their reasoning, to Jones's surprise, was purely negative: "If we can't produce it, then the Germans cannot either." Events later proved the report's accuracy.

The evidence of the military's corrosive prejudice against scientists and the air force's future dependence on technology was overwhelming. Jones, Tizard, and Boyle were convinced of the need for a scientific intelligence service. When the three service directors met in January 1940, Boyle's proposal was immediately opposed by the Admiralty's pedantic deputy director of scientific research, J. Buckingham. Fearing encroachment on the navy's operations, Buckingham loftily insisted that the proposed intelligence agency would duplicate existing work, although Captain Charley in NID 7 was the only scientific research officer working in the naval field. But Boyle's proposal was not killed outright. Instead, Tizard was asked to submit more detailed proposals. Swiftly, he suggested a simple unit of three men from each of the service research departments linked to four scientists attached to the SIS — a total of thirteen scientists. Even before it was discussed by the triumvirate, it was condemned as "clumsy" by officials in the Cabinet Office, who nevertheless admitted "ignorance"[2] about the whole problem. Tainted by that stigma and the Admiralty's continuing veto, the proposal was finally crushed by an SIS objection on the grounds that it was expensive and that it unnecessarily complicated its own operations in Occupied Europe — an eccentric excuse, since the SIS's agent network had been completely destroyed within weeks of the outbreak of war and was to remain valueless as an intelligence source for months to come.

Depressed, on February 29 Tizard sent Boyle a final *cri de coeur:* "Scientific co-ordination is not getting better; it is getting worse. It is almost inevitable that it should. The co-ordinating scientific committees of the CID [Committee of Imperial Defence] have ceased to exist. Scientific establishments and personnel are scattered and personal contacts are more difficult . . . I am surprised indeed that it is thought that nothing useful can be done."[3] But even in that final plea, Tizard unknowingly revealed his own limitations: "We have no reason to be particularly alarmed that the enemy is substantially ahead of us, on the whole, in the technical development of known weapons and equipment. Both sides are however frightened that unknown weapons might be sprung on them." Momentarily, all Tizard hoped to save from the defeat was a polite endorsement for the Air Ministry's continued employment of Jones in combined intelligence, with the possible appointment of an assistant. But even the assistant's appointment was vetoed by Buckingham on the grounds that there was "not enough work to justify the employment of two people."[4] It would take the three services literally years to recognize and then bridge the chasm.

When Captain John Peskett, a former asbestos engineer, reported for duty as the RAF's first technical intelligence officer in September 1939, he was appalled at the dearth of intelligence about the Luftwaffe. "There was not even a complete set of photographs for RAF pilots to recognise their enemy, yet most of the information had been readily available in Spain during the recent civil war. No one had bothered to collect it." During the hectic rebuilding of the RAF during the previous five years, British politicians and the air chiefs had single-mindedly concentrated on the number of German aircraft, not their quality. Consequently, as Peskett soon discovered, RAF pilots were flung into battle with haphazard information about the critical performance of the Luftwaffe's fighters and bombers.

Peskett's own early investigations into the technical advantages and disadvantages of the Luftwaffe's planes were crude and comparatively unrevealing. He had little status and no aviation expertise. Indeed, his only qualifications were fluency in French and German and a large vocabulary of technical phrases learned traveling in Europe trading in asbestos. Others in his group, recalls Peskett, shared his inexperience. They were

> a mixed bag. We had a mining engineer, two garage proprietors, an aeronautical journalist, a patent agent, an Antwerp merchant, a Woolworth manager, the younger brother of an Irish peer, an official from the Bank of England, a Hampshire JP, a steel tycoon. . . . A delightful Evelyn Waugh touch was introduced by the presence of Captain Sumner, a civilian employee of the Air Ministry, who had served in the Royal Flying Corps. His subject was balloons. He knew nothing of superchargers on Jumbo engines or direct fuel injection, but he was useful in steering us through the intricacies of civil service life.[5]

Days after his recruitment, Peskett and his fellow civilian officers were dispatched to inspect the few German aircraft that had crashed in Britain — but, he admits, "We had little idea what to investigate." Based in Harrow, just outside London, the group had been granted official status as Air Intelligence, Technical — or A.I.1(g) — under a regular air force officer, Squadron Leader James Easton, a Cranwell graduate who had spent the previous two years as air armament adviser to the Department of National Defense. Easton had been handed a title but not a blueprint for an intelligence operation. Similarly, Peskett's arrival in March 1940 as the RAF's token enemy crash intelligence officer in France was symbolic rather than part of a calculated strategy: "I dashed around France in the weeks before evacuating back to Britain only confirming our ignorance about German planes."

It is debatable whether, even on the eve of the Battle of Britain, the British air chiefs realized that the struggle for air supremacy would be tilted by whatever technical advantages the plane manufacturers could incorporate. Yet the clash between Spitfires and Messerschmitts would be critically influenced by the most marginal boost in speed and the slightest advantage in maneuver, gunfire, and protection for the pilot. Discovering those details of Luftwaffe planes depended largely upon Easton's forty-man unit, strategically placed around the country so they could swoop on wrecked German aircraft before souvenir hunters removed vital evidence. Under Easton's tutelage, they were expected to scrutinize each plane to establish new inventions and identify new developments of engines, fuel, oil, radio, radar, and bombsights, and the quality and type of ammunition used. Constant improvements and amendments to German planes, especially to the armor plating around the fuel tank, led to a change of ammunition for the Spitfire's guns and modification of the firing sequence. For Easton's small band, charred flesh and a smell similar to that of roast pork became a part of normal working conditions. Luftwaffe officers, dead or alive, invariably carried personal belongings that disclosed the location of their units, while the plane's production plates revealed the rate and sites of German aircraft production. "Occasionally," remembers Easton, "there was a bonus. A complete service manual forgotten by an engineer." Interrogation of surviving Luftwaffe aircrew in POW camps whetted the investigators' appetite, but the RAF's German-speaking interrogators were still too inexperienced and technically handicapped to induce the Germans to explain the latest developments. Easton's team was also hampered by the prisoners' "conviction of Hitler's inevitable victory."

Yet by the end of summer 1940, Easton believed that A.I.1(g) had become a more credible intelligence unit. "It was when they began ringing for more information that I felt we had been recognised by the Air Chiefs as important for the RAF's success." The tally of the unit's discoveries steadily lengthened: throat microphones, inflatable dinghies both for the crew and for the planes (to allow time for the crew to escape), one-inch armor plating around the pilot's seat, the positioning of the fighters' machine guns on the propeller boss to improve the rate and accuracy of fire, three-bladed metal rather than two-bladed wooden airscrews to improve performance, and the impressively superior German bombsights. "Discovering fuel injection in German planes," Easton remembers, "was a major breakthrough. Overnight, it had given the Luftwaffe an important speed advantage over our carburettor-engines which we had to meet. Portal [Sir Charles, chief of the Air Staff] rang me immediately after reading our report and arranged for Rolls-Royce to copy the German invention." But Easton was unaware that Roy Fedden had proposed fuel injection six years earlier; and that although most of his unit's "discoveries" were delivered to experts at Farnborough's Royal Aircraft Establishment, the government-funded center for aircraft research, for analysis, many windfalls such as the optical bombsight could not be adopted because British manufacturers were unable to copy German workmanship. But one discovery was taken up with alacrity. In mid-1940, in a wrecked bomber, one of Easton's investigators found tangible proof that German radar was superior to Britain's — a state of affairs that by the end of the war had been reversed, in a saga that revealed not only the strengths of Allied scientific and intelligence resources but also their paralyzing human weaknesses.

In 1933 Dr. Hans Plendl had begun to develop a spectacular radar system, the "X-Geraet." Using a separate system of inter-secting beams transmitted from continental Europe, Plendl's system could guide a German bomber with astonishing accuracy to the target and calculate the exact moment for the bombs to be released. In London, early rumors and reports of his achievement had been casually dismissed because, like the "death ray" scares, they seemed too farfetched. Pride in prewar development of radar in Britain had encouraged politicians, the military, and even some scientists to believe that the Germans could not have invented anything similar, far less a system that was more advanced. Their prejudice was fostered by Lindemann, who disputed the possibility that shortwave signals could actually bend around the curvature of the earth, while Tizard was equally dubious that, since the British had not developed a device to perfect accurate nighttime bomb-ing, the Germans had mastered the technique. Their sense of superiority was reflected in Churchill's panic after the evacuation from Dunkirk when a prototype British radar set was abandoned in Boulogne and seized by the Germans. Both Tizard and the prime minister would have been shocked by the German investigator's report, which contemptuously dismissed the captured British radar system as a crude copy of an early German design.[6]

For Jones, the SIS's failure to observe German radar development, even when displayed during the bombing of Warsaw, was further proof of its prejudice against scientific intelligence and its conviction of German incompetence.[7] Yet more damning, British intelligence had also failed to spot the glaring evidence of "Knickbein" — a simplified system based on Plendl's idea — despite the prewar erection of three gigantic transmitters, 100 yards wide and 100 feet high, aimed directly across the Channel, one of which was sited, uncamouflaged, on the German-Dutch border.

Nine months after the outbreak of war, Jones delivered an impressive dossier containing his accumulated evidence about the German beam system to Lindemann. Not for the last time, Churchill's enigmatic adviser rejected proof of German scientific achievement. But as Goering's devastating blitz on Britain intensified, personal prejudices began to mellow. Politicians wanted answers and solutions. Jones was summoned, nine days later, on June 21, to the Cabinet room in Downing Street to explain his version of the Luftwaffe's secret weapon to Churchill, Lindemann, Tizard, and the complete hierarchy of the British air force. During those intervening days, Jones had collected an avalanche of new evidence from downed Luftwaffe pilots and from a perilous cross-Channel flight by an unarmed Anson aircraft with radios tuned in to the suspected transmitter. At the start of the meeting, Tizard's argument that the German bombers were not guided by radar beams prevailed — but by the time Jones left the Cabinet room, he had convinced everyone present that the Germans did indeed possess a unique weapon. A few hours later Tizard resigned.

Unemotional about a patron's demise, Jones began to orchestrate his brilliant battle of the beams, a series of countermeasures that neutralized Goering's advantage. However, in the breathtaking struggle of deception and decoding that followed, Jones's experts relied more upon their enviable talent for rapid improvization than on any technical superiority.

On September 7, 1940, when the London docks and the city bore the brunt of the Luftwaffe's first massive bombing raid, British defenses against the German beams were still crudely dependent upon trial and error, jamming, and the transmission of decoy signals. Two months later the inadequacy of British countermeasures was felt by Coventry, the unsuspecting victim of an unopposed fire raid, which confirmed that Britain was relatively defenseless against the Luftwaffe's pinpoint accuracy. Basing his prediction on intercepts and simple mathematical deductions, Jones "guessed" that the Luftwaffe's next target would be Wolverhampton, in the Midlands. On his advice, the city's anti-aircraft defenses were urgently reinforced. Fortunately, his calculations were correct, and in Berlin, on the eve of the bombers' departure, Goering was told that German reconnaissance aircraft had spotted the reinforced defenses. Wrongly believing that the complete X system was compromised, the Reichsmarschall canceled the raid, abandoned the X system, and authorized the introduction of the new Y-beam system. Jones at once entered into a new battle of wits and skillfully directed the transmission of phony, disorienting Y-beam signals from the BBC's Alexandra Palace transmitter, to the utter bewilderment of German pilots. By May 1941 Germany's third beam system had been scientifically neutralized and the blitz defeated. Jones could justifiably claim a major contribution to that military victory. He had also scored a professional and political triumph. Senior scientists had won the right, on their own initiative, to query and influence military strategy. Implicitly, both groups had finally acknowledged at least some German achievements, but their belated recognition of the truth remained grudging.

Ironically, Jones's success reinforced Sir Arthur "Bomber" Harris and Henry Tizard (who was still influential as a consultant, despite his resignation) in their conviction that the beams were not of decisive aid to the German bombers. British "precision" bombing of Germany, they argued, had been very successful without beams. Harris was still serenely confident that "the bomber will always get through" and, Jones remembers, as late as 1940, he scornfully referred to radar as an "adventitious aid." But on November 15, 1940, after a series of raids over Germany marred by heavy losses, Churchill minuted Sir Charles Portal: "No results have been achieved which would in any way justify or compensate for these losses. I consider the loss of eleven aircraft out of one hundred and thirty nine — i.e. about 8% — a very grievous disaster at this stage of our bomber development."[8] During 1941, Bomber Command's losses continued to increase. Lindemann, now elevated to Lord Cherwell, shared Churchill's anxieties, and in summer 1941 he independently commissioned an investigation of Bomber Command's effectiveness, posing a simple question: Were Britain's nightly bombing missions hitting their targets?

Cherwell's initiative was hailed as unprecedented. Yet one of the extraordinary aspects of the development of scientific intelligence during the early days of the war was that the military was continuously reinventing World War I innovations. In 1916 Lord Tiverton, a member of the British Air Mission in Paris, had undertaken an investigation into the success of Allied bombing. But twenty-five years later, Tiverton's comparatively efficient work and its depressing conclusions had been forgotten. Cherwell's research, undertaken by D. M. Butt of the Cabinet secretariat and delivered in August 1941, was based on 650 photographs taken on 100 separate raids over 28 different targets where the returning crews on 48 nights had claimed success. Butt's analysis proved that, at very best, only 10 percent of Britain's bombs were falling near their targets. It was a damning indictment of the air staff's policy and of their unsupportable assumptions; the unpalatable truth was that the amount of industrial resources and manpower needed to bomb Germany was inflicting greater economic harm on Britain than on the enemy.

Portal received Butt's report with a terse note from Churchill: "This is a very serious paper and seems to require your most urgent attention."[9] Unapologetically, Portal and his staff rejected Butt's results outright, although they were based on Bomber Command's own photographs. It is a frightening example of military self-delusion that Portal could find no plausible explanation for Bomber Command's enormous casualties, yet it still did not occur to him that scientific and technical intelligence had a vital role to play in aerial combat.

Unknown to Portal and the RAF, Goering's experts had adapted their anti-aircraft guns so they could be directed by radar. Unaffected by cloud cover, the Würzburg radar system could calculate the distance a British bomber would travel after the shell was fired and amend its direction. Once caught in the radar net, the bomber activated a master searchlight, which was difficult to shrug off. In theory, the kill followed soon after — and spiraling RAF losses corroborated the Würzburg system's potency, diminished only by the RAF pilots' challenging battle of wits with the German controllers.

Cherwell realized that British anti-aircraft batteries were noticeably less effective than the Germans'. Elementary statistical analysis had revealed that anti-aircraft gunners were exaggerating their number of hits. Basic "Operational Research" — which in the light of Butt's findings appeared to be an accurate if unglamorous judge of warfare — also showed that along the coast, reported and accepted hits by anti-aircraft guns needed 50 percent fewer shells than those reported by batteries sited inland. Superficially, it seemed an impressive record, but closer investigation revealed that, while all batteries exaggerated their successes, coastal battery hits could not be checked because any German planes brought down would be lying on the seabed. By the end of 1940 the comparative ineffectiveness of British anti-aircraft units had become a serious cause for anxiety. German bombers would soon be flying beyond the reach of searchlights, reducing further the number of British successes. These factors had been barely considered by the Air Staff — yet here was a glaring example of the need for technical intelligence and innovation. In combating such adversities, the first cracks in the old prejudices against scientists, scientific intelligence, and German scientific achievements appeared.

In Britain, since there was still no possibility of producing anything as sophisticated as the Würzburg system and since British gunners under Anti-Aircraft Command lacked the skills to operate even the imperfect equipment that the laboratories provided, a group of technicians, recruited by Pat Blackett, an Admiralty scientist, sat alongside the gunners in the fields around London to operate improvized radar sets.[10] The primitive equipment produced meager results, but the principle was established, and the civilian scientists, dubbed "Blackett's Circus," ranked equal to soldiers in combat, albeit stationed in Richmond Park.

The second and more important crack in the prejudice against scientists followed the delivery, in late November 1941, of RAF reconnaissance photographs showing a Freya (the next generation of Würzburg) radar site at Saint-Bruneval on the French coast, near Le Havre. It was part of a giant defensive network planned to stretch from Denmark to the Atlantic coast. For the British Air Staff the discovery could not have come at a worse moment. On November 7, Bomber Command had dispatched four hundred aircraft over Europe, of which thirty-seven had failed to return. Hardly any bombs had hit their targets. In Berlin, nine inhabitants had been killed against 120 aircrew lost. It was the climax of an awful year in which one British aircraft had been lost for every ten tons of bombs dropped.[11] Bomber Command faced extinction, and the

Freya network would undoubtedly hasten that inevitability. In contrast, Jones and other scientists were thrilled by the discovery. For them, it was the first critical opportunity to enter the sanctum of German scientific expertise.

On February 27, 1942, with the approval of the Chiefs of Staff, a combined operations assault group of commandos with a scientific adviser was dropped near Saint-Bruneval by parachute to penetrate Freya's secrets. "Operation Biting" was the war's first "military-scientific raid" and a blueprint for future operations. After fierce fighting, the group returned with the electronic heart of the antijamming circuitry and also with a German radar operator — a major step toward hunting for the architects of all German equipment.[12] Although Jones's battle with the beams continued throughout the war, the Saint-Bruneval raid marked an important turn in the fortunes of the Allied air offensive. Germany's prewar preparations had withered, and the radar war was a stalemate.

But in the air battle above Europe, Britain held few advantages. Despite its efforts, in two years Easton's intelligence group had won only limited influence over Britain's aircraft designers. While Easton's investigators had diligently delivered everything and anything discovered in German wrecks, his team was still insufficiently trained and informed to ask the questions that would have extracted fine detail about new German aircraft designs. Unlike the radar specialists, Air Intelligence was still amateur and even, on occasion, leisurely. The ingrained prejudice still remained, sometimes producing unfortunate shocks.

In July 1942, Hector Morrison, a former jobber on the stock exchange, was sent by Easton to investigate a crashed Junkers 88 at Uckfield, in Sussex. Sifting through the wreckage, Morrison discovered what seemed to be new German radio equipment. Two days later, Morrison heard that the recovered "radio" was Britain's latest "Gee" navigational system, introduced during the previous months to direct British bombers over their targets. German scientific intelligence had recovered and analyzed a Gee set from a downed British bomber and was returning it on a probing mission. Yet the RAF failed to respond to the discovery. The following month, a wave of British bombers using Gee radar fell victim to a swarm of Luftwaffe night fighters guided to their targets by the RAF's own radar transmissions. The British invention had cost British lives.

But there was already some change in the RAF's complacent belief in British aviation's superiority.

In June 1942, Portal received the first detailed report about the FW 190, a new German fighter first noticed at the end of 1941. Intelligence reports had given no advance warning, nor was there any information about its specifications. For six months after its first appearance the RAF, reassuringly supported by A.I.1(g) reports from Easton, assumed the new fighter would not pose a serious challenge to British aircraft, although at that time British aircraft losses were four times greater than the Germans'.

An FW 190 force-landed in Wales in June and was inspected by Easton's officers.[13] To their surprise, the plane combined high performance with heavy armor and armament, and was markedly superior to any equivalent British or American plane. In Whitehall, the plane's arrival "achieved considerable notoriety,"[14] especially among Portal's staff, who had nonchalantly assumed that Germany, like Britain, would not spend resources on major aircraft developments and would merely "stretch" existing types. With no end to the war in sight, Portal suddenly realized that the RAF needed a new generation of aircraft, which to date had not even passed the drawing-board stage. The revelation marked an abrupt end to Easton's leisurely style. The RAF's reliance solely on information collected from crashed aircraft had to be abandoned. Monitoring and anticipating German developments were finally acknowledged to be serious intelligence business. Easton was promoted and replaced by Wing Commander G. Proctor. Air Intelligence was expanded and a new section, A.I.2(g), established to collect intelligence that would anticipate new developments. Proctor was ordered to exploit every available source of intelligence: intercepts, agent reports from Europe, photo reconnaissance, captured documents, and intensive POW interrogation. Still unknown to Portal, because of the absence of any technical intelligence, the FW 190 was the first product of a phenomenal expansion program. In Germany no fewer than forty different aircraft types were under development, with a further two hundred possible variations under consideration.

The reshuffle coincided with the arrival in late 1942 of the first Air Intelligence officer in North Africa. David Nutting, an electronics expert, was the solitary RAF representative covering the vast area. Before leaving Britain, Nutting had hoped that he would be allowed to cooperate with similar French army and navy teams, but Wing Commander R. E. de Vintras, chief of French intelligence, rejected his request. Air Force Intelligence, insisted de Vintras, was to remain "self-contained." Without so much as an RAF regiment in support, Nutting admits, his work in North Africa was limited: "Our own troops, by looting and wanton rampaging, damaged the intelligence opportunities more than the Germans." Nutting wistfully remembers the fate of his biggest prize, the latest Me 109, in perfect condition. "After a harrowing twenty-four-day journey through the hot desert with a 'Queen Mary' transporter, I stopped for a drink. Suddenly I heard some shooting and looked up. My beautiful plane was being destroyed by an idle soldier who decided to use it for target practice." As Nutting discovered, Allied troops in North Africa barely understood that their own survival and victory depended to no small measure on technical intelligence — a harsh lesson soon learned in grueling tank battles, which cost many lives and destroyed the reputations of several distinguished British commanders.

Until the apocalyptic battle for France in May 1940, Lord Gort, the inexperienced commander of the British Expeditionary Force, and his staff remained unconcerned about the probable performance of their single armored corps, numbering a mere 210 tanks, against Guderian's ten Panzer groups. Yet, even after the massive German onslaught, not one of Gort's staff understood that all the British tanks, with the notable exception of twenty-three Matilda IIs (the most modern in the British army), had been hopelessly outgunned. Only the Matilda's two-pounder had ripped through German armor, and its own 78-millimeter armor had effectively withstood the German 37-millimeter antitank gun.

Among the casualties of the retreat from France was the abandonment of all the matériel of the British armored corps. With the prospect of invasion imminent, there was understandable panic in Whitehall when the Cabinet met on June 11, 1940. Just two hundred impotent light tanks, armed only with machine guns, remained for the defense of the British Isles. Faced with the legacy of prewar confusion over tank design and production, the Cabinet decided that "the immediate task . . . was to expedite delivery during the next five months of everything required to make good the deficiencies in essential items of equipment." The Cabinet also endorsed the decision taken just days before the German attack that, to avoid production delays, the tank program "must not be interfered with either by the incorporation of improvements to the approved types, or by the production of newer models." Four different tanks were at that time in production: the Valentine, Covenanter,

Crusader, and Matilda II, all armed with a two-pound gun. The Cabinet's fateful support for the status quo was given without any attempt to discover evidence of German intentions in tank design. There was nothing unusual in such self-imposed blindness. The rigid pattern had been established during the previous twenty years.

Destiny dictated that the unmodified replacements for the British tanks lost on the cool, rolling plains of northern Europe were next deployed in the sweltering desert. For the Wehrmacht, Rommel's North African war was a comparatively insignificant sideshow: Only four German divisions were committed to Rommel, while a massive 232 Axis divisions fought against the Russians. Yet for the British and later the Americans, the desert was the decisive proving ground where their armies came of age.

Ignorant about weapons development, General Sir Archibald Wavell, the first commander of the British army in Egypt, did not complain in February 1941 about either the Valentine and Matilda tanks, which were arriving from Britain, or the Grants from America. Wavell's silence reflected the prevalent Allied complacency about the suitability of their equipment. In theory, Middle East Command had formed a technical intelligence section in October 1940, but in fact it only amounted to a single officer, Captain R. W. Plowright, an experienced engineer who had proven himself a fearless soldier in Palestine. Plowright, as his faithful deputy later recorded, started from scratch:

> The amount of technical information about the enemy, which was readily available, was at this stage of the war negligible, in addition to which very little information could be relied upon as accurate. The almost total neglect of technical intelligence prior to the present war increased the difficulty of the work, since every individual type of equipment had necessarily to be regarded as entirely new, and no details could be accepted until finally confirmed.[15]

Throughout the winter of 1940–41, Plowright struggled unsuccessfully to discover the technical details of the German tanks and antitank weapons. British intercepts gathered at Bletchley Park were failing to detect Rommel's stealthy eastward advance and were not scrutinized to ascertain the quality of German equipment.[16] Had that been done, the British would have discovered that Rommel's Afrika Korps had arrived equipped with 50-millimeter or six-pound short-barreled guns whose capped, armor-piercing, high-explosive shells could effortlessly penetrate the Matilda's armor. Without a technical intelligence section, the Middle East Command had also failed to establish that the German tanks' armor was face-hardened, making it invulnerable to the standard British shells.

In contrast to the British, German technical intelligence teams had efficiently examined the abandoned Matildas in France and recommended the necessary improvements to the tank designers in the Ruhr. The experienced General Sir Campbell Clarke had warned the Tank Board in autumn of 1940 that the Germans, after inspecting British tanks, would improve their own design — but even he had underestimated their speed and efficiency in implementing improvements, and his warning, repeated in February 1941, was already woefully out of date: "[They] can scarcely catch up the lead we have gained in 1941, but . . . will certainly do so by 1942 unless our designs for tanks for that year are more heavily armoured than their predecessors."[17] Clarke's broadside was dismissed, but that same month British confidence that their presumed lead could be maintained was unceremoniously shattered.

At the end of January 1941, Allied forces surrendered Benghazi and fell back toward the fortress at Tobruk. In London, the General Staff was faced with another military disaster that neither it nor Wavell could fully explain. Other than Plowright, who was some distance from the front, there was no one to report that the unsuspecting British tank crews, fighting in slow, unventilated, uninsulated, and unprotected vehicles, were being helplessly outgunned by Rommel's new Panzers. Only five weeks earlier the director of artillery had rejected the six-pound gun on the grounds that it was "too long for use in a tank." Now the General Staff had reversed its position. Gun manufacturers who had perfected and displayed the weapon four years earlier were ordered to divert supplies to the tank factories immediately. In June 1941, the General Staff bitterly complained that the six-pounders had still not been installed.[18]

The military was now confronted by an extremely disturbing revelation. Inflexible, inefficient, and inept, British tank manufacturers were unable to alter their production schedules in less than eighteen months. Even years after they were declared obsolete, the outdated light tanks abandoned in France were still being produced. Although the Tank Board was presented with a stream of contradictory recommendations about tank tracks that kept breaking, engines that clogged up with sand, and the technical inability of the British steel industry to produce better-quality armor plates, the board could produce no easy remedy.[19] Unlike the infinitely more efficient Ruhr factories, whose ability to constantly adapt and improve German tanks meant they would never lose their advantage in the West, British management and workers could not deliver the military's requirements.

By the beginning of April 1941, Britain's Third Armored Brigade in North Africa had effectively ceased to exist. The surviving British tank crews retreated eastward, still unable to identify what was destroying their armor. It fell to Plowright alone to discover the reason, but it seemed to him that the personnel of Middle East Command in distant Cairo — who were uninterested in technology and could not even understand the importance of collecting German documents — failed to appreciate the importance of his work. Nevertheless, he courageously volunteered to fly to the beleaguered Tobruk fortress to inspect abandoned Panzer wrecks. His dangerous flight was rewarded by a host of technical revelations, although he was unable to identify the secret of the all-important face-hardened armor and the capped shells. After transmitting his report by radio, Plowright boarded a small plane, which took off toward the sea. Moments later, it was shot down. Only on his death did Middle East Command slowly begin to reconsider the need for technical intelligence. Without trained experts either in London or in Cairo who could isolate the succession of problems murderously obliterating the tank corps, the British tanks' weaknesses remained unidentified for a further twelve months.

"Operation Battleaxe," a British offensive that started early on June 5, 1941, with the aim of repulsing Rommel's seemingly inexorable advance, was the first major set-piece confrontation between British and German armor. A succession of new tanks from different manufacturers had been dispatched from Britain with high hopes of success. Yet within days, General Wavell's forces were humiliatingly routed and Wavell himself was dismissed. German tank losses were a mere one-eighth of those suffered by the British. Out of 104 Matildas, only five survived the battle. Not a single British officer realized that the German tanks were firing high-explosive and armor-piercing shells out of the same gun for different tactical purposes: the one to destroy tanks, the other to kill people. Despite the catastrophic losses, the General Staff, three thousand miles away in London, reaffirmed its order that the replacement tanks should again be equipped with the two-pounder gun, because the six-pounder was still unavailable. So far the military crisis, which would eventually burst into public debate, was the subject of only one protest.

On July 1 a letter from Professor Archibald Hill, a scientist and member of Parliament for Cambridge, was published in the *Times*:

> The defeat in Libya is due largely to a single cause, the inferiority of our tanks to the enemy's. This inferiority is due not to bad workmanship, but to a system which has failed to anticipate future tactical requirements in guns, projectiles, armour and performance; failed to collect, analyse, and profit by previous operational experience; failed sometimes even to obey the elementary rule that production must follow, not precede, development. Too many disasters in the present war have been due either to technical mismanagement of this kind, together with unjustifiable optimism, or else to improper or inefficient use of available weapons, resources or material. . . . There is no central technical staff or individual to advise the Cabinet, or the Chiefs of Staff, directly on the scientific and engineering aspects either of operations or production, or to ensure, on their behalf, that design and development are efficient and far-seeing. All such functions are left to departments.

Despite the damning accuracy of Hill's remarks, the principals in the drama strove to protect themselves rather than the soldiers.

General G. N. Macready, the assistant chief of the Imperial General Staff, on behalf of the Army Council blamed the Tank Board for the late delivery of the six-pounders, which were again delayed and would be ready only in June 1943: "The Army at the moment is in the position of having cavalry mounted on ponies in operation against an enemy with full-sized horses." Recriminations, replied the board, would not solve the fundamental problems. But the debate progressed no further.

In Cairo, the catastrophic losses of Operation Battleaxe prompted Wavell's successor, Sir Claude Auchinleck, to establish a technical investigation section, the Armored Fighting Vehicle (Technical) Branch.[20] According to Captain David Evans, Plowright's successor, the latter's untimely death had not been in vain: "The lesson [was] clear. In the initial operations in this Command, lives and even battles were lost because information of enemy equipment was inadequate. The cause was entirely the lack of interest shown in technical intelligence before the war and the most discouraging handicaps under which work commenced." On the eve of the American entry into the war, the British army was still unable either to acknowledge or adequately investigate German technical superiority.

Strategically, "Operation Crusader" — the British bid to relieve the German stranglehold on Tobruk, launched on November 18, 1941 — was a success. The enemy, vastly outnumbered in tanks and supplies, was taken by surprise; even so, British losses were colossal. Only fifty out of the British Thirty Corps' 450 tanks survived the first crucial battle on November 21 and 22, while the Germans lost just seventy-seven tanks and threw Auchinleck's forces into retreat. Many Allied tanks had been trounced by the mobile 88-millimeter anti-aircraft flak guns on whose effectiveness Captain Kenneth Strong had reported before the war, only to be ignored. Two weeks later brave counterattacks by New Zealand forces turned the tide, and Rommel, starved of supplies and replacements, which had been diverted to the Russian front, began retreating.

As the Afrika Korps pulled back, Allied headquarters was able temporarily to conceal its losses. Undisguised, however, was the British reassertion of their equipment's superiority. Soon after the battle, Auchinleck's headquarters reported to London: "While the German armour has not been analysed, the results do indicate that it is not of a quality to prevent holes being made by existing British anti-tank weapons." Their conclusion was subsequently exposed as totally untrue. Without trained technicians in the desert, Auchinleck's headquarters had not yet properly tested the extra armor plates on the German tanks[21] and had still not discovered that they had been face-hardened, or that the special 50-millimeter ammunition could pierce the Matilda's armor at 440 yards. For the first time, however, British headquarters in North Africa was able to ship a large consignment of German equipment and documents to Britain for testing.

Still unscorched by battle, American tank production was also geared to quantity rather than quality, and in the North African desert the American Grant, Sherman, and Honey tanks, with their standard 75-millimeter guns, were as vulnerable as the British vehicles. Assessment of their technical merits and defects was still a British responsibility — but civilian experts were as impotent as the tanks themselves until the military reported their flaws. Inevitably, the complaints started in the ranks, among those who were bearing the brunt of battle. On January 31, 1942, Auchinleck cabled to Churchill about the "short range and inferior performance of our 2 pounder gun compared with the German [50-millimeter] gun and mechanical unreliability of our Cruiser tanks compared with German tanks . . . there are signs that personnel of Royal Armoured Corps are, in some instances, losing confidence in their equipment."[22]

Meanwhile the Germans, aided by British ignorance and indecision, maintained their technical superiority into 1942. New tanks arrived in Africa equipped with extra 20-millimeter spaced armor plating and with a replica of the Russian 7.62-centimeter gun, which the Germans had admired on the T-34 during the advance to Moscow. The Ruhr technicians had also developed two special innovations: "hollow-charged" ammunition, which could destroy the toughest Allied armor, and the Nebelwerfer, a gun equipped with a multibarreled mortar that fired rocket-propelled shells. In contrast, the British were in complete disarray and were also on the verge of forsaking their most deeply ingrained preconception: their superiority to both the Americans and Germans. To America, the British turned for immediate help; as for Germany, this belated awakening was the source of Britain's eventual plan to plunder the enemy's store of technical and scientific knowledge.

3

Unpleasant Realities

MacLEOD ROSS was a member of the British tank-buying mission that arrived at the Aberdeen testing ground in Maryland in March 1942 hoping that American industry could mass-produce battle-worthy tanks for North Africa. Yet Ross's optimistic expectation of unencumbered Anglo-American cooperation was soon dashed. The Ordnance Department responsible for tank development was, Ross heard, obstinately unresponsive to the inquiries and demands of the American General Staff. Any British interference, he was told, would certainly be unacceptable. Ordnance's stubbornness struck Ross as curious. The Grant was outmoded, the new Sherman untested, and the American army had never fought a tank battle. He pleaded that British recommendations be heeded, since they were based on harsh experience as the victims of German tanks. The American army, Ross realized, needed the same baptism by fire before it would understand technology's vital role in military strategy and success. But Ordnance, as one critic commented, was an "entrenched vested interest . . . and allowed no one to enter their sacred precincts."[1] Ross had no option but to bite his lip and remain patient.

In North Africa, Rommel was on the eve of launching a massive new onslaught against Tobruk. The German armor's technical superiority had, for the first time, been indisputably confirmed by Signals Intelligence, or Sigint, intercepts. In Britain, just before the battle, Brigadier J. S. Crawford of the War Office stiffly minuted the Tank Board, which had been reconstituted for the fifth time within two years, that one thousand Churchill tanks had been built, but sixteen major modifications were needed, and not one of the tanks was "battleworthy."[2] From Cairo, Sir Auchinleck cabled that bad assembly of the Crusader tank was "very prevalent," each tank needing two hundred man-hours to make it fit for combat.[3] The outcome of the battle was a foregone conclusion. In the wake of his triumph, Rommel was promoted to field marshal, while in Washington and London the General Staffs began yet another urgent review of the technology of tank warfare. Reports from British technical investigators in the desert to General Levin Campbell, the new American chief of Ordnance, criticized the new Sherman's bad suspension, inadequate stabilizers, lack of a periscope, and ineffective gun. Since modern warfare was still a novelty for the American army, media, and politicians, the inadequacies of the new Sherman went unnoticed outside the Ordnance Department. Shielded from the glare of public criticism, Campbell agreed to accept British help and initiated an exhausting review of the Sherman.

In Britain, the luxury of temperate review had long passed. The mold was setting for the first major Allied acknowledgment of German achievements. Cables from Cairo reported a serious threat to the morale of Allied troops because of sagging confidence in their weapons. From the desert Captain David Evans sent an admiring report describing the new German Mark III tank, armed with an improved gun and remarkable spaced armor: "It came as an unpleasant surprise when firing trials showed it to be face hardened. . . . [It also showed] signs of cracking [only] after repeated attack. . . . I know quite well how difficult it is to design an effective hull mounting. . . . The Germans have done it however, and done it well."[4]

In the House of Commons, Oliver Lyttelton, the Cabinet minister responsible for weapons production, attempting to calm the growing uproar that followed the Eighth Army's defeat, promised members that the new Cromwell tank "would surpass in armour, armament and power anything we have so far produced." The assurance was a politician's bluff. In a secret meeting five days later, A.W.C. Richardson, the director, Armored Fighting Vehicles, told the Tank Board that the Cromwell's gearbox, turret, engine, and suspension were all suspect: "I am reliably informed that difficulties have arisen which may give rise to justifiable concern."[5] At a Tank Board meeting on August 4, his fears were confirmed. General Sir Neil Ritchie, who had just returned from Cairo, briefed the numbed board members about the complete imbalance between Allied and German armor. While the Grant's engine needed replacement after one thousand miles, the new PzKpfw III's engine ran reliably for five thousand miles. Neither the new Cromwell nor the Sherman had the PzKpfw III's winning features. German paramountcy, said Ritchie, even extended to their jerry cans, which were "far superior to our light 4-gallon tin."

By the autumn, Campbell believed that he had rectified the faults of the American tanks. The replacement Shermans arriving in North Africa were equipped with bigger guns, capped ammunition, periscopes, improved armor, and better suspension. Campbell prided himself on his technical prowess and his tanks' contribution to General Sir Bernard Montgomery's epic victory in November at El Alamein. But even in the consequent euphoria, the long-term frailties of the Eighth Army's equipment could not be glossed over. Rommel had been allocated only a handful of the new sixty-ton Tiger tanks, but their brief appearance clearly demonstrated that the improved Sherman was already as vulnerable as its predecessors. "Have seen Tiger running," cabled Montgomery from the Middle East, ". . . it is a formidable animal with exceptional wading properties." A Tiger was shipped to America to persuade Ordnance engineers that the Sherman was outclassed. With British support, Major General Gladeon Barnes, Ordnance's chief of research, suggested to Lieutenant General Lesley McNair, the head of his new tank research department, that in anticipation of German developments, the medium-sized Sherman needed to be replaced by the more heavily armored T-26 tank, which carried a 90-millimeter gun. But once again blind parochialism blocked change. McNair told Barnes, "There have been no factual developments overseas, so far as I know, to challenge the superiority of the M-4 Sherman."[6]

Plainly McNair was ignoring reports from the first Ordnance technical intelligence unit, which had arrived in the desert after El Alamein under Major J. H. Edgerly. As he combed through the battlefield debris, Edgerly had realized that the Tiger tank was equipped with the most sophisticated armor and gun he had ever seen. McNair ignored Edgerly's messages and also the War Office proposal that future American tanks should incorporate the new British seventeen-pound gun to match the Tiger. McNair resolutely insisted that the American six-pound 76-millimeter gun was adequate. The British mission could only bite its lips harder.

In London, the dispute about the superiority of German tanks could no longer be contained behind closed doors. Just one month after El Alamein, Richard Stokes, the radical Labor member of Parliament for Ipswich, launched the outcry that became known as "The Tank Scandal" by exposing the ministerial conspiracy to deliberately mislead Parliament and the country about the parlous state of British armor. On September 20, 1942, referring to the Cromwell, Sir James Grigg, the secretary for war, had told Parliament: "We have now tanks coming into production better than our forces had before. I have seen them and they are better than anything produced by the Germans, Italians or Japanese — better than any tank in the world. The effect of this tank in the war is incalculable." But the latest reports from Tunisia had described the complete destruction of a twenty-strong squadron of American Shermans by the new Tiger. "Is the Right Honourable Gentleman," Stokes shouted at Grigg in the Commons, "prepared to say that in his considered judgement, that tank [the Cromwell] is capable of taking on the German Tiger?" The written record of proceedings in the House of Commons reports that Grigg "indicated assent." Immediately Stokes countered: "I want to get it on the record; I do not want to get it by a nodding of the head." Under pressure, Grigg stood up. Past mistakes, he said, had been resolved. Production of a new tank, superior to the Tiger, was under way. Grigg knew that his answer was untrue. After extensive tests, Middle East Command had just reported that the Tiger was "certainly superior in design and execution to anything we have hitherto imagined."

Eight months later, on September 11, 1943, Britain conceded victory to German industry and its engineers. After months of perpetual changes of policy about the future of tank design, J. F. Evetts, the A.C.I.G.S., recommended to Grigg that the British effectively cease building tanks, blaming

> the rapid advance made by Germany in a remarkably short space of time. Our advance has been slow and by the time that the weapon is in the hands of the troops, it has been outclassed by that possessed by the enemy. I feel that the time has now come when we must certainly face the fact that British cruiser tank design and production has failed both in quality and in the time factor. . . . Prestige is irrelevant. The troops must have battleworthy tanks.

Britain would build railway carriages instead, turning to America for her tanks, and her reliance on the United States would create a competitor rather than an ally in the race to seize German secrets.

Henry Tizard had been among the few at the outbreak of war to realize that Britain, unable to narrow the enormous industrial and technological lead that Germany enjoyed, would need American help. Few others in Whitehall shared his unpatriotic gloom. The service chiefs had viewed Tizard's proposed Anglo-American cooperation with the same distrust with which they had rejected his suggestion of employing civilian scientists. The Americans, they felt, had nothing to offer for future weapons development and could definitely not be trusted with military secrets. When, René Studler, the U.S. military attaché in London, had asked the War Office before the war for permission to inspect a British tank, he had been firmly told that foreigners were never allowed inside a British armored vehicle.[7] Little changed when war was declared. Exchange of scientific secrets remained unthinkable. Just after the invasion of France, Professor Archibald Hill had been sent to Washington as temporary scientific attaché with the uncompromising brief that Britain would not divulge any secrets.

Shortly before Dunkirk the policy changed. An intelligence appreciation blandly entitled "British Strategy in a Certain Eventuality" described the government's options in the event of France's defeat. Britain's survival, it concluded, depended upon American minerals, foodstuffs, machinery, ships, and a vast range of weapons, "without which we do not consider we could continue the war with any chance of success."[8] This judgment was confirmed a few weeks later. In the last ten days of July 1940, eleven British destroyers were sunk or badly damaged. Britain appealed to America for salvation. "Destroyers are frightfully vulnerable to air bombing," Churchill telegraphed to Roosevelt, implicitly condemning the Admiralty's peacetime folly.[9] To save Britain, in return for fifty obsolete American destroyers Churchill offered the president bases on British territory. As an enticement, he also offered the American navy the secrets of Asdic, which was part of a wilder invitation to exchange information that he hoped would dispel any mistrust in Washington and set the seal on his proposal of total cooperation. Roosevelt approved Churchill's package, and Tizard was selected to mastermind the disclosure of Britain's complete accumulation of scientific secrets.

In the boxes and crates that accompanied the British scientists to Washington were prototypes and blueprints for power-driven aircraft turrets, antisubmarine and anti-aircraft weapons, a proximity fuse, a cavity magnetron valve that would revolutionize the use of radar for the remainder of the war, and a set of designs for the Rolls-Royce Merlin aircraft engine, which would transform the sluggish Mustang into an excellent fighter. Most important of all, the group brought a complete summary of British atomic research. "In the early days of the scientific interchange," wrote John Burchard, a senior scientific director on the American National Development Research Committee, "the British gave more than they received."[10]

The British team was greeted by Vannevar Bush, an inventor and engineer recently appointed chairman of the new National Defense Research Committee by Roosevelt. Like Cherwell, Bush was talented, irascible, and arrogant; but unlike Cherwell, he soon commanded a large, well-funded organization that occasionally wielded decisive influence. The NDRC had been created on Professor Hill's advice that the supervision of new weapons development be entrusted to a civilian organization of scientists and engineers. A year later, when the new and more powerful Office of Scientific Research and Development was created with Bush as its director, the Cape Cod Yankee increased his power by stipulating that he be granted direct access to the president. Around him, he gathered a group of enthusiastic scientists and engineers who were willingly convinced by Tizard's team that warfare depended on science — and needed no persuasion that their efficacy depended upon strictly preserving their independence from the military. To guarantee that independence, Dr. James Conant was sent to London as Bush's ambassador to head a growing NDRC liaison and research group. Tizard's mission had laid the foundations of the intense and extraordinarily uninhibited Anglo-American wartime cooperation, which later spread to the investigation of German technical advances. Under Bush's influence, the American military would eventually develop a huge appetite for German scientific secrets, but the prelude was inauspiciously slow.

In 1940 Bush faced the same problems as Tizard and Cherwell — the peacetime legacy of the military's lack of interest in scientific innovations, not least in the navy. There had been a limited Anglo-American exchange of naval intelligence before 1940, but the British had judged that the United States had very little to offer.[11] The American navy, in Bush's view, was infected by stubbornness: "All decisions were made by a top-brass old-fashioned techni- cally . . . decisions, once made, were not reviewed, were not even commented upon, by anyone whatever."[12] Admiral Ernest King had silently watched the Japanese air force effortlessly sink the battleships *Prince of Wales* and *Repulse*, the pride of the Royal Navy, off Singapore in the autumn of 1941 because the Admiralty had waved aside the provision of aircraft protection and insisted that the ships' own guns were sufficient. King would expose the American fleet at Pearl Harbor to the same danger.

Admiral King's "conservatism," as Bush soon discovered, also prescribed that the U.S. Navy would rely on discredited depth charges and Sonar (similar to Asdic) to avoid and hunt for submarines. Bush's early attempts to convert King to the wonders of radar foundered on, in Bush's words, the admiral's "antediluvian conviction that convoying was the only way to combat the submarine. There never was a clearer example of the tendency to fight a war with the weapons and tactics of the preceeding war . . . King had no grasp whatever of the technical revolution which had occurred."[13] Despite the sinking in 1942 of 1,664 Allied ships totaling nearly eight million tons at a cost of only eighty-two U-boats, traditional seafarers were slow to grasp that technical innovation had swept aside many of the navy's historical preconceptions. It was the same blinkered obstructionism that, until 1943, blocked cooperation among the U.S. Joint Chiefs of Staff to create an effective airborne Coastal Command capable of sinking the U-boats that were attacking Allied shipping with impunity just a short distance from the American coastline. "In an acute situation," wrote Samuel Eliot Morison, the U.S. Navy's historian, "where a prompt solution and close teamwork were imperative, neither the Joint Chiefs of Staff nor any other authority were able to find the one or impose the other."[14] Reluctant and handicapped, the American navy was only gradually drawn by the Royal Navy into the frenzied clash of technology that constantly tilted the balance between the combatants in the Atlantic. As the lessons accumulated, both Allied navies' respect for German scientific skills increased enormously.

Germany's declaration of war against America and the abortive invasion of Russia had forced Hitler, at the beginning of 1942, to change his strategy from a short- to a long-term war. Grand Admiral Karl Doenitz's submarine designers began a crash program that pushed technical frontiers far beyond anything envisioned two years earlier. New U-boats were designed to dive to 600 feet, a specification that the Admiralty found incredible since British designers were unable to produce anything similar;[15] special supply submarines, "*Milch* cows," which could replenish the U-boats at sea, were sent out into the Atlantic, permitting the packs to sustain longer operations and saving them the perilous return journey to European ports; in Kiel, the Walterwerke began building a submarine powered by a mixture of fuel and hydrogen peroxide that did not need to surface for long periods to replenish its batteries; and for attack the U-boats were equipped with acoustic and zigzag homing torpedoes, as well as an improved magnetic torpedo pistol. Against that arsenal, the Allies sent long-range Liberator aircraft equipped with shortwave 10-centimeter radar, high-frequency direction-finding equipment, new and more powerful air depth charges correctly tuned to explode at varying depths, and Leigh searchlights, hoping they would halt the submarine offensive. The location of the decisive clash of technologies was at the "Greenland air gap," an area beyond the range of earlier Allied aircraft.

During the first week of May 1943, sixty U-boats had grouped north of the Azores to attack Convoy ONS.5. Considering the fate of its predecessors, the convoy had only a slim chance of an unscathed passage across the Atlantic. During the first twenty days of March 1943, ninety-seven Allied ships had been lost, totaling more than half a million tons, a crippling loss that, if continued, would have been fatal for Britain. Convoy ONS.5's survival depended on the new technology. As predicted, the U-boats attacked, sinking twelve merchant ships; but in return, seven U-boats were destroyed. By the end of the month, in a series of further attacks and counterattacks, a total of thirty-three U-boats had been sunk. Heeding the high losses, Doenitz, already suffering from Hitler's capricious interference and the backlash of the reverses on the Russian front, temporarily withdrew his packs from battle. Allied losses plunged, while a total of 237 U-boats were destroyed. At the end of 1943 German Naval Intelligence appointed highly qualified scientists to investigate the cause of such unprecedented destruction: "It was 10cm radar . . . which caused all the German losses," Doenitz admitted to Hitler.[16] On January 2, 1944, the British intercepted a message from Hitler to U-boat crews: German losses, the Führer explained, were due to "a single technical invention of our enemies."[17] Convoy ONS.5's survival had been won purely by technology, and the victory whetted the appetite of Allied naval staff for more information about German technological ideas.

In the aftermath of the Tizard mission, the U.S. Air Force entered the war with more robust confidence than the army or navy. When

General Hap Arnold, the genial U.S. deputy chief of staff and commanding general of the U.S. Army Air Force, visited Britain in April 1941, he noted that the British were undisputably amiable and brave — but also inefficient. His hosts had insisted that it was impossible to conduct precision daylight bombing over Germany safely because with existing bombsights, a twenty-second run was needed for proper aim. Unsinged by combat over Germany, Arnold was skeptical of British trepidation. Daylight bombing, he was convinced, was possible with the four-engined high-altitude Flying Fortress, with its pressurized cockpit and daylight bombsight. But the British did have something to offer. At Tizard's suggestion, Arnold had seen the first jet engines designed by Frank Whittle. The RAF, Arnold was told, possessed three jet propulsion planes — one ready to fly, one with the engine on a test bed, and a third ready for installation — but production was in utter disarray. Dismayed by lack of progress, Whittle entrusted Arnold with his priceless blueprints for the jet engine and encouraged him to allow American industry to pioneer its development. Arnold returned to Washington, gripped by the technical duel with Germany.

For Arnold and General Ira Eaker, the commander of the U.S. Eighth Air Force in Britain, the intensive bombing of Hamburg starting on July 24, 1942, would confirm the preeminence of American technology as epitomized in the Flying Fortress. Together with Bomber Command, the U.S. Air Force set out on the first of 3,095 sorties over four days that engulfed the whole city in a massive firestorm, sending a temporary shudder through the Nazi hierarchy. "Hamburg put the fear of God into me," confessed Albert Speer.[18] The cost to the Allied air forces, just twelve bombers, was minimal because the German radar system had been wondrously confused by "Window," hundreds of thousands of strips of tin foil calculatingly dropped before the bombers appeared on the screens of Freya network. To Harris and Eaker, their bombers suddenly seemed invulnerable.

Eaker's bombers were now aggressively poised for an all-American attempt to "sever Germany's jugular." The target on August 17 was the ball-bearing factories at Schweinfurt. Since the Hamburg raid, German technicians had, with considerable resourcefulness, produced radar that could distinguish between the Window tin foil and the bombers — and waiting to swarm for the kill were squadrons of new FW 190 fighters armed with revolutionary 21-centimeter rockets. In the ensuing melee, only 30 percent of the target factories were destroyed, and no fewer than sixty of the 376 Flying Fortresses with their crews were lost. This was, in the official history, a "crippling disaster," augmented by "a high tide of tribulation"[19] during a second, equally disastrous raid in October. It was a bitter blow for Eaker and the U.S. Air Force, inducing new fascination for the adversary's technical talents. Moreover, news of the Eighth Air Force's defeat arrived in London at the same time as startling confirmation that, while the Luftwaffe was about to commit jet fighters to the battle over Germany, the prospects for British and American jets were languishing. Churchill was agitated: "We cannot afford," he minuted, "to be left behind."[20]

The first hint of the Germans' development of jet aircraft was a chance sighting, on July 25, 1942, by an alert Mosquito crewman who had photographed an unusual Luftwaffe fighter. Over the following nine months A.I.2(g) gathered sufficient evidence to confirm the flight of the world's first jet fighter, the Me 262. The sighting occurred just seven days after its maiden flight, delayed by two years when Hitler and Goering had ordered that further production should be halted in favor of bombers. For the Allies, it was a lucky decision, since Germany was at least four years ahead of Britain and America.

The maiden flight of the world's first turbojet aircraft, the Heinkel 178, on August 27, 1939, had passed off relatively unnoticed. Dr. Hans von Ohain, the jet-engine designer, had beaten Frank Whittle by two years because he had chosen hydrogen as his experimental fuel. Von Ohain had also profited from greater interest and financial support from German industry. Although Whittle had designed the first jet engine in 1919, he had suffered twenty years of prejudice and bankruptcy until, on the eve of war, David Pye, the Air Ministry's director of scientific research, agreed to state-sponsored development. But the promise of support for Whittle's engine did not include support for a suitable aircraft. At the end of 1940 the secretary of state for air wrote to Lord Beaverbrook urging the construction of a jet plane, the Meteor, but received no reply. Then, in July 1941, Churchill ordered Beaverbrook to investigate the lack of progress, which resulted in an immediate order for three hundred Meteors. Gloster's, the manufacturer, was urged to improve its design. But, at the end of 1942, when he was shown the improvements, Air Staff Chief Sir Charles Portal realized that Gloster's had failed, and he reduced the order to just fifty aircraft. To make matters worse, by 1943 production of Whittle's jet engine at the Rover factory was, according to an unofficial report, in a "chaotic condition,"[21] and production had to be transferred to Rolls-Royce.

Whittle's depression was somewhat relieved by a visit to the General Electric factory in America. General Electric had been given the British blueprints by General Arnold, since both Lockheed and Bell were finding difficulties in producing a suitable plane. The corporation's plan, in 1942, was to produce one thousand jets per month. American designers, like their British counterparts, lacked the wind tunnels and aerodynamic-design skills to produce a shape that would allow the jets to power the airframe to faster speeds, whereas German designers had found the answer — the swept wing. The experimental Me 163 rocket plane could fly a remarkable 623 miles per hour, while the aluminum alloy Me 262 flew at 540 miles per hour. At best, the Meteor, without swept wings, could reach only 480 miles per hour, and a series of American experimental planes failed to even match the Meteor.[22]

Churchill, suspecting that the air chiefs were complacent, impatiently commissioned his son-in-law, Duncan Sandys, to investigate. Sandys could be guaranteed, the prime minister felt, to submit an independent assessment. The Combined Chiefs in Washington had already concluded that "if German fighters are materially increased in numbers, it is quite conceivable that this would make our daylight bombing unprofitable and perhaps our night bombing too."[23] An Air Intelligence report to the Cabinet confirmed German technical superiority. Jets would certainly destroy any Allied hopes for air supremacy.

Sandys's draft report for Churchill was ready in September. It was doom-laden. "The enemy is appreciably ahead of us in the development of jet-propelled aircraft of all the more advanced types. The possibility cannot, in my opinion, be excluded that towards the end of 1944 and during 1945, the Germans may be in a position to put into service, in small numbers, both fighters and bombers of higher performance than those which we will then have available."[24] The report recommended that Britain and America boost their own development work and use technical intelligence agents to discover German methods both from Germany and, "as soon as Italy collapses," from the Campini-Caproni works.

Portal automatically intercepted Sandys's report. Supported by Air Vice Chief Marshall Sir Wilfred Freeman at the Ministry of Aircraft Production, Portal hoped the report could be suppressed.

In an "official" letter on September 6 to Portal, Freeman wrote, "We must be careful to avoid exciting the uninitiated about this sort of thing." On the same day, Freeman also wrote "unofficially" at greater length. "I am seriously concerned about the possibility that we may squander a disproportionate amount of effort on projects which can have no bearing on the course of the present war. . . . We have got to keep technically ahead of the enemy, but it is ONE jump ahead that we want to keep."[25] Considering Britain's strained resources, Freeman's argument had considerable merit. But it assumed that scientific development could be turned on and off as military needs arose. In autumn 1943, for Freeman, jet aircraft existed only on "a remote and nebulous horizon" and were still comparatively unimportant. Portal agreed and successfully convinced Sandys not only to exclude from his report any adverse comment on Britain's languishing jet development but also to recommend that responsibility for further investigation be transferred to the Air Ministry.[26] Sandys's official, sanitized report concluded that while German jet development had made progress, "there will be many problems to solve before they can be regarded as a serious operational threat."

Shortly afterward, Freeman's self-satisfied assurance, based on the belief that British scientists could always, when necessary, match the Germans, was violently shaken. In September, reports from the Bay of Biscay described a successful German attack on a British ship using a radio-guided rocket missile. Launched from a plane, the Hs 293 was guided by the aircrew to the target. A later report from Italy told of a new powerful German bomb, the PC 1400 FX, which was also radio-guided.[27] Surprised by the apparent lack of any advanced warning, the director of Naval Intelligence reviewed previous intercepts and interrogations. To his discomfort, he discovered that relevant messages had been deciphered but ignored because the members of the intelligence staff were not scientists and simply could not understand their importance. Overnight it seemed that the Allied fleet was at risk because of the failure of scientific intelligence. The Admiralty immediately established a scientific intelligence section, NID 7S, to cooperate with the Air Ministry's A.I.2(g). Such a palliative might have satisfied Portal and Freeman, but not the prime minister.

Despite Portal and Freeman's suppression, Sandys privately communicated to Churchill the substance of his fears. On October 6, the prime minister sent Portal an unequivocal command: "Recent evidence shows that the Germans are working hard on jet-propelled aircraft and accentuates the need for the utmost pressure to be put on their development here."[28] When the Defense Committee (Operations) met on October 25, Sandys's warnings of Germany's supremacy had been reinstated, but to little effect. To satisfy Churchill, Freeman proposed a new development team; a maximum of one hundred men were to be detached for six months. In comparison, Messerschmitt's development team numbered 1,400.

By the end of 1943 the superiority of German equipment and the resilience of German industry were acknowledged by Allied intelligence. Yet even those admissions were based on astonishing underestimates of German production. In adversity German industrialists, engineers, and scientists were constantly innovating and producing superior weapons, and the Ministry of Economic Warfare's Enemy Branch conceded that Germany was still turning out armaments "on an exceedingly formidable scale."[29] Within one year, Erhard Milch (the Luftwaffe's general field marshal) and Speer had expanded Germany's aircraft production by a phenomenal 50 percent. Allied intelligence was simply unable to imagine such industry.[30] The Ministry of Economic Warfare estimated that German fighter production in May 1943 was 765; the true figure was 1,013. MEW estimated that bomber production in August 1943 was 435; in fact, it was 710. Allied intelligence estimated that German industry was producing about 1,500 planes per month in 1943–44, whereas production was rising steadily from 2,100 aircraft per month in April 1943 to 4,219 aircraft in July 1944.[31] The mistake was admitted at the end of 1943. According to the official history of British intelligence, "MEW completed the retreat from the expectations that had been harboured in Whitehall during the first three years of the war: the blows sustained by Germany in the first half of 1943 had been heavier than in any previous period, but there had been no corresponding deterioration in her power to fight."[32] Despite the air offensive, German industry was breaking previous production records, while civilian food rations were down a mere 10 percent from prewar levels.[33] It was the Allied recognition of these achievements that set the scene for the most crucial attack on German scientific resources during the entire war. The target was the rocket research center at Peenemünde.

On the night of August 17, 1943, the whole might of Britain's Bomber Command, six hundred aircraft, attacked Peenemünde, thus successfully delaying by months the first arrival of the V1

"Doodlebug" rocket over London and averting a catastrophe on the Normandy beaches the following year. Yet the Cabinet approved the raid on Peenemünde only after enormous strife, with opponents arguing that the risk to Britain's only strike force was excessive. In the event, the casualties were indeed heavy, but the root of their opposition was more fundamental.

For months, British politicians, scientists, and service and intelligence chiefs had bitterly disagreed among themselves as to whether German scientists had developed a rocket. The scientific experts in the Cabinet, led by Cherwell, disputed the possibility that Germany could be the source of a new scientific era. These detractors of the German achievement would have been shocked to know that the V2 had already been successfully launched at Peenemünde on October 3, 1942, and that after Bomber Command's raid, the launches continued from Blizna, in Poland.

Peenemünde had been bought by the Luftwaffe on the recommendation of General Walter Dornberger and Werner von Braun in April 1936. The whole area was effectively sealed off to the outside world while von Braun's team developed a succession of inventions: revolutionary fuel of 75 percent ethyl alcohol in liquid oxygen, a 1.5-ton thrust motor, and the 40-centimeter cross-section wind tunnel. But at the outbreak of war the team was still unsuccessful, and Hitler slashed its funds and its priority claim to materials. Despite its fall from favor, von Braun's team continued to work with almost mystic fervor and deft political opportunism until its first successful launch and 118-mile flight in October 1942. After watching a brilliantly deceptive film of the team's work, Hitler was persuaded to authorize the highest priority for the rocket's mass production. According to Albert Speer, the Führer's previous reluctance had been overcome by a fanatic vision that in a single strike five thousand of the one-ton warheads would soon be dropped on Britain.[34]

Dribbles of clues about German rocket developments had been arriving in London since the "implausible" Oslo report in 1939. These were methodically filed and forgotten. For British intelligence, the early evidence was understandably too tenuous, if only because the Allies had not developed anything similar. Nearly four years later the debate reopened. Two German generals, Wilhelm von Thoma and Ludwig Cruewell, captured in North Africa, were deliberately left in a bugged room. Unwittingly, they revealed their surprise that London had not yet been attacked by the wonder rockets. Their conversation coincided with the receipt in London in March 1943 of a report from a neutral agent who had visited Peenemünde. Within three weeks the Chiefs of Staff had recommended to Churchill the appointment of Duncan Sandys to independently analyze the available intelligence.[35]

As a trained pilot who had also been posted to Britain's rocket research station at Aberforth, in North Wales, Sandys was eminently suited for the task, which was code-named "Bodyline." In the absence of reliable intelligence hunters, the chiefs' nomination of an outsider was an explicit admission that technical intelligence was by now too important to be the victim of vested interests. But for Churchill's personal scientific adviser, Lord Cherwell, Sandys's appointment was anathema — not only because of Sandys's personal relationship with the prime minister, but because Cherwell had long been convinced that a large rocket was a technical impossibility. In submitting his strong doubts to Churchill, Cherwell was supported by Britain's preeminent rocket expert, Dr. Alwyn Crow, the controller of projectile development at the Ministry of Supply. Crow had been appointed by the Committee of Imperial Defense in July 1936 to develop an anti-aircraft rocket. By 1940 he had developed basic but effective short-range two- to five-inch rockets, powered by solid cordite fuel. He had never considered anything more sophisticated, either in size or design. Any development of his cordite rocket to carry a one-ton warhead over one hundred miles would have been gigantic, weighing at least seventy tons. Even if such a monster could have been launched, both Crow and Cherwell dismissed the possibility of inventing satisfactory guidance and stabilizing systems. Cherwell conceded that the Germans might well have perfected a small pilotless plane carrying a bomb, but he vastly minimized its powers of destruction and believed the Germans were more likely to have built special guns firing rocket shells.

For three weeks Sandys pored over reconnaissance photographs of the Peenemünde site, guided by Cherwell and Crow's diktat of the components vital to any successful rocket project — namely, factories to build explosives for solid fuel. Neither British scientist had considered the possibility that von Braun's rocket was powered by liquid fuel, thus dramatically reducing the rocket's weight and requiring totally different production facilities. Misleadingly briefed, Sandys's photoreconnaissance experts were vainly searching for the wrong clues, and at the end of April 1943 Sandys reported. "It is clear that a heavy long-range rocket is not an immediate threat."

Unknown to Sandys, Isaac Lubbock, a modest Shell engineer, was at that time pioneering a very small research project into liquid fuel for rockets. In August 1942 Crow had visited Lubbock's Horsham laboratories and witnessed a successful experiment. But Crow was so wedded to his own solid-fuel development that he stubbornly ignored Lubbock's work throughout the following year and simply did not believe that an effective liquid-fueled rocket could be built, since no Allied engineer had designed a pump that could supply the fuel quickly enough to the rocket's combustion chamber. In fact, von Braun's expert, Walter Thiel, had perfected a revolutionary turbo-pump driven by a gas turbine.

During June 1943 Sandys was inundated with apparently confirmatory photographs of increased activity at Peenemünde, as well as intercepts and agent reports of German rocket developments, including liquid fuels, and, most important of all, a note from R. V. Jones revealing that Sandys's experts had overlooked a rocket in one of their own reconnaissance photographs taken over Peenemünde. Fearful of the enormous cost that a rocket onslaught on London would cause (it was estimated that each rocket would inflict four thousand casualties), Sandys recommended on June 28, 1943, that Peenemünde be destroyed by Bomber Command. Cherwell disagreed with Sandys's conclusion, and the two began to compete vigorously for the prime minister's support.

The following night senior politicians, service chiefs, and experts met in the underground War Cabinet room off Horse Guards Parade to settle the conflicting evidence. With Churchill in the chair, Cherwell resorted to a hoary argument that he had himself contemptuously dismissed in previous disputes. It was impossible, he claimed, to believe that German scientists had so colossally preempted British and American scientists. Churchill then asked Jones to produce his rebuttal. Although the young scientist could still not explain how the rocket was fueled, guided, or stabilized, he produced a torrent of consistent intelligence from divergent sources, which overwhelmingly convinced the prime minister. Churchill ordered Peenemünde to be destroyed at the earliest possible moment. Cherwell was bruised and crestfallen, although the victors had endorsed his own argument of a decade earlier that the course of any modern war would be determined by the possession and use of scientific advantages.

Bomber Command's attack on Peenemünde was a tacit acknowledgment that in the war against Germany, the overwhelming numerical might of the Allies might be neutralized by German scientific developments. Ordered to gamble the entire strength of his forces on the mission, Sir Arthur Harris briefed four thousand Allied airmen not just to bomb the factories but to kill the scientists and engineers. Radar pathfinding equipment was to be used to lead the force to its target, and Window was to be used against German radar, together with a deception plan designed to lure the entire strength of the Luftwaffe's night-fighter interceptors into combat against an apparent raid over Berlin, 120 miles south. The raid was unprecedented; it was also successful. Although several important buildings escaped and among the important scientists only Walter Thiel was killed, Peenemünde ceased to be the central German research station. Production was slightly delayed while a vast underground assembly factory under construction at Nordhausen, in the Harz Mountains, was rapidly completed. By the beginning of November, production of twelve thousand V2s had already started, yet both Cherwell and Crow still refused to accept that the Germans had succeeded in building a rocket.

On August 27, 1943, the Secret Intelligence Service completed a review of Sandys's Bodyline intelligence. The most important sources were 159 agent reports, a sketch from a worker in Peenemünde, and a high-grade agent inside the Waffenamt, the Ministry of Armaments, in Berlin. The SIS review concluded that the Germans were in fact developing not one but two kinds of rockets. Besides the pure rocket in Peenemünde, there was also a smaller flying bomb, or pilotless aircraft, which became known as the V1. Its genesis was remarkable in the light of Hitler's wasted opportunities.

At the outbreak of the war German scientists were developing a new jet-engined plane (the Me 262), a rocket aircraft (the Me 163), and the Wasserfall anti-aircraft rocket. All three, however, had become casualties of the savage financial cuts ordered by Hitler in 1940, when he confidently believed that the war would be over before they could be operational. In the meantime, German engineers had incorporated the jets into a flying bomb with a one-ton warhead, which was designed to be catapulted from ramps into flight. Production of the V1 was authorized after a successful test in early December 1942, with the hope that they would be launched from northern France by November 1, 1943.

When Cherwell and Crow read the SIS review, they might have

been expected to reconsider their views. Combined with photore-connaissance, POW interrogations, intercepts, and Hitler's own speeches promising the German people that a secret weapon would soon exact revenge for British bombing, the review should have been sufficient to convince them that German scientists were more advanced; and their last lingering doubts should surely have disappeared in early October, when Lubbock's assistant, Geoffrey Gollin, described in detail the feasibility of a liquid-fuel rocket. In a series of heated meetings throughout the month, Crow and Cherwell found themselves gradually isolated, but Crow nevertheless ruthlessly dismissed all the evidence: "We are of the opinion that . . . the possibility of such a [rocket] development in Germany can be ruled out."

Toward the end of October, Lubbock hurriedly returned from America to reveal that American engineers had recently designed the all-important gas-turbine pump. At a tense meeting, Crow sourly ignored the news and, with equal self-assurance, dismissed the most recent photoreconnaissance photos of the Peenemünde rockets as "inflated barrage balloons." For a moment there was silence; then Colonel Kenneth Post, Sandys's assistant, asked the government specialist why balloons would be transported on heavy rail wagons. Crow was left speechless. On October 25 Churchill chaired a Defense Committee meeting to consider all the new evidence, especially Lubbock's rapidly drawn but accurate sketch of the possible German rocket. The verbal, intellectual, and personal clash between Cherwell and Lubbock was vitriolic and ruthless. The shocked Shell scientist was castigated by the professor as "a third-rate engineer," meddling in a "mare's nest." Three days later, in Downing Street, the prime minister finally sided with Lubbock. But within three days, frustrated by his own scientific limitations and baffled by the problem of launching a long-range rocket by any method other than from a tube, Crow publicly attacked Lubbock, again insisting that the alleged rocket was technically impossible.[36] In unison, Crow and Cherwell exploited the confusion between the photographic evidence of the ski ramps being built on the French coast (for the V1s) and the alleged launch sites for the V2 rockets located in Peenemünde. Neither could accept that German scientists had developed two rockets. The V1 was, both argued, too small to be dangerous, and both drew comfort from the absence of rocket attacks against Britain. The dispute was temporarily calmed on November 15 when the Bodyline investigation was replaced by "Crossbow," a more intensive Joint Intelligence Committee investigation into all of Germany's long-range weapons.

Until December 1943 the unresolved argument was strictly contained within the British Cabinet. Unwilling to expose their confusion and disagreements, the British only decided to share their dilemma with the Joint Chiefs of Staff in Washington once the existence of the V1 was irrefutably confirmed by photographs of the ramps in France. The threat had now become imminent, and American help was needed. Until the British disclosure, Vannevar Bush and other American scientists had also doubted the feasibility of launching a rocket carrying a one-ton warhead and believed that the secret German threat was bacterial and germ warfare, possibly delivered by rocket. After the briefing in early 1944, Washington agreed to divert a large section of its bomber force to destroy the ramps on the French coast. Hitler could not have wished for a better diversion from Berlin. Hundreds of tons of Allied bombs fell on the fields of France, killing French farm laborers and only temporarily delaying the first V1 attack.

On June 13, 1944, a batch of V1 rockets was fired toward London, just one month after British experts had inspected a crashed specimen in Sweden, which lay at the end of the trajectory from the rocket firing range. Instead of fulfilling Hitler's dream of five thousand flying bombs falling on the capital, during the first night just four landed and exploded — but they were sufficient to accelerate the reluctant acceptance of Germany's scientific achievement. Seventy more V1s followed two days later. The capital, which had enjoyed relative peace since the blitz three years earlier, reacted in terror to the new crisis. On June 19, Sandys was specially recalled by the War Cabinet from France to coordinate emergency countermeasures. Three hundred seventy missiles had landed in London by July 5 and the death toll was mounting toward 2,500. Successful hits on power stations, transport systems, and hospitals had immobilized a quarter of the city. In desperation, Churchill considered retaliating with poison gas, but Sandys suggested that the best form of retaliation was to destroy the storage tanks believed to contain the rocket's fuel, hydrogen peroxide. Peroxide's apparently remarkable qualities filled the British military with awe of German achievements — but only the V1's catapult used peroxide; the rocket itself was powered by aviation fuel. The end of August saw the climax of the V1 assault. Colonel Max Wachtel fired a record 316 rockets at London within just twenty-four hours. One hundred and seven landed, one exploding at Tower Bridge. Londoners were petrified. At the same moment, von Braun had finally perfected the V2.

British experts had in June returned to Sweden to inspect the first crashed V2, buried in a huge crater but leaving sufficient evidence of its pedigree. At a stormy Crossbow committee meeting on July 18 chaired by Churchill, R. V. Jones presented the prime minister with an intelligence summary stating that the Germans had produced about one thousand V2s.[37] Churchill, Cherwell, and Sandys were furious, convinced that Jones had withheld information that would have helped them conclude earlier that Germany did after all possess a rocket. As retribution, Jones was removed as the Crossbow coordinator.[38] The real culprit was of course Cherwell, who subsequently admitted to Churchill that both he and Crow had suppressed a report written in Crow's department proving the feasibility of building a rocket. But it was only now, after analyzing the rocket debris brought from Sweden, that scientists in London realized that von Braun's pride was fueled by liquid oxygen, not peroxide.

On September 8 a sonic boom cracked across London, causing startled confusion. The explosion left no doubts. By the end of the day Jones, Cherwell, and the other members of the Crossbow committee had received firsthand evidence after two years of acrimonious speculation. Examination of the rocket's debris revealed an astonishing scientific achievement. The thirteen-ton missile had been fired into the stratosphere from Holland, two hundred miles away, and its guidance system had brought it down on target with pinpoint accuracy. Officials both in London and Washington realized that their only defense was to overrun the launching sites. But a more realistic objective was to discover the rocket's secrets.

In July, as the Red Army advanced toward the Blizna missile center, Churchill had cabled Stalin, asking him, in the interests of Allied cooperation, to allow inspection by a joint British-American team of specialists.[39] Permission was granted for Colonel Terence Sanders from the Ministry of Supply and the American colonel John O'Mara, together with an assortment of experts, to travel circuitously to Moscow and onward to Poland. On their arrival, on August 19, Sanders and O'Mara were told by Soviet generals that Blizna was still in German hands, although the site had in fact been captured two weeks earlier. Suspicious but helpless, the team finally arrived at Blizna on September 2 to discover that the Russians were unprepared to share their spoils. Members of the mission were able to pack what remained of the rocket debris into crates, but when they opened them in London, they found that they contained rusting aircraft parts. Russian policy for the plunder of Germany had been eloquently revealed.

4

Planning Plunder

ON THE EVE of the Normandy landings, both American and British army chiefs privately acknowledged that their soldiers, fighting with inferior weapons, would suffer an enormous disadvantage. "German equipment," unashamedly admitted Lieutenant General Sir Ronald Weeks, the deputy chief of the Imperial General Staff, "is as good or better than ours."[1] Weeks declared that the immediate seizure of German research, design, and development projects was "one of the most vitally important of our immediate postwar aims. . . . It may be that this is the only form of reparation which [it] will be possible to exact from Germany. Everything possible to ensure that it is exacted must be carefully planned now."[2]

Weeks was concerned that after Germany's defeat, British forces would not be properly equipped to fight the Japanese war, which, according to Allied strategists, might continue for another three years. Pessimistic about obtaining sufficient military supplies from America and about the prospects for British industry's improving its product, Weeks proposed to rearm the British army with German equipment by keeping munitions factories in Germany open after the defeat and selling obsolete British weapons to the newly liberated European Allies — a proposal that one Foreign Office cynic questioned as "selling duds to the natives?" But even Weeks was cautious about the chances of success. It was the first time an army had been intent on seizing ideas as well as material.[3]

By early April, Weeks's plan was developed by the Enemy Research and Development Committee into a blueprint for the seizure of Germany's leading research and development institutes specializing in everything from missiles to guns and from armor to mines. Under the plan, "sealing and holding" parties with priority status would travel with frontline infantry units to seize objectives of "exceptional importance."[4] These were to be followed by specialist "Investigation of Enemy Technique" groups, accompanied by interpreters, to interrogate German personnel.[5] On paper, it seemed masterful — but when Weeks's proposal was formally presented,[6] a mere thirty-eight German targets had been identified,[7] and the manpower requirement was limited to just 150 men. The birth of the plunder operation was hopeful but inauspicious.

Unknown to Weeks, both the RAF and the navy had similar ideas, although their objectives were markedly different. The RAF, still complacent about its technical superiority, limited its targets to radar. In contrast, the Admiralty, which since the disasters of 1940 had bitterly acknowledged German technical superiority in every field except radar, had compiled a detailed plunder list: mines, torpedoes, submarines, guns, detection devices, and communications. Captured German seamen had been scrupulously questioned and their equipment minutely investigated to discover the manufacturers and their locations. These were listed as black, gray, or white targets depending on priority. Nevertheless, the plan lacked manpower and did not have the Joint Chiefs' approval.[8]

Victor Cavendish-Bentinck, director of the Joint Intelligence Committee, was delegated to resolve the disarray. It was a fateful decision, since the JIC's task was to supervise and coordinate the gathering of pure intelligence, and it did not possess the experience to understand or assemble technical details of weapons design and manufacture. Instinctively, Cavendish-Bentinck, in creating a new agency, the Intelligence Priorities Committee, to supervise the operation, described its task in terms of a historic research project rather than a hunt for new technology. The IPC's role, he emphasized, was "to discover the methods used by Germany to increase her war potential, because it is only through the knowledge of the success of these methods that we are able to . . . perfect our intelligence system for the future." Once Cavendish-Bentinck's plans had been approved, the U.S. Chiefs of Staff were invited to become equal partners in the IPC — which thus evolved into the Combined Intelligence Priorities Committee — and were asked to compile and coordinate a "black" target list. But the Americans were even less prepared for the operation than the British.[9]

Since the outbreak of war, the U.S. Office of Scientific Research and Development's mission in London, under Bennett Archambault, had sheltered a steady increase of American scientific intelligence officers who had willingly accepted the free offer of British skills and sent the details back to the States for development. John Burchard, an architect who was studying the effects of bombing, and Dr. Howard Robertson, a Princeton mathematical physicist, organized the insertion of American experts into British factories, and research and intelligence units. Burchard had systematically toured British scientific institutions and factories in order to understand every aspect of war and weapons research, while Robertson developed close links with British tactical units. They were amply rewarded: The motor and fuse of Alwyn Crow's solid-fuel rocket, missile radar, antisubmarine rockets, and torpedo technology were all substantially more advanced than the Americans'. "Great Britain's scientific mobilization for the war," records the OSRD official history, "was extremely impressive, but her engineering resources were not of comparable strength. . . . In terms of usable knowledge gained, it is probable that the United States was the principal beneficiary in the intensive wartime scientific and technical interchange."[10] Nevertheless, Burchard and Robertson's contribution to British scientific investigations was significant. Robertson had sat on the Crossbow committee, and together with Lord Cherwell, the two Americans had painstakingly established that the chemical composition of Allied bombs generated explosions astonishingly inferior to those produced by the Germans.

From their OSRD experience, Burchard and Robertson gained an insight that those in Washington still lacked. To alert the military to the importance of scientific intelligence, Vannevar Bush — OSRD's director — had sent personal letters to all the theater commanders in chief explaining the value of scientific intelligence teams: "Many examples could be cited in which we have improved our equipment because of studies of enemy equipment."[11] The examples he mentioned revealed his own limitations: fuses, a range finder, the addition of stabilizing vents to rockets, and the German 75-millimeter recoilless gun. Bush urged the commanders to allow teams from every service to accompany their assault forces in order to "win the race against souvenir hunters and the destroyers of enemy equipment." The recipients were apparently unimpressed. Bush did not receive a single reply.

Beyond the military, however, one American intelligence operation, the "Alsos mission," was under way that would eventually
sweep through Germany, surreptitiously scooping up a wealth of
German expertise. The Alsos mission's prime aim was to establish
whether Hitler's scientists had made similar progress to the "Manhattan Project," in New Mexico, which was developing an atomic
bomb. The Americans' anxiety was well justified. German atomic
research went back a long way. Just before Christmas, 1938, Otto
Hahn, working at the Kaiser Wilhelm Institute in Berlin, had succeeded in isolating pure uranium 235. Within days, news of his
monumental breakthrough spread among the small international
network of nuclear scientists, but for nearly two years it excited
little curiosity among outsiders. Although Roosevelt appointed an
advisory committee on uranium in 1939, he showed scant interest
thereafter.

It was only after Dunkirk and the arrival in London of Hahn's
former colleagues, Jews who had originally fled Nazi Germany for
France, that British intelligence understood the potential of the
weapon that Hahn's collaborator, Werner Heisenberg, was trying
to develop.[12] By then Germany's advance seemed impossible to
stem. On instructions from Berlin, during the Blitzkrieg in Europe,
German specialists had seized what scientists still believed were
the vital elements for the manufacture of a bomb: thirty-five hundred
tons of high-grade uranium compounds stored in Brussels, the heavy-
water reactor at Vemork, Norway, and a nearly completed cyclo-
tron from Professor Frederic Joliot's atomic laboratory in Paris.
German scientists were two years ahead of the Allies — but, according to Albert Speer, the Führer was not interested: "Hitler had
sometimes spoken to me about the possibility of an atom bomb,
but the idea quite possibly strained his intellectual capacity. . . . In
the two thousand two hundred recorded points of my conferences
with Hitler, nuclear fission comes up only once, and then is mentioned with extreme brevity."[13]

The Allies did not even suspect such indifference until after the
war. What they did realize, however, was the German reliance on
heavy water, especially from the Vemork plant. Its destruction was
deemed vital. Briefed by the SIS, a Special Operations Executive/
Combined Operations attack was dispatched to Norway on November 19, 1942. The two gliders carrying the commandos crashed,
and the survivors were executed. A second attack on February 28,
1943, was more successful, but the plant was not finally destroyed

until November 1943 by U.S. Air Force bombers. Although the Manhattan Project had long since discarded heavy water as necessary for an atomic bomb, the Allied attacks reassured Heisenberg that heavy water was the key to enriched uranium.

In late 1943 broadcasts from Berlin threatened the Allies with new secret weapons. Major General Leslie Groves, in command of the Manhattan Project, feared the worst: "I could not help but believe that the Germans, with their scientific capacity and with their extremely competent group of first-class scientists, would have progressed at a rapid rate and could be expected to be well ahead of us."[14] Groves proposed that Alsos investigators, sworn to total secrecy and led by Lieutenant Colonel Boris Pash, be sent in early 1944 to newly liberated Italy to investigate. The mission returned without any clues. Pash was blamed for the failure, and his nine-man team, easily overwhelmed by the multitude of other Allied intelligence agencies, was criticized for lacking investigative experience.

Hence, when Pash and his colleagues arrived on June 17, at the first Combined Intelligence Priorities Committee meeting in London as part of the American team, they felt themselves wanting in sophistication.[15] The contrast between the U.S. leader, Brigadier General T. J. Betts — from the Anglo-American headquarters, SHAEF (Supreme Headquarters Allied Expeditionary Force) — and the British chairman, Professor R. P. Linstead of the Ministry of Supply, overawed the American team. At their first meeting Linstead laid before Betts a list of targets in Germany and the blueprint for their seizure. The listed targets were those with "such material, personnel and information of military . . . importance, either of great value to the Allies for operational purposes, or constituting a dangerous potential threat in the future, as justify urgent action on the part of the Allies in seizing them both before and immediately after an armistice." Completely unprepared, Betts's team was overly impressed by what Commander Henry Schade, the U.S. Navy representative, who had been on the Alsos mission in Italy, described as "an imperial performance." Schade immediately complained to Washington: "British preparations are well ahead of ours. If we rely on them, we'll get nothing."[16] Samuel Goudsmit, a civilian scientist also on the Alsos mission, sent the same complaint, urging Bush to galvanize the paralyzed Washington desk officers who were "putting obstacles" in his way: "The British part of the committee, formerly the IPC, had made previous extensive preparations. As a result, the Americans, in my opinion, are definitely at a disadvantage, and all the time put before a fait accompli, and have to accept the British point of view."[17]

This image of the suave and competent British was deceptive. Although, unlike the Americans, the British military had already understood the importance of technical intelligence, the appointment of Linstead, an ineffectual and fastidious civil servant, suffocated at birth any possibility of a huge British seizure operation. Unable to give orders to the military, Linstead had interpreted the IPC's role as that of a clearinghouse supplying SHAEF with information rather than that of an executive agency — and, despite the enormous scope of the operation, he appointed a mere handful of secretaries as his total staff.[18]

Within four weeks Betts, claiming the committee was flawed, arranged for its dissolution. The replacement, with Betts as chairman, was called the Combined Intelligence Objectives Subcommittee: CIOS, soon to be unaffectionately known as CHAOS.[19] The harsh reason behind the American coup was the crisis on the Normandy beaches, where Allied troops found themselves equipped with many weapons that were inadequate compared with the Germans'. CIOS was suddenly too important to be the responsibility of a docile civil servant.

Allied officials were appalled by the casualties in Normandy. Between July 20 and August 12, the U.S. Second Armored Division lost 70 percent of its tanks and half its combat personnel. Its weakest spot was the Sherman tank, which was mercilessly outgunned by the giant Tigers and Panthers. One frontline report described how, even when the Shermans got close enough, American shell "ricocheted off the thick armour and went screaming into the air." Another reported that "One Sherman fired fourteen rounds of 76mm ammunition at a Tiger before it had any success at all and the next moment was destroyed by another Tiger."[20] The Allied advance into the heart of France staggered and occasionally faltered. Crews in armored vehicles often hesitated to go forward until they had mounted captured German periscopes and automatic weapons on their own vehicles for protection against snipers. A dispatch to the *New York Times* from France summed up the plight of the Sherman tank crews:

> Why at this late stage of the war are American tanks inferior to the enemy's? That they are inferior, the fighting in Normandy showed. . . . This has been denied, explained away and

hushed up, but the men who are fighting our tanks against much heavier, better armoured and more powerfully armed German monsters, know the truth. . . . This does not mean that our tanks are bad, they are not; they are good. They are the best tanks in the world — next to the Germans.

The British had learned some lessons from technical intelligence and equipped the British Shermans with a seventeen-pound gun that was infinitely more effective than the American 75-millimeter six-pounder, but they had ignored everything else. In a comparison of British and German tanks for politicians, the Tank Board conceded that German tanks possessed better guns in the 88-millimeter twenty-pounders but insisted that the decision was deliberate. The Germans had shown "complete disregard for crew comfort or well-being in any shape or form." As a result, their tanks had less stowage space.

For the vulnerable Sherman crews, comfort was hardly the most important consideration, and word quickly spread among Allied infantrymen that, because of inferior weapons, they too were imperiled. Artillery gunners discovered that while their gun pads disintegrated after firing three hundred rounds, German pads, made of synthetic rubber, withstood 1,800 rounds. The barrel of the American 50-caliber machine gun eroded after eight hundred rounds, while German barrels lasted for five thousand. American bazookas and antitank guns were ineffective compared with the German hollow-charge heavy rockets (the *Panzerschreck*) and high-performance light antitank weapons. Both, according to Allied intelligence, were "being issued on a very lavish scale."[21] During any lull in fighting, American troops would scour the battlefield to retrieve abandoned guns and ammunition. From Field Headquarters, Lieutenant General McNair, Ordnance's chief of tank research, poured out a stream of complaints to his old adversary, Major General Barnes, Ordnance's chief of research, about the worn-out gun tubes, and Barnes spiritedly returned his complaints with reminders about McNair's earlier lack of interest. By then a steady flow of German equipment had arrived at the Aberdeen testing ground from Enemy Equipment Intelligence teams in France, producing reports that confirmed the superiority of German artillery, ballistics, electronics, engineering, opticals, fuses, ammunition, and metal. These findings evoked a hail of protest at Allied inadequacy from both the veterans and the new converts to weapons intelligence.

In Washington, Bush was dismayed by the European command's resistance to new weapons such as radar-directed bombs and rockets designed for aircraft attacks on tanks. "I am much disturbed," he wrote, "that it does not even appear to be included in the basic doctrine."[22] Bush's complaint "that something is wrong somewhere" was unhesitatingly returned to him from Air Force Headquarters. Brigadier General H. M. McClelland claimed that while none of the radar devices, rockets, or bombs were more than experimental and the ground forces were insufficiently educated to use them, "the important thing is, we're doing the job." Bush silently blamed Hap Arnold, who had flippantly retorted during one argument: "Why use a rocket when you can use a bomb?"[23] While Arnold had not understood the greater accuracy of a rocket, McClelland's reply echoed critical observations by Bush's staff that even the few talented senior officers in the army's "top-side" were too overstretched to consider any changes: "I am sufficiently conservative to believe," wrote Edward Bowles, a scientist on Bush's staff, "that in an organization as ponderous as the Army, no simple means, such as intellectual pressurizing, will yield substantial and outstanding results."[24]

The hardened resistance against innovation at the top was not shared by the younger, battle-scarred lower ranks. Plundering Germany's industry had become an imperative, but the predominance of British intelligence still rankled. "It is absolutely necessary," reported Air Intelligence to Washington in a communication that showed the level of American distrust,

> that the US have a complete and independent intelligence agency at the time of and immediately after cessation of hostilities. Participation in a combined intelligence agency with the British is essential to assure that we have access to intelligence that is uncovered in areas other than our own. However, to depend solely upon this combined agency would be dangerous in that, should bargaining develop concerning intelligence matters between the British and ourselves, we would have nothing to trade on and we would not have the alternative of pulling out of the combined set-up and resorting to unilateral exploitation of the German intelligence sources.[25]

There was immediate approval for both the Second and Ninth Air Forces to form intelligence sections. The seeds for postwar competition between the two Allies were firmly planted.

The importance of the prizes to be gained in such competition was more persuasively underlined by the sudden reality of new German jet fighters entering into the battle along the North European coast. On July 13, 1944, the deputy chief of the Air Staff warned Allied commanders that the new Luftwaffe jets were about to attack and that even the successful Mustang would be vulnerable. The assessment correctly stated that although both the Me 163 and the Me 262 were high-performance planes, the Me 163 suffered from "extravagant" fuel consumption, and neither could be produced in sufficient quantities to "interfere seriously with Allied air operations."[26]

In other respects, the assessment was deliberately deceptive. To protect morale, the Air Staff assured commanders that the Meteor, although delayed for another six months, would match the German jets. In truth, the Meteor was crippled by a myriad of design and production defects: Spent cartridges were hitting the plane, the hood came off at high speeds, and the engine was seriously unreliable, producing a top speed of only 400 miles per hour at just 15,000 feet, while the Me 262 flew at 540 miles per hour at 20,000 feet. The more advanced Vampire would not appear before 1946. Production of American aircraft was even more retarded. The Bell XP-59 was a failure and had been relegated to training use, while the Lockheed XP-80A would only be deployed, under the safest conditions, in 1945 to raise the morale of American pilots who had encountered German jets.[27] As the Allies advanced toward Paris, still enjoying overwhelming air superiority, their dilemma prompted two different responses. In Britain, Sir Wilfred Freeman of the Ministry of Aircraft Production recommended "a very drastic reduction" in jet production, which Air Staff chief Portal curtly rejected to prevent the balance from tilting in Germany's favor, while among the Americans, the reports sparked a determination to find the German jet designers.[28]

By August 1944 no fewer than twelve separate Allied organizations had been created. Spearheading the British venture was the 30 Assault Unit, a naval team organized in 1942 by Commander Ian Fleming, the bon vivant creator of James Bond, then serving as personal assistant to Rear Admiral John Godfrey, the director of Naval Intelligence. Fleming's "Red Indians" were intended as a team of intelligence hunters, modeled on a small Abwehr commando team that had successfully penetrated behind Allied lines before the 1941 assault in Greece and the Balkans to capture secret documents and cipher equipment.[29]

After overcoming considerable Whitehall opposition, Fleming's enthusiasm for a British elite technical intelligence group was rewarded, in November 1942, by the dispatch of the first 30 AU team to join "Operation Torch," the Allied invasion of North Africa, under the command of Duncan Curtis, an energetic officer with experience in special operations. But isolated from Operation Torch's intelligence headquarters, Curtis and his five-man pathfinder mission met with disaster. Helplessly marooned on a crippled destroyer outside Algiers Harbor as the first wave of troops rushed onto the beaches, their hope of capturing the French admiralty building intact, together with its secret ciphers, was dashed. Irritated and anxious to prove his importance, Curtis drove eastward, with huge white ensigns flapping, following Rommel's retreat through the desert, toward Bône.

Behaving like "armed and expert looters,"[30] the Red Indians plunged into unsavory controversy amid reports of fights, drunkenness, and thefts. Ironically, the commando group had begun its life self-defeatingly unaware that tactful diplomacy and negotiations with regular fighting units would determine its success. According to the unit's official history, "most of those originally selected lacked the qualifications and aptitude required for the particular type of work envisaged for the unit." Consequently, at the end of the North African campaign, when an inquiry revealed that valuable intelligence had been lost, the culpable "misfits" were returned to their regiments, and in the long term, British planning and headquarters staff were unable to assign the British team the priority rating needed to realize its ambitions.

After an unsuccessful campaign by new recruits in Sicily, the reorganized 30 AU's haul in Italy under the Arctic explorer Quentin Riley improved, but the unit's reputation again plummeted. Following a stream of complaints from regular officers about the "private army's" rampant indiscipline, looting, eccentric dress, and refusal to obey orders, in November 1943 Riley's men were ordered to return to London for investigation and immobilization, leaving the British Chiefs of Staff bereft until D day of any group capable of satisfying their growing appetite for scientific intelligence.

Despite reorganization, instead of parachuting with the airborne divisions hours before the D day landings, 30 AU's 150 men arrived on a landing craft the day after D day — a clear indication that they were regarded as unreliable. Charged with seizing the radar station at Douvres, ciphers and maps, samples of V1 rocket fuel, and the German naval headquarters at Cherbourg, the Normandy campaign started as it ended, in flamboyant style.

A 30 AU unit, "Woolforce," under Lieutenant Colonel A. Woolley, attached itself to the American VII Corps. Driving in jeeps and armored cars, the officers and their marine escort confirmed every Yankee prejudice about English eccentricity and amateurism. As they headed toward Cherbourg, they sent back to England a trickle of radar and rocket equipment, but most of their plunder was lost en route. During the battle for Cherbourg, Woolley was seriously injured. In his absence, his marines uncontrollably enjoyed the spoils of war and behaved like "merry, courageous, amoral, loyal, lying toughs, hugely disinclined to take no for an answer from foe or fraulein."[31] Even Fleming, in London, was impatient with his Red Indians, whom he renamed the "30 Indecent Assault Unit." Furiously, General George Patton ordered Woolforce to leave the American sector.

As the titillating reports of 30 AU's antics passed through SHAEF headquarters, Betts, the chairman of CIOS, recognized that the master plan agreed to by his committee was in tatters. Linstead had not sent the latest and comprehensive target lists, and amid the pressing operational crisis, a directive ordering all commands to establish independent T-forces to seize and guard named targets had been ignored by army commands pleading a shortage of manpower.[32] "For some months," admitted Brigadier G.H.C. Pennycook, the British T-force commander, "T-forces in the 21 Army Group were little more than an idea on paper." British headquarters, he volunteered, "knew little or nothing about the specific whereabouts and nature of their targets and the investigators . . . would know even less."[33]

As the German army retreated toward Paris, the value of scientific plunder was increasingly verified. A British intelligence report confirmed colossal German advantages in the whole range of weaponry on land, sea, and air.[34] German jets were described as "possessing exceptional performance"; the Luftwaffe had flying bombs of "great destructive power"; the radio-controlled Hs 293 and FX bombs had no "counterpart in the service of the Allies"; the Flamingo infrared receiver could allegedly detect aircraft exhaust fumes from a forbidding 16,000 yards; the A4 long-range rocket was "brilliant in conception and . . . difficult to counter"; and two revolutionary types of submarine, extremely fast and practically undetectable, were reported to be under construction, both possessing "abnormal speed" and *"Schnorkels"* that would enable them to recharge their batteries while submerged. The demand for information was enormous, but the Allied machinery to gather it appeared totally disorganized. Too many personnel, recently promoted Major General Kenneth Strong, SHAEF's intelligence chief, complained, lacked qualifications or were unsuited to infiltrate Paris in advance.[35]

Those recruited to the plunder operation believed that the first major opportunity to seize German secrets would be offered by the capture of Paris. The honor of being the first Allied unit to arrive in the French capital was claimed by both the Alsos and 30 AU teams. Pash, the Alsos leader, drove with Goudsmit amid sniper fire, to the laboratory of Dr. Frederic Joliot, the atomic scientist. With mischievous glee, Pash had telephoned Joliot the previous day advising him of their imminent arrival, and the Frenchman was still obediently waiting. But Joliot resolutely denied any German progress in developing an atomic bomb, a conclusion that was too much of an anticlimax to be acceptable by either American.

Similarly, 30 AU had been sure of capturing a wealth of secrets. With bravado and excitement, marine commando units, led by Woolley and T. J. Glanville, sped through the empty Paris boulevards to dozens of German naval quarters. At the Villa Rothschild, the principal German naval headquarters, the marines fought briefly with the defending Germans but found other buildings deserted, their sensitive material destroyed. Reluctant to believe that the Germans could have been so methodical, Glanville blamed French intelligence, claiming, "They got there before us."

The first CIOS field team of fifty-two civilian specialists arrived in Paris two days after its liberation, to be greeted within hours by military complaints of their ignorance.[36] For their part, the CIOS investigators complained that nearly every target they visited had already been cleaned out by Allied intelligence groups, that their passes were invalid, that the target descriptions were wrong, and that they were denied any opportunity to communicate with Britain.[37] Summarizing the fiasco, Strong reported a long list of grievances: no interpreters, no safe breakers, inadequate transportation,

T-forces leaving before the specialists arrived, and no one to meet the CIOS investigators.[38]

As the competition between the two Allies hardened, Strong noticed that whereas Montgomery's headquarters amateurishly allocated T-force duties to the chemical warfare team because they seemed "to be very enthusiastic and active in embarking on numerous treasure hunts," American servicemen arriving in Europe on the same errand boisterously insisted that they were "first among equals" and came equipped for success. Commander Henry Schade, once disgruntled by British preeminence, had returned to Europe as leader of Admiral King's new Naval Technical Mission, staffed by no fewer than two hundred experts, with a promise of unlimited transport and funds to roam Europe, and — to his delight — a personal airplane.

Sensing this shift in fortune, Strong suggested that Britain needed a unit equivalent to the Alsos mission, but his suggestion remained unanswered.[39] Instead, he received a curt dispatch from the U.S. Eighth Corps asking that the "function of 30 Assault Group be clarified considering their activities . . . appear to be creating aggravated situations." Strong replied that 30 AU's duties were well known and should continue. Unimpressed, Twelfth Army Headquarters demanded that the detachment be withdrawn.[40] Without ceremony, 30 AU abruptly returned to Britain, where new demands for the unit's disbandment were again considered but rejected because of Schade's impressive reappearance. By the time 30 AU returned to France, the hunt had become a free-for-all. "Experienced officers in the field," reported one bewildered officer, "are constantly aware of the good stuff they are unable to handle."

Behind the chaos, the investigators suddenly seemed to have touched a nerve. CIOS investigators arriving at their targets in France were curtly told by the French industrialists that they were unwilling to divulge any secrets. Inquiries by British and American rubber manufacturers, keen to discover the remarkable German formula for making synthetic Buna rubber, were resisted by French rubber manufacturers — who coolly pleaded that they had signed secrecy agreements with the departing Germans.[41] A high-level Anglo-American team investigating aircraft factories was bluntly denied access and told that these were private French corporations that, despite wartime collaboration, wanted to protect their secrets from peacetime competitors.[42] The investigators' reactions were mixed. While the American OSRD team simply accepted that the Germans had not trusted the French with high-priority research, the British were more cynical.[43] At SHAEF headquarters, Strong's staff had evidence confirming that the new French government had expressly forbidden their industrialists to divulge anything to the Allies.[44]

In the Netherlands and Belgium, the CIOS investigators faced similar treatment. David Nutting, who led the Anglo-American air force and CIOS team to the Phillips factory at Eindhoven, was not warmly welcomed: "The management kept on giving me excuses why they couldn't show me their latest navigational equipment. When they finally told me that their keys were lost to one box, I just broke it open. Inside was an interesting new radio altimeter." And when Harold Phelps of the Economics Advisory Branch arrived in Brussels to investigate factories producing tires, oxygen, and synthetic fats and soap, the best material had already disappeared. Other manufacturers pleaded secrecy. Disgruntled, Phelps sought help from CIOS but discovered that the organization barely existed.

The British felt that the Europeans were not entirely to blame. Officers at Montgomery's headquarters suspected that Alsos officers and American civilians unofficially attached to the Alsos team were misusing their powers. They were, claimed one irate British official who feared that the Americans were winning unfair advantages, "a bunch of disorganised looters on a par with Goering in an art gallery."[45] The grounds for outrage against private plunder were, of course, entirely justifiable. It was morally indefensible for buccaneering individuals to profit from other people's suffering — and the Allies had agreed that any plunder should be shared by the victors for common good. To prevent private looting, Montgomery's headquarters proposed to bar American industrialists from traveling without British "observers." The plan was rapidly discarded when American industrialists complained that their British competitors were putting out a smoke screen to conceal their own illegal plunder.[46]

Nevertheless, British suspicions seemed confirmed when a message sent from Paris by Sosthenes Behn, a director of the giant ITT telephone company, to his New York office was intercepted. Throughout the war, Behn had covertly and illegally maintained contacts with his empire's activities in Occupied Europe, having established close relations with important Nazi personalities and politicians before the outbreak of war. With Hitler's defeat imminent, Behn, like every other Allied investor, wanted to reassert ownership and control over his assets. But only the most intrepid — some would say the most ruthless — had, like Behn, managed to create the opportunity to realize their schemes. Dressed as an honorary colonel and described as a "special communications expert for the Army of Occupation," the tycoon successfully manipulated a passage to liberated Europe, making him possibly the first Allied civilian to land there. The message the British intercepted revealed that Behn had just clinched a secret and highly profitable deal with a French telephone corporation.[47]

Charles Peake at SHAEF headquarters was alerted to Behn's activities, but the communications magnate had already left Paris for Spain. His activities, however, had not ceased. Another intercept in December, this time from New York to an ITT agent in Madrid, revealed that Behn had skillfully arranged with his contacts in Washington for an ITT representative to be among the first to arrive in Berlin. The Foreign Office concluded that ITT was poised to simply absorb Siemens, Germany's leading telephone manufacturer. "If the American Titan can swallow and digest the German," commented an alarmed Foreign Office official, "I doubt whether British interests will get much of a show." At the Treasury, Edward Playfair admitted that the British were helpless: "I find it hard to think of anything which we ought to do, beyond of course, making sure when we get to Berlin that our arrangements do not permit Sosthenes Behn to send his people in to do what he likes, when he likes."[48]

By then it would of course be too late. The British already acknowledged that in the race for plunder, the Americans possessed many advantages. "Commercial information is what we want," Colonel Mountain and Colonel Keith — both British industrialists clad in uniform — told Mark Turner, a senior official at the British Control Office for Germany. "The scent is now hot and it will belong to the person who gets his hands on it first." Both "colonels" wanted to mobilize MI6 agents and intelligence units throughout Europe, especially in Switzerland, to seize German assets ahead of others. To their irritation, Turner was cool to the idea, refusing to violate Allied agreements despite the apparent breach by America in the case of Behn.[49] But Behn's seemingly maverick escapade was part of a calculated scenario. In November, the Joint Chiefs in Washington had established the Technical Industrial Intelligence Committee to hunt for both military and civilian industrial secrets.[50] Organized plunder teams were to be sent to Europe, among them two specialist groups approved by the Joint Chiefs, whose mission was to seize the German personnel who had secretly developed synthetic fuel. This target was chosen not out of scientific curiosity but, in the words of John McCloy, the assistant secretary of war, in order to protect "the legitimate interests of the United States" — namely, the Texas oil industry.[51]

Christmas, 1944, brought further vindication for those who, like Vannevar Bush, had pleaded the importance of science in warfare. On December 16, Field Marshal Gerd von Rundstedt had led a spectacular German offensive through the Ardennes forest against the weary and depleted U.S. First Army. Spurred on by the advantages of total surprise and bad weather, which grounded Allied planes, the German tanks sliced a murderous path toward the Meuse. Once again, the Shermans' armor appeared to be no stronger than cardboard, and most of the American guns were inadequate against the Panzers. New high-velocity ammunition with a tungsten-carbide core had arrived from America in November, but throughout the remainder of the war, supplies amounted to a derisory monthly allocation of two rounds per gun. Eisenhower's troops steadily retreated, waiting for the weather to improve and for salvation by the air force.

When the weather cleared, the air force was given special permission to use the proximity fuse bomb for the first time. Over the following days, its high-incendiary blast and shrapnel devastated the German ranks. Bush and others subsequently claimed that the fuse swung the balance decisively toward the Allies.[52] It was an exaggerated boast, but politically it served to embellish Bush's achievements.

For the American army, the way was now clear for the crossing of the Rhine, aptly code-named "Operation Plunder." What remained totally obscure was the amount of reparations and booty the Allies would extract from Germany. Britain's reserves had been exhausted in March 1941; since then, the war had cost a further $27 billion, financed by Congress's Lend-Lease Act. A new source of economic and industrial recovery was therefore vital.

The first serious discussions among civil servants about reparations had begun in November 1942, when William Malkin, the Foreign Office legal adviser, chaired an "interdepartmental com-

mittee on reparations and economic security." Mindful of the ap-
palling legacy of the onerous reparations imposed on Germany in
1919, Malkin wanted to destroy only those German industries that
produced military hardware and strategic chemical products.
Quoting history and statistics, trade and industry officials opposed
to Malkin passionately argued for stiffer retribution. Unless plans
were made to deprive Germany of her wartime loot and destroy
her dominant industrial and commercial grip over Occupied Europe, they argued, "Germany will be in such a position that she
will have 'won the peace' . . . in spite of military defeat."[53] Germany's economic disarmament, held the eminent economist Lionel
Robbins, was vital for Britain's trade.

Finding a balanced solution to these competing and contradictory requirements eluded even the brilliant economic triumvirate
of John Maynard Keynes, Lord Vansittart, and Hugh Dalton, the
labor minister for economic warfare. "I see no virtue," wrote Dalton, "in 'moderation', either in doing justice or in taking steps to
prevent a repetition of the German crime. Nor is it easy to defend
compensation for things carried away intact by the enemy, but not
for similar things destroyed by them in battle."[54] In contrast, the
Ministry of Economic Warfare argued that, regardless of Allied
policy, there would be a quick return to full employment in Germany, since it would be impossible to prevent wartime industrial
facilities from being converted to peacetime production. In Britain,
as in Germany, former baking-machinery factories were turning
out gun carriages, railway workshops were producing tanks, and
elevator manufacturers anti-aircraft guns. Conversion in the opposite direction would be no more difficult.

Malkin's lengthy and reasoned report of August 1943 excluded
all extremist demands. Malkin recommended a soft peace based
on the Atlantic Charter: Germany should be deprived of the means
to start another war but should eventually be able to become a
prosperous neighbor. "Nothing is more important or difficult,"
wrote Malkin, "than to ensure that any such system framed in the
atmosphere of total war . . . shall continue to appear to them, ten
or twenty years after the war, sufficiently just."[55] But Malkin conceded that principled generosity could be the Allies' own undoing:
"As the war itself has demonstrated, Germany is an immensely
efficient industrial organisation, capable of vast and sustained output." British industry compared miserably with the German com-

petition. Research on aircraft production showed that the German work force was up to twenty-five times more efficient than the British, and the German motor and shipbuilding industries were even more productive.[56] There was no doubt in Malkin's mind that if German industry was able to sustain similar efficiency in peacetime, bankrupt Britain would never recover. But ruthlessness was eschewed. Malkin's recommendations were confined to the complete destruction of Germany's aviation, armaments, and synthetic oil industries and to the severe limitation of her machine-tool industry. German reparations, suggested Malkin, should be small, since the lion's share would inevitably go to Russia and would be financed by Britain's subsidizing of German imports. His principles were blessed by Churchill, who declared, "It is not the purpose of the Allies to leave the people of Germany without the necessary means of subsistence."

Eighteen months later, after the liberation of Paris, to many people Malkin's view seemed too soft. In general, the British public was angered by the constant stream of reports about German atrocities, weary of the long war, and fearful of perpetual bankruptcy. Opinions in Britain hardened against excessive concern for the well-being of Germany as opposed to the well-being of her victims.[57] Germany, it was felt, should not be allowed to recover at Britain's expense. Representatives of the military and industrial departments who had not been members of the Malkin committee demanded destruction rather than reparations, especially of the competitive German shipbuilding, optical, and clock industries.[58] For those Allied governments exiled in London, the drift toward a tough policy was worrying. German industry, their ministers argued, was vital to Europe's recovery and would be the best source of weapons for the war against Japan.[59] One possible compromise, suggested by Whitehall's think tank, the EIPS (Economic and Industrial Planning Staff), was for British industry to extract Germany's superior technological know-how.[60] The only problem, wrote Mark Turner of the Control Office for Germany, was that British industrialists did not recognize their own shamefully "low standard of efficiency."[61]

Hugh Dalton and the trade ministry temporarily won the argument over reparations. Britain was second only to Russia in demanding huge quantities of German machinery and raw materials, and Arthur fforde, a civil servant, was ordered to compile a list of British demands. Seven weeks later, reflecting fears that a

German industrial revival would severely harm Britain's recovery, fforde produced a short report predicting £500 million worth of British demands over the following two years, and asked for suggestions regarding items of plunder.[62]

With the end of the war in sight, the sentiments that had been so carefully repressed during the fighting were now unleashed. Encouraged by an instruction that "departments should compile their estimates arbitrarily,"[63] government departments, industrialists, and the three armed services flooded fforde's committee with demands. The Admiralty listed not only the latest weaponry but bakeries, office and kitchen equipment, floating docks, and salvage vessels, too, while the Board of Trade wanted 59 million combs, 20 million pencils, and more than a billion boxes of matches. Daily Britain's list grew longer — and disappeared into the realm of fantasy when the Stationery Office submitted demands including 120 million buff envelopes, 120 million thick buff envelopes, 40 million sheets of greaseproof paper, and 100 million sheets of carbon paper. What Britain would ultimately receive depended entirely upon the agreement of Russia and America. But, as in Britain, ideas in Washington were confused.

At the end of June 1944, American embassy officials in London asked the Foreign Office to start negotiations on restitution and reparations.[64] The State Department's Committee on Postwar Programs had just completed a report that reflected many of Malkin's earlier proposals but that was substantially less developed. Before the first meeting could even be arranged, Henry Morgenthau, the U.S. secretary of the treasury and Roosevelt's neighbor and friend, dramatically intervened. On a visit to London, he had seen the SHAEF handbook, which contained a simplistic guide of Allied policy toward Germany. Morgenthau was appalled at its deliberate evenhandedness. On his return to Washington, he convinced the president that the Department of War's plans to rehabilitate postwar Germany were outrageous. At a White House meeting on September 2, Morgenthau unveiled his own Draconian proposals for the complete deindustrialization of Germany. What remained would be a harmless, pastoralized nation of peasants and cuckoo-clock manufacturers. Eleven days later, Morgenthau's plan was apparently endorsed by Roosevelt and Churchill in Quebec. But at the end of the month there was a complete volte-face. Both leaders withdrew their approval, and Roosevelt banned any further postwar planning for Germany. So, when Roosevelt and Churchill arrived in Yalta in February 1945, neither government had an agreed policy on reparations and returned home with nothing decided. Roosevelt's death added to the confusion. When Allied officials returned to the Soviet Union just weeks after the war to settle the reparations issue, the American team, led by Edwin Pauley, a power-seeking oilman, decided to ignore past agreements and policy considerations. Pauley was confident that he could decide Germany's future alone with the Russians. In the event, the Russians ignored him, leaving Germany open for plunder by those on the spot.

In London, the head of OSRD, Bennett Archambault, was by now totally dissatisfied with CIOS. Linstead had chaired ten meetings and resolved practically nothing. U.S. Army T-forces, on the verge of occupying Cologne, were complaining that despite the previous year's CIOS promise that "a complete list would be ready by August [1944]," six months later they were still waiting.[65] Despite Linstead's plan for a spearhead of three hundred and later one thousand investigators, Pennycook, commander of the T-forces, protested that it was still "astonishingly difficult" to get accurate information about targets.[66] Since Linstead stubbornly rejected all complaints, Archambault asked for a special meeting to resolve the crisis.[67] On February 28, thirty-two representatives of the rival American and British interests met in London under an American chairman, Colonel Bryan Conrad. Instead of reaching an agreement, the long meeting broke up in acrimony, with frustrated complaints about SHAEF's bureaucracy and only one decision: 30 AU should not be allowed to operate independently.[68]

For Archambault it was the last straw. Months earlier, his staff had tried to persuade Strong, the head of intelligence at SHAEF, to cooperate in "ferreting out" from Germany all the secret "scientific and technical subjects which can be beneficial to the Allies" but had despaired because there was no reply.[69] After the February meeting, with the agreement of the American military commanders, Archambault was allowed to establish an organization that would look after America's interests. OSRD experts were to accompany forward combat units to quickly judge the value of newly discovered technical secrets. These Consolidated Advance Field Teams (CAFT) would report back separately to Victor Fraenkel and Dr. Howard Robertson, who would then decide whether an officer from the new American agency called FIAT (Field Information Agency, Technical) was needed to interrogate a particular German scientist or analyze seized documents.

Leading the pack were eager American air force engineers. A memorandum to Churchill justified their excitement: "The United States and Britain are outstripped technically by the Germans . . . immediate steps should be taken to re-establish our position. This can be done only by a major effort of reconstruction."[70] The following intelligence summary bears witness to the extraordinary feats of German technology even in the eye of defeat. The report declared: "Owing to high speed, the enemy has been able to use his jet fighters in a fighter-bomber role successfully and with comparative immunity from Allied fighters. The Me 262 is equally excellent as an interceptor."[71] Another Air Intelligence report from Holland stated that a crashed FW 190 had been armed with "an entirely new rocket projectile" that was faster and better than British rockets.[72] Also from Holland came an analysis of the latest German 30-millimeter anti-aircraft weapon, the MX 108. Only forty-two inches long, it was "unique," and tests had shown that its ammunition "had great effect." Comparative production statistics showed that despite all the Allied bombing, estimated monthly production in the protected underground factories would have risen to 214 Me 262s by June 1945, in contrast to a mere thirty Meteors and sixteen Lockheed 180As.[73]

"If Germany has not been beaten before July 1945," Sir Charles Portal was told, "she will have dominance in the air over Germany and above the armies during the period of good flying weather."[74] The situation, Portal reassured the prime minister, "may be serious but should not be disastrous,"[75] since there were still few German jets and a very limited number of skilled pilots left to fly them. Yet as a stunt, Portal sent a scratch squadron of Meteors to Belgium in order to answer newspaper criticisms in Britain and to prevent the U.S. Air Force from capturing the headlines by landing the first Allied jets in Europe. But while Portal's preoccupation was to save the RAF's reputation, American air force teams were already scouring Germany to snap up every item of German expertise.

5

The Hunt

WHEN THE FIRST U.S. INFANTRY swept toward dense woodland outside Brunswick in North Germany in early April 1945, the frontline detachments feared desperate and vengeful SS soldiers were concealed in the undergrowth. But, to their surprise, there was neither shooting nor any sign of the enemy. Instead, slowly driving up the forest road toward the small village of Volkenrode, they discovered, cunningly camouflaged under one thousand acres of thickly planted trees, a large complex of low stone buildings. Zigzagging through the area, smashing down the doors, the soldiers found workshops, laboratories, parts of airplanes, engines, and huge earth-covered mounds, which they were later told were wind tunnels powered by electricity cables buried deep underground. As they swung their rifles, glass tubes splintered, microscopes crashed, and bundles of files scattered on the floor. Although the area was deserted, the unit soon discovered that it had arrived at the Hermann Goering Aeronautical Research Institute, the most sophisticated and advanced of its kind in the world. News of the find quickly reached G2 — U.S. Army Intelligence — and the CAFT teams behind the front lines — yet when the first intelligence officers arrived, none could quite understand what they had unearthed. Reference back to G2 confirmed that no Allied expert had ever heard of an aeronautical research institute at Volkenrode, and it was not marked as a target on any CIOS list. Unknown to the Allies, the institute had been established in 1935 and was operational at the outbreak of war. Its anonymity was damning confirmation of the failure of Allied scientific intelligence and the inherent weakness of the Allies' own research.

In early May, Colonel Donald Putt, an eager test pilot who had campaigned in the mid-thirties for the U.S. Air Force to adopt Flying Fortresses, arrived to inspect Volkenrode. Putt, who was leading "Operation Lusty," an air force search and plunder mission, was amazed. Walking through the complex, he realized that he was in the midst of probably the most magnificent and lavish research facility ever constructed. The sheer abundance and extravagance of the instruments, subsidiary tools, and testing equipment were awe-inspiring. In the aerodynamic section there were low-speed, subsonic, supersonic, and trans-sonic wind tunnels; the engine section was equipped with a camera that could take one thousand pictures a second to study the growth of a flame and that could simulate altitude conditions up to 50,000 feet; the armament section had two firing tunnels, 400 meters long, built to study the effect of 500-mile-per-hour crosswinds on missiles in flight. Among the first German scientists Putt met was Adolph Busemann, the inventor of the swept wing, who had been responsible for the supersonic wind tunnels and the rocket test station in Trauen. Busemann told Putt that throughout the war he and his fellow scientists had been granted every demand, regardless of expense, and that there was a similar institute in nearby Göttingen.

Days later, Theodore von Karmen, a U.S. Air Force scientific adviser, arrived to interrogate Volkenrode's directors. He too was astonished by such overwhelming evidence of German superiority. Busemann told von Karmen that he had given lectures about sweptwing jets as early as 1935 and that Volkenrode's wind tunnels were not the only ones. In a hillside in Kochel, a picturesque Bavarian village thirty-five miles south of Munich, was another wind-tunnel complex. Von Karmen's colleague, Dr. Fritz Zwicky of the California Institute of Technology, had already arrived at Kochel and reported that the Germans were "many years ahead of all other countries."[1] Dr. Rudolf Hermann, Kochel's director, had obligingly dug up his reports hidden two months earlier and, with his colleague, Dr. Hermann Kurzweg, proudly presented their impressive experiments on supersonic flight. Zwicky showed surprisingly little interest in the rumors that both Germans had been long-serving members of the SS, were ardent Nazis, and had held daily party rallies for their research team. Of much greater interest to him was the news that American troops had found a range of high-altitude test beds at Oberwiesenfeld, where jet engines were run at full speed in "normal flying conditions" — a huge advance on the cumbersome Allied practice of fixing the engines to flying planes.

The three Americans began discussing how to make best use of the German expertise and soon agreed that the most sensible solution was for the Germans to be transported across the Atlantic. Putt wrote at once to General Wolfe at Wright Field, in Ohio, and to Major General Hugh Knerr, deputy commander of the U.S. Strategic Air Force in Europe, reporting that he had discovered five German scientists "who would be of immense value in our jet engine and airplane development program," advancing the American program by at least two years. Wolfe and Knerr, Putt suggested, should lobby for permission for the five to be evacuated to Wright Field. After five years of unceasing anti-German propaganda and with the newspapers full of the newly publicized horrors of the concentration camps, it would not be an easy task. Nevertheless, Knerr, who had already received several similar requests, reported to General "Tooey" Spaatz, commander of the U.S. Strategic Air Force in Europe: "Occupation of German scientific and industrial establishments has revealed the fact that we have been alarmingly backward in many fields of research. If we do not take the opportunity to seize the apparatus and the brains that developed it and put the combination back to work promptly, we will remain several years behind while we attempt to cover a field already exploited." In common with many Allied scientific experts, Knerr presented an uncompromising demand: The Germans should be treated as fellow scientists, not as Nazis. They should be well paid and allowed to travel with their families, and critics who argued that the Germans were enemies should be told that "pride and face-saving have no place in national insurance."[2]

Spaatz passed Knerr's request to Washington, where the military was already distancing itself from the euphoria gripping the public. Now the priority was to defeat Japan — but there was also the longer term, and the air force, in particular, urgently needed to plan for the future. Early in 1945 General Hap Arnold — the commander of the U.S. Army Air Force — had asked von Karmen, his scientific adviser, to provide him with the "scientific ammunition" to launch a congressional campaign for adequate funds for postwar research. The mood then at the Pentagon was openly self-critical, and there was no attempt to hide the unpleasant truth that, while British and German research had forged ahead, in America "research and development of new weapons . . . for the period 1939–45"[3] had been "unsatisfactory." Other countries' success, wrote Arnold, had arisen out of "a different national psychology" toward research. It was therefore imperative that "necessary steps . . . be taken to permeate the entire AAF structure with a whole-hearted conviction and acceptance of the necessity for understanding the scientific way of doing things." Recently converted to the strength of von Karmen's case, Arnold urged the secretary of war that in future the air force, not private industry, should control the nation's research program. In the next war, air power would be the first-strike weapon, America the first target: "The United States must [therefore] be the world's first power in military aviation."[4]

There was no sense of boisterous bravado in Arnold's message; it was an earnest plea for support following the annihilation of a group of B17s on the very eve of Germany's surrender. Diving at 700 miles per hour out of the sun, six Messerschmitt 262s had attacked an unsuspecting raiding party of Flying Fortresses traversing Germany toward Berlin. Within minutes fourteen B17s had been destroyed, the victims of Germany's R4/M missile. Each German jet was armed with sixty of these missiles, which had first, and devastatingly, been used against American bombers over Schweinfurt in October 1943. Eighteen months later Allied aircraft still possessed no equivalent. For the Germans, the brief moment of glory was sparse comfort in the dying battle, but for Hap Arnold, the incident was a telling indictment of his air force's technical inferiority.

Throughout the war, neither Britain nor America had understood the importance of aircraft guns. As a result, aircraft armament did not figure on the investigators' priority lists. Both air forces had spent a great deal of time overcoming problems in this field that had been with them since World War I. Gun mechanisms froze at high altitudes, so antifreeze lubricants were needed; blocked cartridge belts meant renewed research to produce a power-driven belt; and research was also needed into the absorption of recoil. The design secret of the fast-shooting German guns — electrical firing of the cartridges — was rejected by experts in England and America alike as unreliable. Gun design, even for aircraft, was the monopoly of the army, and the army remained obdurately unimpressed by a Luftwaffe invention.

As the war ended, the German aircraft-gun design teams at Mauser and Rheinmetall-Borsig and the designers of the R4/M aircraft rocket prepared to offer their services to a CIOS team. Unable to appreciate the advanced technology, the Americans spurned the approach. Five years later, at the beginning of the Korean War, the same Germans were quickly recruited and spirited to the United States — but by then other members of their team had equipped the Russian MiG fighters with the world's best aircraft guns.

Arnold's ambition for a scientific air force was still a proposal pending political approval when, in May, Eisenhower's staff at SHAEF headquarters in Paris asked the U.S. War Department why its request for a definitive policy regarding the exploitation of German science and research remained unanswered.[5] Germany was already under Allied control, and the plethora of competing intelligence missions needed to be coordinated and monitored. Officially, SHAEF's policy was to close all German research stations and arrest their personnel, who were to be released only after exhaustive interrogation.[6] Some Allied investigators found that policy inflexible and self-defeating: It was vital, they felt, to keep the laboratories open in order to obtain information — and releasing the scientists might mean losing them forever. The crude remedy was imprisonment. Internment camps (code-named "Dustbin," "Ashcan," and "Backporch") for war criminals, important Nazis, and a few scientists had been established successively in Paris, Bad Kissengen, and lastly Kransberg Castle, near Frankfurt. Germans named on arrest lists were incarcerated to await the waves of military investigators, representing every interest, who passed through the camps, often asking the scientists the same questions and receiving the same answers. Arresting important Germans seemed the only possible course — but the absence of any policy allowed individual officers carte blanche to exploit national and sectarian interests.

The last frantic weeks during the eclipse of the Third Reich gave the Allies a breathtaking opportunity to grab German secrets. Intelligence that a few weeks earlier would have been priceless poured into Allied headquarters. Reports from more than two hundred American secret agents from the OSS who had infiltrated into Germany; from resistance groups, frontline units, and intercepts; and from sightings by reconnaissance aircraft produced a detailed, if not always accurate, picture of the Nazi plans to conceal whole government archives, laboratories, patents, prototypes, and underground factories. Sympathetic railway workers, hotel staff, and telephone operators supplied Allied agents with an endless list of sightings. At Mühldorf, east of Munich, there were "10,000 men at work day and night building repair shops above and below ground"; Heinkel blueprints had been hidden in "a tunnel entrance thirty meters from highway on east side of mountain at Fügen in the Zillertal";[7] at Eichach there was a "subterranean Messerschmitt factory," and there was another at Straubing Prison. Flash messages reported sudden intensive security measures around villages and remote areas where monasteries and mansions had been requisitioned by "unknown government agencies" or for weapons factories.[8] It was a golden harvest for the technical intelligence teams traveling close behind the front line.

By far the earliest and most staggering discovery of the first intelligence teams to arrive in Germany was that scientists at I. G. Farben had secretly developed a new strain of lethal nerve gases, against which Allied troops had no protection. The discovery of this invincible weapon, which, had it been loaded onto a V2, could have destroyed the population of London with ease, was not made public until years after the war — first, to avoid alerting the Russians, and second, because American investigators were concluding a series of secret deals with the I. G. Farben scientists.

The revolutionary nerve gas, Tabun, had been invented in 1936 by Dr. Gerhard Schrader. Even a minute quantity of Tabun could kill within twenty minutes, and its derivative, Sarin, could kill five times more effectively. Commissioned by the Wehrmacht, Otto Ambros, a brilliant chemist and senior director of I. G. Farben, had in 1940 secretly built a factory at Dyhernfurth, in Breslau, Silesia, for mass production of the two lethal gases. Tests on animals and painful experiments on concentration camp inmates confirmed the new chemicals' fatal efficacy. The first critical discussion about its use probably took place in Berlin following the Wehrmacht defeat at Stalingrad in 1943. Ambros was summoned by Hitler and asked whether sufficient Tabun was available for use against the advancing Russian army. Production, said Ambros, was increasing, but he suspected that the Allies also possessed Tabun, since international technical journals had discussed the compounds before the war. Moreover, the Allies could together produce more gas than Germany alone, and he feared that I. G.'s only deception, codenaming its gases Trilon (the name of a common detergent), had been unsuccessful. Until his death, Hitler, who harbored a marked aversion to gas warfare, apparently shared Ambros's delusion. In fact, although Allied intelligence was aware of the name, throughout the war it never discovered its true significance.

In 1941, an MI10 assessment had confidently asserted, "It appears that the Germans have no new gas of surprising effect."[9] For the next two years the possibility that the Germans might launch a chemical or biological attack on the Allies surfaced occasionally for discussion, only to be dismissed. Allied intelligence assumed that the Germans possessed only the type of mustard gas used in World War I, which had proven unreliable when used over large areas. Although Churchill was not totally averse to the notion of gas warfare as a last resort, Britain's resources were so depleted that upon the outbreak of war the country lacked sufficient phosgene to initiate an attack. In contrast, the U.S. Chemical Warfare Service was public, expansionist, and sufficiently powerful to openly lobby Congress to prevent the ratification of the Geneva Protocol banning gas warfare. Between 1940 and 1942 American expenditures on chemical rearmament zoomed from $2 million to $1 billion a year.

The first suspicion of Ambros's development emerged in 1943 from an intercept about the issue of new gas masks to Wehrmacht units and from a German POW who, under interrogation, gave a precise description of a new odorless and colorless gas that possessed "astounding properties." But the alarm soon subsided. Lack of more concrete evidence reassured Allied intelligence that there was little likelihood of a chemical attack, though fears persisted that Hitler might, in a moment of despair, order a suicidal holocaust. As a precaution, chemical warfare teams were attached to frontline units invading Germany. Allied fears were not groundless. In January 1945, on Hitler's orders, stores of Tabun were hastily evacuated from Silesia and later loaded onto barges on the Elbe and Danube, in preparation for launching a final attack from the Bavarian "last redoubt." Lieutenant Colonel Paul Tarr, the intelligence chief of the Chemical Warfare Service, led the hunt for the stores and the plant where the gas was produced.

Traveling with fifty other experts, Tarr joltingly drove across France in armored weapon carriers, passing through bomb-damaged towns and villages, creeping over Bailey bridges, and avoiding a never-ending torrent of humanity, before finally crossing the Rhine at the end of March, hours before the last German defenders fell, surrendered, or disappeared. While the battle was still raging, despite complaints from the Twelfth Army headquarters that "investigators are currently proving a nuisance to the armies . . . pressing too hard on the heels of the combat soldiers,"[10] Tarr's team broke into the I. G. Farben factories in the Ruhr and farther south. Finding the factory in Ludwigshafen heavily damaged, Tarr and Edmund Tilley, an air force interrogator whose fluent German and investigatory skills were to prove invaluable over the next months, ordered cowed German technicians and industrialists to lead the American soldiers to the homes and hiding places of their colleagues. Those who showed reluctance were summarily locked up. Within a day Gerhard Schrader, the inventor of the new gases, had been located, promptly opened his safe, and willingly confided the secret Tabun and Sarin formulae to the Americans. Momentarily Tarr and Tilley were ecstatic — until Schrader volunteered that the I. G. Farben production factory at Dyhernfurth had been captured intact by the Red Army. It was some comfort when Schrader added that he believed a counterattack had later destroyed most of the plant. In fact, the Russians had not only captured the Dyhernfurth factory intact, they had also found the laboratories' notebooks and documents hidden in a mine shaft at Rudesdorf. With the threat of a German attack receding, the first priority for Tarr and the Chemical Warfare Service was now to counter the Russians' new advantage.

By the end of April, when Tarr's top-secret reports had been circulated in Washington and London, several other intelligence agencies were looking for Ambros and the other I. G. Farben directors. Colonel Bernard Bernstein, a Treasury official from Washington, was given the assignment of destroying I. G.'s iron grip on European industry. Bernstein set himself the task of interrogating the industrialists, exposing their camouflaged stranglehold over their European and American competitors, and tracing I. G.'s enormous wartime plunder. Another group of American officers — war-crimes investigators seeking evidence for the proposed international trial of Nazi leaders at Nuremberg — wanted to extract from I. G.'s directors information and confessions about their prewar financing of Hitler's regime and their intimate complicity in his subsequent crimes. Ambros could answer all their questions since he had, with Himmler's help, masterminded the construction of I. G. Farben's factory in Auschwitz, where tens of thousands of concentration camp inmates were literally worked to death by I. G. Those exhausted by the work were callously diverted by the terse jerk of a thumb to the gas chambers. But Tarr showed less interest in Ambros's genocidal career than in his scientific expertise.

Soon after the German surrender Ambros was located at Gendorf in Bavaria, but it took two weeks for the information to percolate down to Tarr. In the meantime, Tarr had tirelessly interrogated other gas warfare experts. From them, it rapidly emerged that with Ambros's connivance the new gases had been tested on human beings with fatal consequences. Inmates from the Natzweiler concentration camp had been used by Dr. Karl Wimmer, a Luftwaffe doctor, and Professor August Hirt, from Strasbourg University, to test the effect and possible antidotes. After excruciating deaths, the human guinea pigs were dissected and pathologically examined.[11] Eyewitnesses told the Allied investigators that Hirt and Wimmer had, over the open cadavers, gleefully congratulated themselves on their pioneering work, which was in turn praised by the health directorate of the German air force.[12] Accordingly, when Tarr finally met Ambros, I. G. Farben's complicity in the human experiments was beyond doubt. The atmosphere at their introduction resembled countless other first encounters between Allied experts and similarly qualified German scientists. The war was over, and the Germans' past attitude toward the Nazis was irrelevant to the extraction of their often unique knowledge; like many other Americans, Tarr had no interest in Ambros other than the scientific. By all accounts, Ambros was responding enthusiastically and was beginning to form a binding relationship with his interrogator when, in July, an edict from SHAEF headquarters ordered Ambros's arrest and transfer to the Dustbin internment camp for intensive interrogation.

By this time, Colonel Bernstein had compiled a chilling indictment of the I. G. directors' intricate involvement at the highest level in the planning and management of the war; and the war-crimes investigators had uncovered incontrovertible documentary evidence of the I. G. directors' complicity with the SS in enslaving and gassing millions of innocent victims. Most of the directors of the I. G. board were already being held at Dustbin when Tarr set off with Ambros from Bavaria to Kransberg — then suddenly diverted to Heidelberg, ostensibly for forty-eight hours' questioning. While Ambros remained in Heidelberg, Tarr frantically flew between Frankfurt, Paris, and London, at first trying to negotiate, then demanding the release into his custody of all the German chemical warfare experts from Dustbin. The reason remained obscure, but at every level his request was denied. Finally, amid accusations that Tarr was forging release orders, Ambros suddenly disappeared; days later, he reappeared at Villa Kohlhof, his home in Ludwigshafen, by then in the French zone.

It eventually became apparent that French investigators had followed Tarr's team to the I. G. factory and, in the prevailing chaos, scooped up more than five hundred major reports and arrested the technicians, including Karl Wurster, a senior I. G. director and known war criminal. Since the German surrender, the French had adamantly protected "their" Germans from the American and British investigators.[13] Among those demanding access was Major P. M. Wilson, a British officer responsible for tracking down German scientists. In August, when Wilson eventually arrived in Ludwigshafen with an arrest team, he found Ambros installed as head of the I. G. Farben factory by the French military government. Wilson reported at once to London "the friendly treatment being given to this man who is suspected of war criminality."[14] Cheekily, Ambros even wrote to the British that he was "regretfully unable to meet in Heidelberg because I have to attend important meetings with high-ranking French gentlemen." By then he had been named for questioning by the Allied prosecutors at Nuremberg, but the French ignored their requests. "This man is thought to be far too dangerous and undesirable to be left at liberty," protested Wilson, but Tarr refused to reveal the circumstances of Ambros's escape, and Wilson suspected that he had "taken steps to assist him to evade arrest." Tarr's denial of French bribery seemed to Wilson unconvincing, but he never considered the alternative, more probable, scenario: that in return for divulging their secrets to the Chemical Warfare Service, Tarr may have guaranteed the Germans their freedom. It was another eighteen months before Ambros was finally delivered to the American prosecutors and Wimmer handed over the detailed pathology reports on his human guinea pigs. He was never prosecuted.[15]

Personal deals were not confined to either the Chemical War Service or the air force. Similar "understandings," for different reasons, were being made in the north of Germany, where a race was under way to plunder the German navy. Brian Urquart, commanding a British T-force, had reached Hanover in mid-April to find the town enveloped in a thick alcoholic haze. Liberated slave workers had consumed the contents of the town's largest cellar. Traveling with Urquart was an Anglo-American naval team under the command of Duncan Curtis and Ian Aylen from the Royal Navy's 30 AU group and an American naval captain, Albert Mumma, later promoted to admiral. These three pioneers of technical intelligence were closing in on Kiel, Admiral Doenitz's sanctum and the hub of the German naval inventions. En route, little had been found. Retreating German garrisons had methodically destroyed classified material, and liberated concentration camp inmates had ransacked vital laboratories and administrative offices, both in anger and in search of loot.[16] Only in Lübeck did the team find a taste of the riches to come: a prototype of a 50-knot hydrofoil, human torpedoes, and a unique two-man midget submarine.

On May 5, escorted by a small Special Air Service detachment and soldiers from the Fifth King's Regiment, Curtis, Mumma, and Aylen reached their goal — the Walterwerke, where the revolutionary high-speed peroxide submarines and torpedoes had been developed and built. Despite intensive bombing, the factory was practically unscathed, and its production lines had halted only two days before. Two new peroxide-driven submarines, the U-1408 and the U-1410, lay shattered by the jetty: "They looked like gigantic fish rather than conventional submarines,"[17] Aylen remembers. To Aylen's surprise, thousands of German naval officers and seamen meekly surrendered to the small Allied naval group.

Finding Helmuth Walter, the owner of the factory — "a heavy, flabby-cheeked man," according to Aylen — was easy, but at first he was reluctant to talk. Walter, a committed Nazi, sullenly claimed that he had just completed two days of destroying and concealing the results of twelve years' work. Although his factory was filled with torpedoes and submarines under construction, their vital combustion chambers were missing. Walter doggedly insisted that his allegiance was still to the Third Reich, not to the Allies. Only when Doenitz agreed to individually sign forty copies of a written order to Walter that nothing was to be withheld were Aylen and Mumma's frustrations relieved. On May 7, Walter began his revelations, starting with the admission that prior to their incineration, all the documents had been microfilmed and the cans hidden in the coal cellars. "For the first two weeks," recalls Aylen, "we found new weapons at the rate of two a day. Combustion chambers were hauled up from flooded bomb craters, key torpedo data dug up from underground, a miniature twenty-five knot U-boat salvaged from the bottom of a lake, parts of a Messerschmitt jet engine from a train on the Danish border, and there were prototypes of dozens of new and ingenious weapons: long-range guns, mine-sweeping devices and jet-powered grenades." Six hundred workers, paid by Walter, were ordered to rebuild two U-boats, types 17 and 18, watched by visiting American and British naval teams. Among them was a joint team of torpedo experts that went to inspect the Eckerneforde research station. "A visit will certainly provide a shock of surprise," reported Captain Maitland Dougall. "The magnitude of German torpedo development effort impresses all beholders." Equally remarkable was the "astonishing willingness" of the German officers and scientists to answer questions and volunteer information.[18] The booty was equitably divided. A type 17 submarine was shipped to America, while the type 18 went to Britain for trials. Equipment from Hamburg's internationally famous experimental ship tank was stripped, the building destroyed, and the tank itself filled with rubble.[19] The only ones left out seemed to be the Russians.

Until earlier that year, Mumma, like most young Allied combatants, had been anxious to cooperate with the Soviets. Disillusion set in when the Russians suddenly reneged on an agreed visit by an Anglo-American naval team to the former German torpedo research center at Gdynia, in Poland. The Admiralty believed that Stalin had approved the visit at Yalta. Mumma was a member of the Allied team. After protracted negotiations about whether the team's route from London should be via Sweden, Rumania, or Iran, Mumma realized that he would never arrive in Gdynia. "They were supposed to be our Allies and we were just double-crossed," recalls Mumma. "After that, everything was coloured and we never forgot it." While the Walterwerke and the submarines were rapidly stripped of equipment, the Admiralty embarked on a deliberate deception. A top-secret cable from London gave instructions that if the Russians inquired about the survival of the equipment, Allied officers should issue bland rebuttals. Three prototype U-boat hulls were on no account to be sunk, but "if Russians ask questions about these vessels, they should be informed that they were scuttled and their machinery sabotaged. . . . Anything likely to emphasize the importance of these vessels should be avoided."[20] Pleased with the Machiavellian guile of their "denial policy," the Admiralty informed Washington: "No important naval unit has fallen undamaged into Russian hands and all surviving U-boats and important surface ships have been captured."[21] As the Allies later discovered, it was a wildly optimistic message. Soviet agents in Gdynia and Berlin had already seized the blueprints of all Germany's important maritime designs, which would form the foundation of Russia's huge postwar naval expansion program.

Between Russian stealth and American resourcefulness, within weeks of victory British interests were already being squeezed. Two months before the surrender, the American Advanced Communications Section had established a daily train, which became both the envy and the bane of America's allies. Dubbed the "Toot Sweet Express," it carried plundered equipment from Germany to a Paris depot and then across the Atlantic. For Harold Phelps at the Board of Trade, who with admirable prescience had realized a year earlier that Britain would never be able to compete in the stripping of Germany, the alternative solution was obvious: "Bring over here the key scientists and technicians . . . settle them down into British industry . . . [and] send out industrial missions to spy out all that Germany has been doing."[22] One of those "key" Germans was Karl Doetsch.

Doetsch's war ended quietly and pleasantly at a Luftwaffe air base at Travemünde, in northern Germany, on Good Friday, 1945. Only after landing had he been told that the base's fuel-storage tanks were empty. Nevertheless, he felt some compensatory satisfaction. He had survived the war and had successfully obeyed his last orders from Berlin, which were not to fall into Russian hands. Doetsch was a *Flugbaumeister*, an elite breed of German test pilot that brilliantly combined the expertise of a highly skilled, trained engineer with the flair of an experienced pilot. "A week later, the Allied front line passed by the base. No one seemed interested in me, so I began cycling south to my family in Bavaria." In fact, Doetsch's special understanding of aeronautics was eagerly sought by all four Allies.

During the war, no more than seventy German aeronautic graduates had qualified as Flugbaumeisters at the Adlershof aviation research center in Berlin. Like Doetsch, they were determined, stubborn pioneers on whom the Luftwaffe's astonishing aircraft developments had ultimately depended. To qualify at Aachen University in the early 1930s, Doetsch had built his own aircraft, incorporating his own innovations, and then flown it. "By the end of the war," he recalls, "I had flown about seventy different planes, pushing all of them to their limits, looking for solutions to a whole range of problems."

Doetsch had also flown every type of Allied aircraft, looking for ideas that the Luftwaffe might copy, and was scathingly critical of them:

> Wartime aircraft development was about German engineering and science versus Allied improvisation. Throughout the war, we learnt nothing from the Allies about plane design. The Spitfire's frame was cloth-covered while the Me 109 was metal. We laughed at the Blenheim bomber with all its beautiful bronze screw caps. We couldn't believe it. The Flying Fortress was far too heavy and unmanoeuvrable. But we couldn't beat the Rolls-Royce engine. We had already copied the Russians' very clever air-intake design, but engines remained our weak point.

In the course of the war, Doetsch had invented and tested advanced navigation and autopilot equipment and pioneered the development of precision instruments that could test planes in flight — technology still undreamed-of in either America or Britain. Among Doetsch's last projects had been an autostabilizer for the guns of the Me 262. It was characteristic of the difference in approach between the Germans and the Allies that whereas the Germans recognized the importance of building the fighter-interceptor around the gun, Allied plane designers just stuck the gun onto their pride, the plane itself. Consequently, while German fighters were armed with a lethal mixture of six 30-millimeter or 50-millimeter guns, some firing at a rate of 1,100 rounds per minute, most British fighters at the end of the war were still equipped with four 20-millimeter shell guns, while even the Mustang relied on an outdated one-half-inch machine gun.

Doetsch consoled himself with the thought that the Allied air forces had won air superiority through sheer volume of production, apparently effortless replacement of airmen, uninterrupted fuel supplies, and the mounting dislocation of German aircraft production caused by relentless bombing. But he was certain that even during the last days of the war, Allied Air Intelligence investigators sifting through crashed Luftwaffe aircraft would be amazed by the stream of improvements that the manufacturers were still building into their latest models. Someone, he felt, would eventually make him an offer, but for the moment all he was concerned about was survival.

By the time Doetsch reached his family in Bavaria, Donald Putt's enthusiastic reports from Volkenrode and elsewhere had arrived in Washington, encouraging teams of American investigators to flood Germany. Their efficacy was noted by the British investigators, comparatively few in number, whose indignant reports reveal their jealousy and awe of the Americans' vacuum-cleaner tactics, which netted everything and everyone available.

"The scale on which science and engineering have been harnessed to the chariot of destruction in Germany is indeed amazing," wrote W. S. Farren, the director of Farnborough. "There is a tremendous amount to be learnt in Germany at the present time." Like Putt, Farren was overwhelmed by Volkenrode, which possessed "a magnificence in layout, structure and furnishing that beggars the imagination of anyone who has seen similar institutions in the U.K." Farren had arrived in Germany with eleven senior British aviation experts for his first visit on July 9. It had taken a month just to clear formalities. By then American investigators had either left a trail of debris and tantalizing gaps or, even more irritating, were deliberately excluding the British. The Messerschmitt factories, Farren discovered, were packed with American specialists, spending weeks in a single plant learning everything they could from the Germans. "The British representation at these targets appears unsystematic, hurried or in many cases non-existent,"[23] he noted. Farren was limited to simply collecting statistics. Heinkel Aircraft had managed to design, test, and fly the He 162 within three months, "an outstanding achievement and worthy of special study."[24] Design had taken 200,000 man-hours due to enormous enthusiasm, whereas in Britain it would have required 600,000 hours, and the job would have "gone sour due to tedious delays in the design and development stage."[25]

The gushing reports from Germany were read in Britain with a mixture of astonishment and even disbelief. With the war over, few wanted to believe the wisdom of the comment made by Roy Fedden, the brilliant engineer, after the event: "How fortunate we were," he wrote, "that the war ceased when it did . . . had hostilities gone on a year or so longer, we should have been faced with a crop of entirely new problems."[26] Fedden had flown to Germany in early June on a mission sponsored by the Ministry of Aircraft Production. The aircraft builder had never hidden his admiration for German engineering, and despite the chaos and destruction he was "deeply impressed." Traveling around Germany in his personal Dakota, with two jeeps on board, he complained that British aviation industrialists were being "lamentably slow" to fly over and take advantage of the information available. "Americans," wrote Fedden, "have adopted exactly the opposite tactics and have 'fine-combed' the country removing considerable quantities of drawings, technical records and actual equipment direct to the States." So much "excellent" equipment was there for the taking, yet it was "deteriorating for want of attention or . . . being pilfered." During his visit to Volkenrode, Fedden witnessed an audacious example of American plunder: He could only stand and watch openmouthed as two trucks that he had loaded with books were cheerfully commandeered by a USAF team.

Fedden was exasperated. When he urged the importance of learning from German achievements, RAF officers and British experts — especially those from Rolls-Royce, who had failed to deliver jets during the war — arrogantly dismissed his admiration of German achievements. "We won the war, didn't we?" was their constant retort. They shrugged when Fedden pointed out that in the spring of 1945, despite all the bombing and military defeats, German factories were producing between two thousand and three thousand jet engines a month, while Britain produced barely a hundred. Even the great Sydney Camm, the designer of the Hurricane fighter, derided swept-wing planes, while others stolidly professed their conviction that German jet aero-engines were inferior. Many of the people he spoke to were self-made men who had risen from apprenticeships. Proud of their own achievements and those of their country, they could not accept that they had been outstripped by a foreign competitor or that their own wartime innovations were already of only historical interest. During the war those same engineers had been unable to revolutionize their production methods, because — although the aircraft industry itself was young — the work practices were encrusted with legacies from earlier crafts.[27]

Fedden, in contrast, was a restless innovator impatient to take advantage of German knowledge — but his protests in the previous decade had antagonized so many people that, despite the validity of his arguments, he was now once again ignored. Depressed to see so much equipment, which British designers had only dreamed of, lying abandoned and unused, he telephoned the Ministry of Aircraft Production in London, suggesting that British scientists come over to Germany and work in the research institutes alongside their former enemies. In the conclusion of his report from Germany, he sadly noted:

> Britain has lost a remarkable opportunity, during the last two months, in not accumulating as much information on aeronautical, and in fact all engineering matters, as she might have done. The mission regrets that British industry has almost entirely ignored the opportunity which should have been open to it, to explore the research and production potential of Germany in all aeronautical matters, while this has been done so enthusiastically and so successfully by our American Allies.[28]

Fedden's report got an icy reception in London. Officials were swift to deny most of his complaints but conceded that not enough experts had visited Germany. Among those who arrived in the wake of Fedden's report were two aircraft designers from Farnborough, Morien Morgan and Handel Davies. "We were genuinely amazed," recalls Davies. "We realised within five minutes that all our design work on the Meteor and other planes was obsolescent. Swept-wing jets were the future." Davies was exceptionally farsighted compared with most of his fellow Britons. "At the outbreak of war, I'd been very concerned about their advantage. At the end of the war, I was raring to discover what they had achieved. We knew that they were ahead of us in nearly everything."

Morgan soon discovered that Germany's leading swept-wing designer, Adolph Busemann, and the foremost German delta-wing designer, Alexander Lippisch, had been spirited away from Volkenrode (which was in the British zone) by U.S. Air Force expert von Karmen and Hap Arnold and taken to the American zone. A third expert, Dietrich Kuchemann, who had developed the swept wing after 1936, had refused American offers to leave Göttingen. Morgan and Davies were determined to make the remaining member of the trio an offer he could not refuse and to lure him to Britain — but first they had to win the approval of the Ministry of Aircraft Production. "There was a lot of table-thumping," recalls Davies. "The British were both prejudiced and amateurish. Prejudiced, because they could not believe that the Germans were better than us. Amateurish, because compared to the Americans, our approach was sloppy. The American teams were led by regular officers who were dynamic and effective. They were conscious that they had to get the best for America."

British prejudice and amateurism had plenty of energetic perpetrators in Whitehall, among them the chief scientist at the Ministry of Aircraft Production, Ben Lockspeiser, a chemist and, some believed, an impractical man. The complicated calculations of wind flow over an aircraft's wing and fuselage were understandably foreign to him. Morgan realized that he would find it hard to convince Lockspeiser of Britain's need for German scientists since, until Lockspeiser could test the swept-wing theory under laboratory conditions, he was unwilling to commit himself to scrapping the Meteor.

Nevertheless, Morgan returned to Oberammergau, in southern Germany, to search for the scientists and technologists not yet scooped up by the Americans. They were now no longer conveniently grouped around an institute but were scattered throughout Bavaria, often having been evicted from their homes by the American army or living in temporary shelter. His first targets were the test pilots who had flown the new Messerschmitt jet. Like so many of the investigators, Morgan was forced to learn the skills of the chase quickly. Driving in an ammunition carrier, after two days of fruitless searching Morgan had to admit that his morale was "at a low ebb." But his persistence was finally rewarded when, to his delight, he found Karl Bauer — Messerschmitt's chief test pilot. With pride, Bauer recounted the history of Messerschmitt's jet development after the first experimental flight, described some of the problems encountered — such as the jet's vibrations, its drag, its instability and snaking — and explained to Morgan Messerschmitt's attempted solutions and conclusions. Bauer's criticism of the plane's fuselage and rudder convinced Morgan that he needed to find Karl Doetsch, who during an early interrogation in London had been mentioned by Hans Multhopp, Focke-Wulf's stability expert. Morgan believed that Doetsch "had the answers to so many questions" and was "really pleased" when he found him at Trauchgau. Doetsch did indeed prove to be an "extremely useful man" and was singled out for further interrogation, if possible in Britain.

But the omens of American competition were already depressingly obvious. At the end of his tour, Morgan was told by Colonel Gifford, the leader of the American team at the Messerschmitt works, that seventeen sealed crates of Messerschmitt blueprints unearthed by American investigators had been "sent to London" for joint Allied use. Morgan happened to know that they were already over the Atlantic, destined for Wright Field. Gifford, like so many U.S. Air Force officers, had acted on his own initiative, confident that his enthusiasm and patriotism would be unhesitatingly endorsed by his superiors.

6

Compromises

BRASH, ENTHUSIASTIC, AND UTTERLY DETERMINED to ful-
fill his mission, Major Robert Staver, a twenty-eight-year-old mechanical engineer, followed the front line of the U.S. First Army
into Nordhausen in the Harz Mountains on April 11, 1945. "Task
Force Welborn" had engaged in a fierce battle for more than a day
with six companies of SS troops before the road into the picturesque valley had been cleared. Avoiding snipers and land mines,
with the assistance of a detailed and very accurate map supplied
by British intelligence he was the first Allied technical officer to
arrive at the underground factory where the V2 rocket had been
assembled. Staver had been given an aggressive brief from Colonel
Holgar "Turtle" Toftoy, the swashbuckling and congenial chief of
the Ordnance Department's technical intelligence mission in Paris,
to "get the scientists who were years ahead of us and could teach
us from their success." "The German foremen's cups," he recalls,
"were still warm when we arrived." Staver harbored only one fear:
that the British would grab the German scientists first and sabotage Toftoy's dream of securing their services exclusively for America. But on the first day, that danger had not arisen. Not surprisingly,
only a few Germans had remained behind at Nordhausen to be
captured. Nevertheless, Staver was completely bewitched by what
he found. Dug deep into the heart of the mountains were giant
tunnels with hundreds of abandoned V2 rockets in various stages
of completion. Twenty years' brilliant research and innovation were
laid out on the production line, waiting to be plundered.

Appointed in 1942 to work in the American rocket program, until
that moment Staver had proudly regarded himself as a veteran of
the "rocket business" — but the rocket developments with which

he had been associated were pitiful compared with what he saw as he walked through the musty underground tunnels. No one in Washington or London had ever imagined a development such as the Mittelbau at Nordhausen. Yet Staver had been in the forefront of U.S. rocket research, which had started because of the immense enthusiasm generated by Theodore von Karmen at the California Institute of Technology. In the early 1930s the Hungarian-born scientist had recruited a handful of engineers and technicians to study the possibility of a liquid-fueled rocket for space exploration. Until December 1941, the Jet Propulsion Research Project had been severely handicapped by the military's lukewarm interest. Only after America's declaration of war, with the inheritance from Henry Tizard of the successful results of British tests on solid-fuel rockets, could von Karmen's National Defense Research Committee convince the military of the feasibility of rockets as strategic weapons. Within weeks, the projects were given extra funds, although the amount remained paltry. The situation would have barely changed throughout the war had not one of von Karmen's regular pleas for more support been read by Colonel Gervais Trichel, the ambitious head of the rocket branch at Army Ordnance. In a bid to intensify the American program, in July 1943 von Karmen cited an equivocal British intelligence report on German rocket development as a reason for greater investment. In London, the report had been virtually ignored, but Trichel was immediately persuaded. Overnight, he overwhelmed von Karmen with enthusiastic appeals to establish the American equivalent of the German V2 project.

Trichel's fervent ambition was to mastermind and control a missile program, and in the midst of the rocket bombardment of London, he fueled the appetite of service chiefs and politicians for an American rocket program to gain support for his plans. By early 1945, he had successfully commissioned his department's own firing range at White Sands, New Mexico, although its immediate use was limited, and in March a Joint War Plans Committee survey of special weapons that could be used against Japan concluded that missiles were "highly desirable" in order to destroy Japan's "industrial heart" and hasten victory. But the same report acknowledged that the development of the only available American missile, the JB-2 Buzz bomb, was so retarded that its development was highly "unlikely"[1] before the end of the war. The Peenemünde scientists, Trichel recognized, could simultaneously provide the solution to this problem and the key to his personal success. The plan for the capture and development of long-range German missiles was code-named "Project Hermes."

As a first step, Colonel Toftoy, Trichel's executive agent in Paris, was given urgent orders to ship one hundred completed V2s to White Sands. The obvious source was Nordhausen, which had been identified as the V2's underground assembly plant in August 1944 by a captured German electrician and confirmed by photoreconnaissance. Allied experts, however, had decided that the natural protection of the Harz Mountains would shield the plant from even a thousand-pound Tallboy bomb, so they ruled out the possibility of an aerial attack. Consequently, when Major Staver arrived in Nordhausen, he found the Mittelbau intact.

Staver, who had never forgotten the sensation he felt when a V2 exploded near to where he was standing in London, began the hunt for the rocket scientists the following day. Unknown to him, the majority had joined Werner von Braun in Bavaria, but some had remained in the area and, before Staver's arrival, had already been arrested by army units. To his fury, a few had even been jailed. "I was furious," he recalls, "that they had been so badly treated. They were scientists after all." Staver was quite emphatic about the treatment of the rocket scientists. In briefing his team, Staver stressed that they should be treated civilly: "I wanted them treated as normal, friendly human beings, in the same way as if our situations were reversed and we were captured. Otherwise we wouldn't get their cooperation." Staver's approach was not a ploy: He sincerely believed there was no difference between a German designing weapons of war and an American weapons specialist like himself. "It's even steven," he said.

The soldiers who had fought to liberate Nordhausen adopted a different attitude. As they swarmed through the complex of barracks at the mountain entrance, the frontline tank group reeled in horror at the sight of emaciated men, many unable to stand, dressed in tattered, striped clothing. Strewn around like debris were hundreds of corpses, the bodies of those who had died in the past days, still awaiting cremation; and by the crematoria hundreds more were stacked like timber. "It was a fabric of moans and whimpers of delirium and outright madness," remembers Staff Sergeant Donald Schulz. "Here and there a single shape tottered about, walking slowly, like a man dreaming." It was a scene that would be encountered time and again throughout Occupied Europe during the last weeks of the war as concentration camps were liberated. This was Camp Dora, which housed the thousands of slave workers who had tunneled through the mountain and then assembled the rockets. The camp was too small to merit even the barest mention in the numerous accounts of Nazi atrocities written over the next weeks and months, yet further investigation revealed monstrous crimes perpetrated in the name of science and warfare. A seven-strong war-crimes investigation team was summoned to Nordhausen soon after the plant's capture. Its interpreter was William Aalmans, a young Dutch officer attached to the American army. Aalmans stayed there for five days, appalled by the "stench, the tuberculosis and the starved inmates." Inside a makeshift hospital tent he took statements from barely audible survivors, only able to drink diluted milk. "Four people were dying every hour," he remembers. "It was unbelievable."

Yet when the war-crimes investigators left the camp, "we had all forgotten about Nordhausen by the time we arrived at the next investigation." Like the work of all war-crimes investigations at that time, theirs at Nordhausen had been patchy and inconclusive. Pressed for time and ill informed, Aalmans's team was unable to establish who was ultimately responsible for the crimes committed there or to unearth any documentary evidence — save one item, the Mittelbau telephone list. At the very top, listed as management, were Georg Rickhey, director of production, and Arthur Rudolph, deputy production manager. The names meant nothing to the Americans, but they attached the list to their report — which, together with the accompanying statements, completely crushed the idealized image harbored by Staver and other American scientists about the working conditions underground. Among these statements was an account of a short interrogation with Albin Sawatski, a Danzig-born engineer who was Mittelbau's technical director. Sawatski confessed that inmates had been hung and that he "kicked some of the workers from time to time" but claimed that he had "frequently complained to the direction concerning the mass executions."[2] Sawatski also told the interrogators that Rudolph was responsible for the "hours of work" and that Rickhey had returned to his old home in Saalfeld, but the information was ignored. Shortly afterward, according to legend, Sawatski was shot by outraged American troops. In any event, his "death" became an accepted fact among the surviving Germans, and thereafter most of the responsibility for the crimes committed at Nordhausen was attributed to Sawatski.

Hitler's approval for the construction of the vast Mittelbau factory had followed Bomber Command's successful attack on Peenemünde in September 1943. The exposed peninsula site was clearly too vulnerable, and both the scientists and the Wehrmacht readily agreed to transfer production — though not research — to safety underground, about 250 miles to the southwest. The records of the ensuing negotiations and planning were destroyed in 1945, but there is no doubt that the rocket pioneers fully accepted the necessity of slave labor, since only Himmler and the SS could provide the organization and manpower to transform a mountain into a factory and testing station. The negotiators on behalf of the rocket team were Werner von Braun and General Walter Dornberger, the Wehrmacht officer who with remarkable foresight had a decade earlier recognized the genius and potential of the German rocket enthusiasts. The use of slave workers did not inhibit either man, and a large contingent had already been used at Peenemünde. Moreover, since von Braun and Dornberger were anxious to see their efforts bear fruit quickly, an agreement with the SS was a considerable advantage, and neither of them was particularly appalled by Himmler. Indeed, von Braun had willingly accepted the rank of captain and then promotion to major in the SS. Others among his closest confidants and associates were also committed Nazis — including Herbert Axster, an accountant; Kurt Debus, responsible for rocket launching; and Arthur Rudolph, the deputy production manager. All of them were striving to perfect the rockets not merely to satisfy a passion for scientific achievement but as a major contribution toward German victory.

Among the first engineers to arrive at Nordhausen from Peenemünde was Arthur Rudolph, then age thirty-seven. Like all von Braun's close associates, Rudolph, a farmer's son with a rudimentary education, had been mesmerized by the possibilities of space travel from his early youth. In 1930, he had watched helplessly as his mentor, the rocket pioneer Max Valier, died while testing a rocket car. The following year, Rudolph joined the Nazi party. "I read *Mein Kampf* and agreed with a lot of things in it," he explained fifty years later.[3] "Hitler's first six years, until the war started, were really marvellous. They were the best years in Germany. Everybody was happy. Everybody got jobs." Rudolph also joined the SA (the Brown Shirts) and marched through the streets of Berlin in uniform singing the Nazi party's "Horst Wessel Lied," which includes the line "When Jewish blood spurts from the knife, then all goes twice as well." Rudolph was unashamedly attracted by both the party's challenge to Communism and its discrimination against the Jews. Peenemünde offered him an enormous challenge, which he fully met, and he was Dornberger's natural choice to direct full-scale production at Nordhausen.

By the time Rudolph arrived in September 1943, the first batch of sixty thousand men, transferred from the Buchenwald concentration camp, had begun transforming the small ammonia mine into a warren of forty-six 220-yard tunnels, 14 yards wide and up to 30 yards high, bisected by a pair of two-mile tunnels. At least twenty thousand men would die there before the end of the war. Working without power drills or mechanical excavators, the slaves were constantly threatened and beaten while they dug, hammered, and heaved their pickaxes. Since there was scarcely any food or water and no sanitation or medical facilities, life expectancy rarely exceeded six months. During their daily tour through the tunnels, the Peenemünde scientists felt the extreme humidity, the chill gusts of air, the dusty atmosphere, and intense depression. Despite the constant arrival of new labor, the number of workers never increased. On average, one hundred men a day died of exhaustion, starvation, and disease, or were murdered by the SS guards, either on a whim or as punishment. Their emaciated bodies were usually disposed of in the crematoria at Camp Dora; those who were hanged as punishment were left at the end of the rope for days, successfully intimidating the survivors. Replacements supplied by the SS from other concentration camps arrived on demand from Rudolph or Werner von Braun. Neither scientist was directly responsible for these conditions, but they accepted the situation created by the SS without demur.

Survivors, like the French resistance hero Yves Beon, swear that although the SS officers' function was to control the work force, they acted only on the scientists' instructions. Among the fragments of documents that survived the war, American investigators discovered the record of a meeting at Nordhausen on May 6, 1944, chaired by Georg Rickhey, Mittelbau's general director of production. Twenty-eight men — including officers from the SS and the Wehrmacht as well as engineers — had been summoned to decide how to overcome a particular bottleneck in the production of steering assemblies. Among those present were General Dornberger, von Braun, Rudolph, and others from the Peenemünde group who would eventually work in America. Next to them sat notorious SS officers who would later be prosecuted for their crimes. Clearly, it was a regular meeting that, without any special formality, agreed that the ideal solution was to take prisoner 1,800 skilled workers in France, who would be housed in the Dora camp and treated as concentration camp inmates. Everyone agreed that after their abduction from France, they should be distinctively clothed in striped suits. Twenty years later, few would associate von Braun, who was then managing America's future moon landing, with grisly discussions about kidnapping Frenchmen and condemning them to certain death underground. Rudolph later admitted, "I knew that people were dying."[4] Incontestably, Dornberger and von Braun also realized that the Frenchmen would suffer maltreatment, although it was Rudolph who witnessed their daily torment. Together, they managed a factory to produce rockets in which the SS were, at most, equal partners.

There can be no doubt that it was the civilians who received the daily reports on production, labor statistics, and sabotage. Workers who were sick were disposed of by the SS, while those suspected of sabotage were reported to the SS by the scientists, who were the only people qualified to recognize sabotage. The consequences of such a report were inevitable, although of the Peenemünde team probably only Rudolph and a few others were present at the regular weekly hangings as described by eyewitnesses.

On one occasion, according to a survivor, "Fifty-seven were hung. An electric crane, in the tunnel, lifted twelve prisoners at a time, hands behind their backs, a piece of wood in their mouths, hanged by a length of wire attached at the back of their necks to prevent them crying out."[5] Work was temporarily halted for those hangings; afterward, the survivors returned to their place in the tunnels to continue rocket assembly. Another survivor, Yves Beon, recalls that those hung would be left for days afterward dangling from the rope, their trousers fallen on the ground below, mixed with excreta, while "the German civilians just passed by without looking, without any sign of emotion."

Strangely, Major Staver, intent on Project Hermes, was insensitive to the atmosphere at Nordhausen. He admits that he saw the bodies stacked by the crematoria, but there were "only a couple of hundred" and everyone else "was alive, so there's no way so many could have died." Assigned to the hunt for scientists and not for Nazis, Staver ignored the moral considerations: "My side of things was technical. These were brilliant men, geniuses who were twenty-five years ahead of us down the road." As for the scientists who remained at Peenemünde, Staver maintained that they were completely isolated and knew nothing of conditions at Nordhausen. The few who did know, Staver believed, were "just obeying orders, doing what they were told, oppressed like every other German by the Nazi state." It was a scenario that von Braun himself was at that moment methodically cultivating with his captors in Bavaria.

Werner von Braun had spent the previous six months carefully planning for that moment. Isolated on the Baltic coast, von Braun and his colleagues had spent considerable time since the end of 1944 discussing their own predicament. Unlike the aviation experts scattered throughout Germany, the rocketeers at Peenemünde were conspirators with a single mutual aim: to offer their services to the highest bidder. By the new year, when Peenemünde was on the verge of falling to the Russians — unattractive future employers — their evacuation westward was efficiently executed.

On February 17, 1945, the first train left Peenemünde, with 525 scientists and their families heading south for Bleicherode. The equipment and records for the V2 rocket and the Wasserfall anti-aircraft missile were packed up and transported by barge. To the sound of Russian artillery fire, a demolition squad planted dynamite haphazardly among the installations and fled, negligently abandoning considerable quantities of the most valuable equipment intact. Within weeks it would be transported eastward, to Russia. As the evacuees headed south, the fighting intensified. Fourteen tons of documents, the summary of thirteen years' research, were hastily buried in a mine near Goslar. Smaller bundles were hidden as von Braun's team, with the blessing of the SS, headed ever southward to Oberammergau, in Bavaria, Hitler's fabled last redoubt. In comfort they waited, joined by other rocket experts, confident of surviving the remainder of the war and believing that their secrets were secure for the highest bidder.

Commander Henry Schade, the leader of the American Naval Technical Mission, whose impatient zeal and apparently limitless resources had so irritated Professor Linstead and the British investigators, arrived in Oberammergau on May 1. Schade's Navtech team was already well briefed about the leading scientific personalities. Soon after his capture, Dr. Werner Osenberg, an SS officer and engineering professor specializing in naval research, had voluntarily presented the Allies with a comprehensive list of fifteen thousand leading German scientists, together with brief individual descriptions of their work and truckloads of documents. Schade's chief quarry in Oberammergau was Dr. Herbert Wagner, described by Osenberg as the designer of the Hs 293 guided missile bomb, which had effortlessly and devastatingly destroyed several Allied ships. For the American navy, the quest for the secrets of the missile had become an obsession. The following day Schade excitedly cabled that Wagner had been found and interrogated, and was surprisingly cooperative. Schade recommended that the German be evacuated via Paris, "directly to US for complete interrogation and utilization." Hewlett Thebaud, the director of Naval Intelligence in Washington, immediately asked the War Department to approve Schade's request.[6] To Schade's surprise, Wagner did not surrender alone. With him were von Braun and Dornberger, who, with the whole Peenemünde team, were patently eager to be discovered by the Americans.

Richard Porter, an employee of General Electric on contract to the U.S. Army Ordnance Department for Project Hermes, arrived with CIOS team 183 a few days later. Following Staver's guidelines for securing the Germans' cooperation, Porter's team was overtly friendly to their former enemies. Porter knew that Toftoy, unlike the British, was determined to extract as much help as possible from the Germans, who, it seemed, were amiable but cautious. Von Braun later claimed that while the battle was still raging, his team was already plotting for its negotiations with the Americans and had conspired to withhold information until the Americans had made an acceptable offer: "We were interested in continuing our work, not just being squeezed like a lemon and then discarded. A three-year contract, we felt, would reflect long-range intentions on the part of the US, but such a contract could not be [immediately] attained."[7] As part of their bargaining tactics, von Braun and Dornberger decided to retain military-style control over their team — a tactic that did not pass unnoticed by American intelligence officers. "Dornberger and von Braun were in a position to bargain," recalled Walter Jessel, an intelligence officer, "to exercise pressure and attempt blackmail. Security clearance of the group as such [was] an obvious absurdity."[8] Oblivious to the conspiracy and delighted to be the only representative of private industry with access to the Germans, Porter gratefully settled down amid the lush Bavarian countryside to gradually build up a relationship by means of gentle questioning interspersed with meals and games of chess. Offering contracts could be taken care of by the government.

At Nordhausen the pace was more frantic. Like Staver, Major William Bromley, a recovery specialist dispatched by Toftoy, was dedicated to the fulfillment of his mission. Nordhausen lay in what was shortly to become the Russian zone, and June 1, the deadline for the U.S. Army to withdraw westward, was less than three weeks away. Bromley's task was to seize everything of value inside the "magician's cave," but the secret authorization for mass plunder did not arrive until May 22, which left Bromley with little time to clear the tunnel entrances and then track down and retrieve thousands of rocket parts. In a spectacular operation, Bromley hired the newly liberated slave workers to salvage four hundred tons of equipment — then, requisitioning trains and wagons, and trucks summoned from as far as Cherbourg in France, over a period of eight days he moved the equipment to the port of Antwerp for shipment to White Sands. In Antwerp, British officers spotted the crates of rocket parts and demanded that Eisenhower call a halt to the shipments. But the Supreme Commander refused. Among the jubilant American team a rumor circulated that, as a measure of despair, the British had dispatched a frigate to intercept the shipments.

The British witnesses to Bromley's blitz operation were CIOS team 163, led by William Cook, Dr. Alwyn Crow's deputy from the projectile development team, and John Elstub, a frustrated British pioneer of liquid-fueled rockets. Their mutual wartime antagonism disappeared when they became aware of the daunting scale of rocket production inside the mountain. Both arrived in Nordhausen four days after its liberation — four vital days, during which Staver and Bromley had established themselves. For Elstub, as for almost everyone, the first, overwhelming impression was of "the indescribable stench and evidence of inhumanity. I was most shocked how the head of the administration proved the accuracy of his calculation that the most cost effective use of slave workers was to keep them alive for just six months." Accompanying them as they toured the production lines were the engineers who had not joined von Braun. Before Elstub and Cook left, many quietly asked them whether there was a chance of continuing their work in Britain. The Britons could give no reply. They left, however, with boxes of valuable components, packed onto a truck by an American expert, Edwin Hull, a General Electric employee. "We never saw that lorry again," grumbled Elstub forty years later. "Hull just shipped it straight back to the U.S. I felt sour that the bird had flown." It was the Britons' first taste of knife-edged competition between the Allies. Staver had taken one glance at Cook and instantly distrusted him: "He gave me a fishy-eyed look when I asked him what he'd found." The habitual reserve of the Englishman seemed sinister to the more extroverted Americans, especially to Toftoy's cowboys. While Cook traveled to Bavaria to question von Braun, Elstub returned to London keenly aware that British rocketry needed hefty political and military support. The prospects for a British rocket program seemed hopeful. After all, London had just suffered a year's rocket bombardment.

At that moment von Braun was equally available to the Americans and the British. Indeed, had the British possessed the same resolution about rocket technology as they were showing at that same moment in Hamburg and Kiel about submarine warfare, there would have been little opportunity for Project Hermes, the American plan for achieving missile expertise, to have achieved such instant success. But British experts were, despite the overwhelming evidence of the success of liquid-fueled missiles, still obsessed with solid fuel. Crucially, in Britain, unlike America, none of the three military services sought missiles for their armory, while civil servants lacked both the information and the foresight to appreciate their true importance. Almost before it started, Britain was set to lose the missile race.

Throughout the long and bitter wartime arguments in London about whether the Germans had succeeded in building an effective rocket, Alwyn Crow's damning skepticism had undoubtedly been at least partly due to his own failure to construct or even design a rocket with a diameter of more than four inches. Admittedly, solid-fuel rockets had successfully been fired against the Luftwaffe and submarines, but in Britain they were regarded as a new type of shell rather than a completely new science. Lacking vision and of only limited ability, Crow had stolidly obstructed any investigation into liquid fuels capable of powering a large rocket, and without the imagination to become excited about the German discoveries, he soured others' interest. Crow's indelible legacy was to leave the British government without a senior, informed expert on missiles. There was no British equivalent of Toftoy, eager to embrace and develop the new weapons within his own service.

A year before the German surrender, the British Joint Chiefs, recognizing that there was no central control of the country's limited scientific manpower and resources, had established a War Cabinet committee composed of the three services and civilian scientists to decide on future research and development priorities. When the committee first met on May 10, 1944, the representatives of the three military services had independently warned that they would not tolerate any interference by others in their own exclusive projects;[9] and the meeting was dominated by a heated discussion as to whether Britain should develop an anti-aircraft missile similar to the German Hs 293. The army and navy's interest in missile development was not shared by the RAF, which feared that missiles would render its service redundant and was adamant that air warfare should be limited to manned flight.

The War Cabinet committee reported on the possibility of a guided anti-aircraft projectile (GAP). Unenthusiastically, Crow stated that its development was feasible as a "long term" project, which could take four years to complete, using a significant proportion of Britain's meager resources, and would obviously not be ready for use against the Germans.[10] Crow's accurate yet desultory message annoyed both General Weeks of the Imperial General Staff and Admiral Charles Kennedy-Purvis. Although isolated, both demanded the rejection of Crow's recommendations but were rebuffed by Ben Lockspeiser, Crow's immediate superior. Justifiably, Lockspeiser, the chief scientist at the Ministry of Aircraft Production, argued that if British scientists could not produce a jet plane, then a guided missile was far beyond their capabilities. The compromise was to make a slow start, employing no more than four people under Crow's control, without Air Ministry support.[11] Weeks was dissatisfied. On his return from America in November 1944 he suggested that Britain critically needed a single "missile agency." Again, Lockspeiser, supported by more senior officials from the Ministry of Supply, successfully undermined Weeks's case: They were "against the concept of setting up an organisation in advance of needs." By December, as V2s began to rain on London and demands for new defenses grew, Churchill insisted on increased effort to develop British missiles. Lockspeiser partially retreated, but his resistance to any coordination effectively neutralized the prime minister's spirited intervention.

Paradoxically, throughout that year, a grid of high-minded committees scattered throughout Whitehall were pontificating on a myriad of future British policies in Germany. Complicated arguments were being scrutinized, and ideas were postulated that would never be implemented, including estimates of the reparations Britain should demand from Germany. Yet no one was considering how to exploit the Peenemünde scientists who were wreaking such havoc on the capital. Consequently, when Cook and his team arrived at Oberammergau, they were motivated by little more than scientific curiosity.

While Cook was still patiently completing his own investigations, further north, Staver managed during the interrogation of Karl Fleisher, a Peenemünde engineer discovered near Nordhausen, to extract the location of the documents hidden in the Goslar mine. It was May 20. Staver's race was now not against the Russians but against the British, who, on May 27, were to assume control of the area. Frantically, Staver hired miners to move thirty-five feet of rock blocking the mine entrance and, in the meantime, flew to Paris to solicit Toftoy's help. Soldiers were needed to guard the fourteen tons of documents, as well as a small army of trucks to move them, without delay, to the American zone. In Staver's absence, Cook was inveigled into leaving the mine entrance without suspecting what treasure was hidden a thousand feet inside. Soon after, Staver returned with trucks and, a week later, led the fully loaded convoy to Paris. Flushed with success, Staver nevertheless realized that no one in America was equipped to understand the complexity of German technical documents. Ideally, he felt the army should also ship the scientists in Oberammergau to New Mexico as a temporary arrangement. But unknown to Staver, the scientists were already being methodically interrogated by U.S. Counter Intelligence Corps investigators.

Both von Braun and Kurt Debus, the small, dynamic rocket-launch expert, reluctantly admitted that they had joined the SS in 1940. Understandably, Debus did not mention that at Peenemünde he was often to be seen wearing his SS uniform and that in 1942 he had denounced to the Gestapo as an "anti-Nazi" a colleague who did not share Debus's view that the British started the war and who disputed the merits of *Mein Kampf*. Debus's denunciation resulted in his colleague's arrest and conviction by a special court. With considerable charm, both he and von Braun explained that they had reluctantly bowed to intolerable pressure and that their party membership was purely symbolic. The American interrogators were skeptical. And about Dornberger, their skepticism was positively vehement: "He should be interned," scribbled the interrogator, "as a menace to the security of the Allied Forces. He is a technical member of the German General Staff with extreme views on German domination and wishes for Third World War etc." As for Rudolph, the interrogator's note read: "100% Nazi, dangerous type, security threat, had to leave SA in 1934 when entered Waffenamt. Suggest internment." When asked whether he had anything to do with slave labor at Nordhausen, Rudolph emphatically denied any responsibility or knowledge.[12] Having made their recommendations, the interrogators departed. Under occupation laws agreed upon by the Allies, every former SS officer and active Nazi was automatically to be arrested pending investigation. Loath to antagonize the scientists, Colonel Trichel of Army Ordnance decided that their temporary imprisonment, albeit in the comfort of Garmisch-Partenkirchen, in Bavaria, satisfied the regulations.

Meanwhile, in Paris, Staver composed a message to Toftoy recommending that the rocket team be offered short-term contracts and brought to America for further interrogation. His cable to the chief of Ordnance in Washington was enthusiastic and in part dishonest.[13] He claimed that U.S. forces were holding more than four hundred top rocket scientists whose "thinking is twenty-five years ahead of U.S." and urged that the top one hundred scientists be evacuated to America, where they could complete the drawings of the Wasserfall anti-aircraft missile within three months and, shortly afterward, put it into production for use against the Japanese. Staver knew that the timetable was impossible but felt he had to offer senior officers in the Pentagon the bait of some immediate benefit. Staver also suggested that the scientists' recruitment would deny "whole or part of this group to other interested agencies." To lend color to the threat of competition, Staver added that Russian agents had set up loudspeakers along the River Elbe and were broadcasting enticements to German scientists. This fanciful and naive fabrication was probably the invention of one of the scientists, keen to improve his chances of immigration to the United States. But in the chaos of the German collapse, Staver was working unsupervised and uncontrolled, with unlimited enthusiasm and, apparently, unlimited power.

Finally, knowing that officers antagonistic to recruiting Nazis would oppose the proposal on principle, Staver ended the message with an intentionally deceptive flourish: "future scientific importance outweighs their present war guilt." Staver never believed that any of the rocket scientists were tainted by war crimes; this parting shot was simply an astute device to "smooth the idea" and mitigate the inevitable perception in Washington that the Germans were war criminals.

In Washington, Toftoy mulled over Staver's cable and Bromley's reports from Nordhausen. Thousands of crates of blueprints and unassembled V2s were crossing the Atlantic, and the only people who could assemble the rockets were their German designers. U.S. Army newsreel film had already shown a beaming von Braun, with his arm in plaster, standing outside a whitewashed house surrounded by his friends Axster, Dornberger, and Debus. All were laughing. Toftoy's immediate problem was not only his colleagues' antipathy toward Germans, but their conviction that the threat of another war was remote. Nevertheless, both politicians and officials at the War Department were by then anxious to grasp at anything that might shorten the war in Japan, and Staver had offered a temporary expedient. The only likely obstacle was the State Department, especially the visa section, whose permission for entry into the United States was required by law.

Howard Travers, a visa section official, had already become aware of the problem in March. Representatives from the chemical industry had discreetly inquired about the possibility of recruiting German experts, whose knowledge was undoubtedly the most advanced in the world. Travers was aghast at the prospect, interpreting the suggestion of such recruitment as a surreptitious attempt to place Nazi intelligence agents in America. "We should do everything we consistently can," he told colleagues, "to prevent German chemists and others from entering this country."[14] Other officials, as yet unaware of the horror of Nazi atrocities, were not alarmed. Cogently, Kermit Gordon, another State Department official, presented the national defense argument in favor of admitting the Germans: "The remarkable achievements of German science before and during the present war were largely responsible for Germany's achievement of a degree of military power entirely out of relation to her population and raw material position." Gordon argued that if the Allies attempted to ban scientific research, history would repeat itself. In 1918 German scientists had fled to neighboring countries to continue their work and returned fully equipped to launch Nazi Germany's armament industry. "The main purpose of encouraging their immigration [to the United States] would be to assure that they shall not work in this field for another power." The memorandum suggested that the scientists were mostly "politically passive" and could safely be admitted to America, where "it would be possible in time to alienate their loyalties to Germany and assimilate them to the American community."[15] It seemed that the State Department would offer no barrier to any reasonable request by the military, which had, after all, made enormous sacrifices for the nation and was still committed to a war of attrition in the Far East.

The military, on the other hand, was for the most part in a state of confusion. On May 15, the same day Eisenhower urged the War Department to send him a cable stating its policy about the future treatment of German science, General Brehon Somervell asked the chief of staff in the War Department to sanction the admission of thirty-eight German scientists. Remarkably, all of them were either theoretical scientists or ship designers. Not one of them could be of any immediate use in the war with Japan.[16] Over the following two weeks, most sections of the War Department and the army acted in a thoroughly confused and uncertain manner, leaving Somervell's request unanswered.

As far as the rocket scientists were concerned, however, Army Intelligence, or G2, knew what it wanted. Major General Clayton Bissell, assistant chief of staff (destined in later years for an intriguing career in the CIA), adopted a more subtle approach than Somervell. On his orders, on May 22 two colonels visited Frederick Lyon, an assistant secretary at the State Department, and politely informed him that G2 intended to bring forty rocket scientists into America under military custody as a matter of urgency. Since they would technically be under arrest, State Department approval for visas was legally unnecessary. G2, Lyon was told, had heard that German rocket blueprints had been passed to the Japanese, and it was vital that the Germans be interrogated by experts. Bissell's ruse seduced Lyon into believing that the Germans would be returned within four to six weeks. "One can readily appreciate the necessity of having these men work here for a temporary period," wrote the beguiled official.[17] It was the first of many lies the army would tell the State Department.

Four days later, Bissell received a detailed proposal from the chief of Military Intelligence for two sites able to accommodate fifty to one hundred German scientists. For the moment, it was relatively uncomplicated to bring the scientists to America without "formally consulting" the State and Justice departments. But Military Intelligence still felt concerned about avoiding "promiscuous travel" by the scientists, which would arouse "unfavorable publicity" and inevitably cause problems.[18]

Indeed, an outbreak of public fury was the politicians' greatest fear. On May 28, Robert Patterson, the under secretary of war, approved Trichel's plan, based on Staver's recommendations, agreeing that every possible aid should be used in the war against Japan. But his letter reflected the politicians' sensitivity to considerations that the military had apparently ignored: "These men are enemies and it must be assumed that they are capable of sabotaging our war effort. Bringing them to this country raises delicate questions, including the possible strong resentment of the American public." Bearing this in mind, Patterson wrote that as much information as possible should be extracted "within Germany and only those should be brought here whose particular work requires their presence here. It is assumed that such men will be under strict surveillance while here and that they will be returned to Germany as soon as possible."[19] A week later, the British were told that the U.S. Chiefs of Staff had informally agreed to import German scientists as a temporary measure to help with the war against Japan. The British were assured that the scientists would be screened to "eliminate war criminals and undesirables" and were asked to agree quickly so the scientists could be "removed during the SHAEF period."[20] The approval from London arrived with two conditions: first, that only Germans who would be useful in the Japanese war would be recruited, and second, that the two countries establish a negotiating committee to eliminate competition.[21]

Trichel had, in fact, already anticipated approval of the plan. On June 1, Staver began to select a group of rocket technicians, rather than theorists, who would be given six-month contracts to work in America provided they were willing to cooperate. During their absence, their dependents in Germany would enjoy privileged conditions. With fervent zeal, an American ordnance group led by Staver and Porter, with active help from von Braun, began scouring the Bleicherode area in search of the remaining Peenemünde and Nordhausen evacuees. Dozens of vehicles were requisitioned, and officers with lists of names and addresses drove through the area amid the postwar chaos, delivering this simple message: "Either accept immediate evacuation or remain at your peril in the future Soviet Zone." Ernst Stühlinger, an important theoretician, was among those given a few hours' warning: "An American captain came and told me to leave Thuringia before midnight. I told him that I had no transport. He replied: 'Just take the mayor's car. From tomorrow, he won't need it.' " Others left in a massive convoy. Only hours before Russian troops were expected to arrive, on June 20, a train carrying one thousand scientists and their families crossed the river Werra into the American zone. Many scientists decided not to leave their homes, and later Porter was insistent that "we used no threats or force of any kind." Subsequent investigations would prove otherwise.

As ordnance officers and Porter patiently started negotiations with the Germans in Garmisch-Partenkirchen about their terms of employment in America, some State Department officials began voicing their doubts about the apparently unquestioning support that Kermit Gordon had promised in April. The focus of their anger was William Clayton, an assistant secretary at the State Department who had drafted a letter to John McCloy, the assistant secretary of war, supporting the admission of the Germans "in the national interest," since otherwise they would "find their way to other countries."[22] Clayton's letter was not sent. Al Clattenburg in the department's Special War Problems Division objected because it seemingly allowed the Germans into America without any restrictions either on the scientists or on the army itself. His objection triggered a major departmental meeting to review policy on June 27.

Officials arrived in the conference room nursing a variety of irreconcilable interests, passions, and grievances. Throughout the war the department had been split on numerous issues but on none more so than the treatment of the Jews and, specifically, the admission to America of Jewish refugees from Europe. Subsequent investigation proved that senior State Department officials had deliberately played down, and even suppressed, eyewitness reports of Nazi persecution in order to resist the pressure for more Jewish immigration. Irate officials — especially the handful, like Seymour Rubin, who were Jewish — were moved by the daily postwar exposure of German atrocities to atone for their colleagues' suppression of the truth. Reading through Gordon's presentation, they were uneasy about his assumption that the scientists were "politically passive." They were simply no longer prepared to tolerate the presence of any German in the American hemisphere who had collaborated with the Nazis during the war. Within weeks there would be a clear schism between pro-Jewish and other officials, but for the moment those arguing against the military's proposals rested their case on less emotive grounds. Throughout the War Department, officials had been concerned about the pro-German bias of the "neutral" South American states, especially Argentina. American security, it was felt, had been threatened by Germans developing new weapons in the neutral countries for Hitler's benefit. At the State Department meeting, the antiscientist faction argued that the United States should now convince the South Americans to repatriate these "dangerous individuals" to Europe, where they would be imprisoned with other pro-Nazis while their future was considered. Agreement proved impossible, and the meeting ended in acrimony, leaving the department without any policy.

With the State Department in disarray, the Joint Chiefs and McCloy came under pressure from impatient officers to approve their plan of bringing the Germans over under military custody as prisoners of war. By late June, the criteria for admitting the Germans had been agreed upon and seemed to those with political sensitivities to be sufficiently strict. Only an "essential minimum" of "indispensable" volunteers, none of them suspected war criminals, were to be "temporarily" transferred to Fort Strong, on an island near Boston, where they would be held for interrogation. A War Department study conducted by Major General Gladeon Barnes, in charge of the Ordnance technical division, stipulated that "only the most compelling argument should bring a German specialist to this country for interrogation. . . . It must be emphasized that this procedure is in effect a form of exploitation of chosen rare minds whose continuing intellectual productivity we wish to use."[23] As Bissell noted, the essential criterion was their "indispensability to the successful accomplishment of the most vital research program."[24] On July 5, Toftoy was told that his plan had been approved. Brusquely, the British chiefs were informed that since the scientists' exploitation was only a "temporary . . . priority matter," further discussions were unnecessary and British cooperation was desired and expected. The exploitation program was officially sanctioned on July 19 by the Joint Chiefs of Staff as "Operation Overcast," allowing 350 German scientists, without their families, to be brought to the United States on six-month contracts that could be renewed for another six months. Ordnance was allowed to bring in one hundred rocket scientists, and von Braun's team was expected to arrive within six weeks. Only eight weeks earlier, Bissell's emissaries to the State Department had told Assistant Secretary Lyon that the limit would be forty.

Soon after, Toftoy — who had now taken over the selection of the scientists from Trichel — arrived in Witzenhausen to begin choosing the best scientists and negotiating their contracts. Asked to explain how taking German scientists to America for war research was compatible with the Joint Chiefs' directive to Eisenhower expressly forbidding any dealings with ex-Nazis, Toftoy claimed that he was acting on superior orders from the president.[25] Despite the Joint Chiefs' limitation, he listed 115 names. Von Braun was offered $750 per month; the others, commensurate salaries. While the Germans seemed impressed by the high rate of pay, they were all worried about leaving their families behind in Germany, although they would be housed and protected by the army in a special compound where they would receive substantial privileges. Toftoy tried to allay their fears, but other American agencies suspected that the families issue was a smoke screen concealing a more crucial question. Colonel Ralph Osborne, a scientist and chief of FIAT, less enthusiastic about the Germans than Toftoy, was convinced that the Germans "were running rings around the Americans." By mid-September clear evidence had emerged of von Braun's devious schemes.

Three Peenemünde scientists, all anti-Nazis who had refused American contracts, confided to Osborne that the rocket team's strict hierarchical structure under Dornberger, Axster, and von Braun had remained intact despite the German surrender.[26] Before every interrogation, each German was carefully briefed by the triumvirate and their lieutenants about what could and could not be disclosed. The guidelines were explicit: divulge no more than required to arouse technical and scientific curiosity and avoid going into technical detail that would render employment by the Americans unnecessary. Whenever pressed, the Germans were either to plead the absence of documentary material or refer questions to other members of the team, in order to create the impression that a larger number of scientists were "indispensable." After every interrogation, each German was debriefed in the presence of his colleagues, so that the others knew precisely what was the Americans' current state of knowledge. Osborne also discovered that those scientists who criticized or failed to obey Dornberger's edicts were punished. Toftoy breezily dismissed Osborne's findings, including evidence that the triumvirate was deciding who should or should not be allowed to accept American contracts. Excluded were those scientists, regardless of qualifications, who had rebelled against the clique's authority; included were the faithful, despite lack of scientific expertise, among them the group's artist, Gerd de Beek, as well as von Braun's chauffeur, and Axster.

While Toftoy was patiently trying to persuade the Germans to accept his terms, Crow successfully argued that the British had the right to question the team before it left for America. After all, the British were equal partners and also had the right to develop rockets; indeed, other than the obstacle of Britain's financial predicament, there was no reason the British should not take the lead in European rocket development. Reluctantly Toftoy agreed. Von Braun, Dornberger, Axster, and others were flown to Inkpot, the Beltane School in Wimbledon, requisitioned as an internment camp for scientists. Crow wanted their advice about how to establish a British rocket center and help with "Operation Backfire," a British plan to assemble and fire a series of V2s in Cuxhaven. Von Braun claims that his team — probably with Toftoy's encouragement — was polite but deliberately unhelpful.[27] In fact, Crow put no great pressure on the Germans to be otherwise; in July 1945 British rocket policy was still in astonishing confusion. In the end, von Braun was flown back to Garmisch-Partenkirchen while Dornberger and Debus were taken directly to Cuxhaven, the desolate site on the coast of the North Sea where five hundred Germans and 1,500 British military personnel were already building a brand-new V2 assembly plant and launching pad. Rudolph and about eighty others from the team had already arrived.

Operation Backfire had been informally approved by Eisenhower on May 10. Major General Alexander Cameron, then chief of SHAEF's air defense division, and his staff had convinced both Eisenhower and the War Office that the British should test-fire a series of V2s for experimental purposes. Crow concurred. Squads of interrogators and investigators from the Twenty-first Army were dispatched throughout Europe to collect and assemble the equipment and German personnel. Dozens of trains and hundreds of planes brought the equipment to Cuxhaven, where new roads and railway lines were being laid and huge assembly sheds erected. With Eisenhower's personal support, the enormous cost and vast resources needed for Operation Backfire seemed to be the prelude to a British breakthrough.

The U.S. War Department was skeptical about the idea and strongly protested Eisenhower's freeze on shipping V2s to White Sands. The British, it seemed, were more interested in learning how to fire a rocket than mastering the scientific knowledge to build one. Curiously, London had asked Eisenhower's headquarters to send just four V2 rockets to Britain while Washington wanted one hundred. The British had abruptly increased their request to match the Americans', but their initial modesty was interpreted by the Pentagon as proof that the British would not seriously contest their control over the von Braun team.

Proprietary about "my Germans," Toftoy was furious about the British operation. He felt that the British were deliberately scuttling Operation Overcast and demanded the immediate return of twenty-six of the Peenemünde experts, claiming that they were vital for the Japanese war. To his relief, the British were cooperative, indeed, quite conciliatory. Fourteen of the scientists and technicians were released immediately, and the return of the remainder was promised after the firings. The British Deputy Chiefs had already decided that, because of their heavily reduced defense budget, rocket development would be limited to LOP/GAP, an anti-aircraft missile smaller than the V2.[28]

On October 2, amid considerable excitement, the first British V2 was ready for firing. Hundreds of spectators had assembled to witness the event, yet several of the most important Britons were absent. William Cook, Crow's deputy, and John Elstub, the British rocket pioneer, were not invited. "It was the military's operation," says Elstub, "and had no technical importance"; for Cook it was simply "a waste of time." Nor was Crow, who had a new title, director for missile development, or Lockspeiser, from the Ministry of Aircraft Production, present.[29] These two displayed an amazing lack of interest. Although Cook and Elstub had chosen Westcott — an abandoned airfield northwest of London — as Britain's rocket research center, both had been denied access to British staff files, and Crow refused to allow recruitment of any Peenemünde scientist until such time as government policy was agreed upon. Cook was astonished how, in a matter of weeks, some in Whitehall had come to regard rockets as historical relics rather than weapons of the future. But in Britain, unlike America, lobbying of the military by civilians was considered unsavory.

During Cook's absence, on October 15 senior British, American, and Russian officers with the German experts watched a V2 fire its engines and fly toward Denmark. It fell short of its target, but all agreed that it had been "a good show" that convincingly removed most doubts about the future of rocketry. Everyone then disbanded. In January 1947, Major General Cameron delivered to the War Office an impressive five-volume account of the operation. By then, not only was it redundant, but both Cook and Elstub were about to resign in anger, frustration, and disgust.

For the Germans, Operation Backfire lived up to its unfortunate code name: It furnished ample proof that the British could not offer an attractive future. Rudolph expressed his contempt for British amateurism; and in Washington the operation was ignored. On their return to Garmisch-Partenkirchen, Rudolph and his colleagues discovered that von Braun and a small advance team had left for America in early September. They had flown from France to Wilmington, Delaware, and then via the Aberdeen proving ground to El Paso, Texas, where they arrived by the end of the month. Over the next three months 118 of the Peenemünde group arrived in Texas. They were well looked after — for a forty-eight-hour week they were paid six dollars per day tax-free, with free medical care, sick leave, accommodation, and food. There were no checks to discover whether any of those selected were ardent Nazis or war criminals. "The checks," concedes Staver, "were crude." Looking down the list of arrivals, others would later say they were nonexistent.

Only Walter Dornberger failed to arrive in America as planned. During the preparations for Operation Backfire he had been flown to London — ostensibly for consultations, but instead he was taken to the London Cage, an interrogation center for suspected war criminals. Politicians wanted a scapegoat for the bombardment of London. Toftoy was outraged. All his suspicions of British perfidy were confirmed. Dornberger, he thundered, was needed in America. Dr. Howard Robertson, chief adviser to Osborne, the head of FIAT, disagreed:

> Dornberger is a regular soldier of 30 years service, is not a first rate technician and . . . wields great power over his subordinates, including Prof v. Braun. I am convinced that Dornberger is a most dangerous man, and that he should in any case be shorn of all influence over and even prevented to have contact with his former Peenemünde subordinates."[30]

For the next two years Dornberger was held with other high-ranking Nazis at Bridgend, in Wales, but he was neither charged nor interrogated about the V2. In Cook's words, "Dornberger was the SS's man. He knew nothing about rockets." Washington felt differently. When he was eventually released, Dornberger was flown directly to Texas, where he was accorded a hero's welcome.

7

Competition and Confusion

JUST FIVE DAYS before Japan's formal surrender, on August 14, 1945, the Joint Chiefs finally agreed on a detailed scheme for German scientists to enter America — guardedly referred to as "temporary exploitation." The Joint Intelligence Committee was authorized to set up an "interim procedure" to coordinate the government's activities until a "long-range" policy had been agreed upon by the all-powerful State-War-Navy Coordinating Committee (SWNCC).[1] The formalized agreement had barely been printed, numbered, and circulated to those entitled to see it when the atomic explosion at Hiroshima ended the war and gave a particular piquancy to the spectacular new arms race, henceforth based entirely on scientific knowledge. But just then the importance of science for warfare was so dramatically confirmed, the War Department lost its most important pretext for admitting German scientists to America — namely, to assist in shortening the Japanese war.

Major General Bissell immediately grasped the unfortunate juxtaposition. Werner von Braun's arrival was imminent, and Military Intelligence feared unpleasant political repercussions should word of his arrival be leaked before it could be officially announced. In the aftermath of the war the public had been shocked by reports of Nazi atrocities, and any unplanned leaks would certainly provoke "misguided protests"; but the blanket top-secret classification imposed on Overcast restricted the army's ability to prepare the public. In May Bissell had agreed that the scientists should be kept out of public view to avoid "difficulties with the State and Justice Department, to say nothing of the reactions of the general public." Major Staver was insistent on strict secrecy, since publicity "would have been deadly. In the furor, they would have all been sent back to Germany." Bissell agreed that the "avoidance of unfavorable publicity" was essential but feared that total secrecy might inflict greater damage, which, with sensitive handling, could be avoided.[2]

On October 9 he authorized a press release that was deliberately terse. In compliance with the Joint Chiefs' criteria that each German listed must be verified as "indispensable to the successful accomplishment of the most vital military research program,"[3] it baldly stated that "certain outstanding German scientists and technicians are being brought to this country to ensure that we take full advantage of those significant developments which are deemed vital to our national security" and that the Germans, who had been "carefully selected" and "brought on a voluntary basis," would be properly supervised during their "temporary stay." Press officers in the War Department were ordered to "play this story down" and were not to release the names or pictures of the scientists or mention where the Germans were "permanently housed."[4] Bissell's avoidance of publicity was nearly successful. Although von Braun arrived unnoticed, on September 29 the *New York Times* had reported the disembarkation of sixteen "Reich technicians" from a troop ship in Boston who had come "for the Transportation Corps." The only adverse reaction seems to have been the booing from a crowd of the returning GIs, standing alongside the ship rails, as the "jovial group . . . came down the gangplank to an Army bus." In the future, the army had at least some grounds for pleading that there had never been any intention to deceive the public, but in the short term, a more pressing problem — British allegations of "double-dealing" — needed to be resolved.

Back in May 1945, the British had been skeptical about Washington's demands that America should have first claim to the German scientists "because of the Japanese war." But in the interests of "good relations" and in the hope that later a more formal agreement could be negotiated,[5] the American request was quickly approved. At the time, dozens of German scientists were arriving in Britain in total secrecy for "indefinite interrogation." Dr. George Madelung, an expert on bomb design, was taken to England from Ruit; Dr. E. Kutzscher, an infrared expert, was flown in from Kiel; Kurt Tank, Focke-Wulf's chief designer, arrived from Hamburg; Gerhard Lindner, a Messerschmitt jet test pilot, was brought over, together with an Me 262, from Lechfeld, and Dr. Karl Waninger, a ballistics expert, from Dusseldorf. The fact that Waninger — "an ardent Nazi" — was now secluded in relative comfort at Inkpot (Wimbledon's Beltane School)[6] passed without comment. To Eisenhower's query about the control of German scientists and laboratories, the British disarmingly replied that they wanted time to interrogate important scientists to determine whether they should be given "special treatment."[7]

Their temporizing lasted only four weeks. Faced with the pressures of American recruitment, a three-power concordat in Berlin which agreed that all German war-research establishments would be closed early in 1946, and the growing realization that there was much more to learn from the Germans than was possible during short interrogations, on June 25 the War Office held its first official meeting to formulate a policy for the long-term employment of German scientists on defense projects. In marked contrast to the Pentagon, the British military could not even partially conceal its intentions from civilian government officials. The obstacles seemed formidable: security, public sensitivity, and, above all, opposition from the Home Office.

A modest program, limited to one hundred scientists "of outstanding ability," was proposed to the Deputy Chiefs by Admiral Charles Kennedy-Purvis. During the war, of the three armed services, the navy had been the most diligent investigator. New reports from Germany suggesting that fierce competition had broken out between the Allies, the aggressive American campaign to recruit the Peenemünde scientists, free-lance kidnap attempts launched by the British, and the wholesale corralling of Germans from the Soviet into the U.S. zone all made Kennedy-Purvis anxious to reach a quick agreement with the Americans. The Royal Navy was not overly concerned with whether or not the Peenemünde team went to America so long as the German naval experts at Kiel ended up in Britain.

Kennedy-Purvis was well aware of the weakness of his position in negotiating with Washington.[8] Britain's lead in weapons development was eroding fast, and there were not even sufficient planes to fly all the investigating teams to Europe. At first it seemed advantageous to draw on the wartime relationship: The British chiefs proposed that all information extracted from the Germans should be fairly shared between Britain and America — and that both the French and Russians should be automatically excluded.[9] The suggestion was readily accepted in Washington, but simultaneously, the British Deputy Chiefs realized that the important category of industrial information must not be included, since American industry could not, as in Britain, be compelled to hand over information. They therefore decided quietly to renege on their own proposal.[10] As far as military information was concerned Kennedy-Purvis set about fashioning an agreement among the conflicting departments in Whitehall for presentation to Washington, from which Russia and France were to be deliberately cut out.

On July 21 Kennedy-Purvis presented a draft policy statement entitled "The Exploitation of German Science and Technology" to the Deputy Chiefs as "a matter of urgency." It was unequivocal: "We consider that our object must be to obtain from Germany the maximum amount of scientific and technical intelligence by way of personnel, equipment and information which would be of general advantage to the Defense Services of this country."[11] The plan was for "a small number of high-grade experts" to be brought to Britain for six months' probation — then "encouraged" to "prolong their sojourn" together with their families. The security risk was considered "fully justified," since the scientists would need express permission to leave Britain, which the British felt there would be no obligation ever to grant. Kennedy-Purvis tentatively suggested that "a very provisional total of 150" experts should be brought over: twenty-five for the Admiralty, forty for the Ministry of Aircraft Production, and eighty-five for the Ministry of Supply.[12] They would be experts in hydrogen peroxide engines, supersonic aircraft, wind tunnels, missiles, fuels, ceramics, fuses, and ballistics.

Judiciously, he then set out the arguments against his own proposals: The most dangerous part of German war potential would be kept alive; Britain would disqualify herself from protesting against her allies doing the same; and there would no doubt be public criticism of employing Germans who had recently been working for Hitler against Britain. For Kennedy-Purvis, the advantages easily outweighed any disadvantages, but his hopes of rapid approval were soon dashed. Both the Home Office and the Joint Intelligence Committee were critical of the security risks. The JIC feared that, since the Germans could not work in a vacuum, they would quickly discover Britain's latest scientific and technical secrets; and because it would be impossible to isolate them from Germany, no regulations could prevent them from returning to rebuild new munitions industries:

It makes little difference whether one of these scientists is a convinced Nazi or not. It has been abundantly proved during this war that Germans both here and in the United States, whether they be Social Democrats or Jews, maintain their fundamental loyalty to the Fatherland and that if there were any possibility of Germany's regeneration they would be as likely as any to take advantage of it, so long as it was not Nazi.

On the other hand, if they married and settled in Britain, it would be equally impossible to force them to leave. Even those who stayed would be a danger, because they would inevitably be in close contact with German scientists in America. The JIC recommendation was to bring the Germans for a maximum of one year, to "suck them dry," and prevent them from working with industrial teams planning future designs.

Even the JIC's compromise was rejected by the Home Office as "fraught with danger." Wartime memories were too fresh, and the conviction that all Germans were dangerous was still deep-seated among officials whose task for nearly six years had been to preserve the nation's internal security. For both the JIC and the Home Office, the insuperable obstacle was that a brilliant German scientist would inevitably become "indispensable" and therefore dangerous. Kennedy-Purvis was faced with an apparently unanswerable security argument. His solution was to seize on a genuine problem and blow it up so as to create an "alarming crisis" just before the Chiefs of Staff met at the end of August.

The British chiefs were already irritated by Colonel Toftoy's pressure to return twelve Peenemünde scientists working on Operation Backfire, at Cuxhaven, before the launch. With the end of the Japanese war, the British chiefs signaled Washington: "We cannot believe that a delay of less than two months could seriously inconvenience the US Chiefs of Staff." Two days before Kennedy-Purvis presented his report to the decisive meeting, he heard of a disagreement at Volkenrode, now under permanent British control, over whether Britain or America "owned" Dr. Bernard Goethert, a German aeronautic designer. According to an American intelligence report, Lieutenant W. A. Rosenbauer arrived at Volkenrode to collect Goethert, who, he claimed, had already been assigned for departure to America. Rosenbauer later stated that Goethert had suddenly "disappeared" — "kidnapped" by Roy Goody, the British commanding officer, who had left a note saying, "The Ministry of Aircraft Production have an interest in Dr Goethert and he must not be removed from the neighbourhood of Göttingen without letter permit."[13]

Kennedy-Purvis's version to the chiefs was very different. Goethert, he insisted, was not named on the Anglo-American list of wanted German scientists and had in fact been kidnapped by Rosenbauer, who had returned to take away between two and four other Germans, including the famous aerodynamics expert Adolph Busemann. Solemnly, Kennedy-Purvis circulated to all the chiefs a brief description of the incident, characterizing it as an American attempt to kidnap four top German aeronautic designers from Volkenrode. It was, Kennedy-Purvis claimed, the second attempt and was only foiled at the last moment. "Originally the Americans stated that the scientists in question were required 'at Wright Airfield for immediate work directly connected with the prosecution of the war against Japan.'" Accordingly, "in view of the end of hostilities . . . the activities of Lt Rosenbauer should be brought to an end and . . . no further action regarding the removal of German personnel should be taken by the Americans pending the negotiations arising from the decision of the Defence Committee."[14]

Kennedy-Purvis hoped that the incident would convey the intense competition for German scientists and thus influence the security services to relax their opposition and approve his proposal to Washington. Ten days later, his tactics were rewarded. A very extensive compromise was hammered out with the JIC and the Home Office, which were both convinced that if Britain did not grab the scientists, her allies would certainly do so.[15] Security demands were emphasized — although in an attempt to satisfy both sides, they were noticeably contradictory. It was admitted that "there would be virtually no adequate safeguard against leakage of defence secrets," since the scientists' movements and correspondence could not be controlled and their access to secrets could only be restricted, not prohibited. Therefore, since "leakage of information on the long-term trend of secret weapons would indeed be serious," the agreed compromise was to severely limit their numbers and their length of stay. The basis on which they were to be employed was also revised: In anticipation of trade union criticism, a condition was added that no German would be brought to Britain if his job could be done by a British subject, and the Home Office was given final discretion regarding conditions of entry, plus the task of spying on the Germans' activities. Ironically, at that very moment, despite the Deputy Chiefs' opposition, the JIC also recommended that all foreign scientists, mostly refugees, who had worked on secret defense projects during the war "should be removed immediately" in the interests of long-term security.

Anxious about American pressure, the Cabinet's defense committee approved the compromise on August 31.[16] Kennedy-Purvis was authorized to offer Washington a deal providing for the scientists in both zones to be pooled, then shared out by a combined Anglo-American allocation committee. Tongue-in-cheek, the British also proposed that the results of their work be exchanged, and reinforced the offer with a personal telegram from the prime minister to President Truman. With a list of more than one hundred wanted German scientists, Kennedy-Purvis waited for a reply, not realizing that the machinery of government in Washington had become practically paralyzed.

The detailed management of Overcast had by then been transferred from Bissell to Colonel Ernest Gruhn, who had been appointed director of the Joint Intelligence Objectives Agency. Operating from a few rooms in the Munitions Building in Washington, Gruhn and successive directors of JIOA would become passionate advocates of America's need to recruit the Germans and deny them to the other powers. More sinisterly, they would deliberately conceal their irregular and unauthorized activities from civilian government departments. Their duplicity started less than four weeks after Gruhn's appointment.

The British proposals arrived in Washington just after the Japanese surrender. Peace and the election of a new president had created a mood of confusion and uncertainty among the American Joint Chiefs. Eisenhower had been told by the War Department that, now that the pressures of war had dissolved, Overcast was being reassessed "with a view to reducing requests to minimum numbers of key personnel in most essential fields."[17] The message left the Joint Chiefs unsure about the conditions for admitting the Germans. President Truman clearly favored plundering Germany and in June had ordered the Department of Commerce to organize the publication of as much of the hitherto secret German scientific information as possible for general use.[18] But that fell considerably short of approving the entry of Nazi scientists. In peacetime, as War Department officials realized, the military's ability to steamroller unquestioning acquiescence from other departments would inevitably disappear. New allies were needed, and American industry, whose support could be canvassed with the promise of military help for the plundering of Germany, was clearly an important potential partner. Two weeks after the Joint Chiefs asked Gruhn and their intelligence staff to study the British proposals, Gruhn recommended approval of the proposed machinery for sharing the Germans but criticized the British stipulation that the program should be restricted to scientists involved in military projects as excessively "limited."[19]

Gruhn's recommendations for Pentagon staff included a draft letter to Henry Wallace, the secretary of commerce, inviting his participation in Overcast and suggesting that he dispatch a representative to Frankfurt to recruit Germans.[20] Gruhn also reiterated previous arguments and two hitherto apparently uncontroversial assumptions: first, that "informal inquiries" had revealed there would be "no real difficulties with either the State Department or the Immigration and Naturalization Service of the Department of Justice in securing permits for temporary entry," and second, "no known Nazis, irrespective of their scientific or technical qualifications, should be brought to the United States."

While it was certainly true that the War Department had obtained informal State Department agreement in April and May, by September Gruhn undoubtedly knew that many State Department officials were strongly opposed to the Germans' entry. The evidence also suggests that, fearing rejection, Bissell and later Gruhn deliberately made no attempt to secure Department of Justice approval. Since May, the army had assumed that bringing the Germans into America under military custody exempted them from Department of Justice control.[21] The second assumption, the explicit ban on Nazis, also posed a problem. Von Braun had just arrived, and whatever cosmetic treatment would be used in the future to conceal his SS membership, his presence in America was an indisputable breach of the War Department's undertaking. Accordingly, Gruhn was asked to rewrite his memorandum.

Gruhn's revised recommendations, considered on October 11, judiciously removed all reference to the informal agreements with the State Department and the Department of Justice and included the proviso that "only in exceptional cases will a German specialist whose record indicates that he was a convinced Nazi be brought to the United States for exploitation otherwise than in an interrogation center operated by the War or Navy Department."[22] To

Gruhn's surprise, the attempted reconciliation created fresh problems.

Unpredictably, Michael Strauss of the Department of the Interior vehemently opposed the distinction between pro-Nazi and anti-Nazi: "This Department's whole concept and goal in the matter is what we are to get out of the Germans."[23] Strauss wanted their technical and scientific knowledge regardless of their politics. Another bombshell arrived from John Green, an ebullient lawyer appointed by President Truman in June to mastermind the use of German scientists by American industry and the dissemination of German expertise through the Department of Commerce.[24] Bringing scientists to the United States temporarily, as prisoners of war, he told Gruhn, "does not appear sound." Green wanted fifty scientists to come to America, but only as permanent immigrants and only those "whose opposition to Nazi principles can be demonstrated." Topping Green's list of desirable scientists was Dr. Walter Reppe, a director of research at I. G. Farben; shortly afterward, Reppe would be arrested by American investigators as a suspected war criminal and held at Nuremberg.[25] Irritated and impatient about the civilians' contradictory moral arguments, Bissell — to Green's embarrassment — summarily excluded the Department of Commerce and American industry from any further involvement in Overcast. Moreover, the operation suddenly faced a grave and possibly fatal obstacle: The majority of State Department officials now opposed Gruhn's proposed reply to the British.

"The State Department finds itself in a very difficult and embarrassing position," wrote Paul Hutton at the beginning of a lengthy internal memorandum on October 31, describing the personal animosity that bitterly divided officials: "It is a long and sad story." The acrimony had started earlier in the month. Until Gruhn drafted his letter to the secretary of commerce, the State Department had reluctantly succumbed to the War Department's argument of military need. JIOA's proposed expansion of Overcast to include industry confirmed many State Department officials' suspicions that the compromises involved were excessive. Other officials were skeptical for different reasons, reflecting the deep policy divisions and diversity of personal feelings that had permeated the department during the war and now persisted in discussions about the country's postwar policies.

Since April these disagreements, albeit muted, had prevented the State Department from starting discussions about the German scientists in the influential State-War-Navy Coordinating Committee. After the arrival of Gruhn's revised proposal on October 11, the discussions could be delayed no longer. As a preliminary, Hutton called an interdepartmental meeting. After two hours during which "strong partisan views" were heard, only one official, Kermit Gordon, still supported the military; among those who changed sides was Frederick Lyon. Two weeks earlier Lyon had been in favor of JIOA's proposals — but at the end of October he confessed that if industry did not want the Germans, then the risk to the national interest of admitting them for the military alone was too great to take. Hutton summarized the officials' consensus as follows: National security would be jeopardized by admitting the Germans, since neither their movements nor their acquisition of American secrets could be controlled; there would be an outcry from the public and press; and the department's current attempts to persuade South American governments to expel Nazi scientists would be ridiculed. State's unity, however, was an illusion; there was, in fact, no consensus.[26]

When SWNCC met on November 9 to discuss the question for the first time, Lyon proposed that the only safe policy was for the United States unilaterally to announce that no scientist should be allowed to emigrate from Germany to any other country. Other officials vociferously urged different solutions, either fearing a huge influx of young Hitlerites or loath to countenance an absurd waste of talent clearly needed in America. Seymour Rubin, who had originally opposed Overcast inside the State Department, tried to effect a complicated compromise — a "paper to end papers" — by suggesting that the military's list of wanted scientists should be referred for critical scrutiny to Vannevar Bush of the Office of Scientific Research and Development.[27] His attempted mediation merely reopened old wounds and intensified divisions, paralyzing any opportunity for the Joint Chiefs formally to send the British a reply.

For Bissell and Gruhn, this latest round of the disagreements at Foggy Bottom, combined with the contradictory policies demanded by others, augured ill for Overcast's future. To make matters worse, the Germans at Wright Field were complaining that the security restrictions placed on them constituted a contradiction of the promises made in Germany. Some even expressed a preference for returning to Europe. Major General E. R. Quesada wrote to Bissell suggesting that the Germans receive "a more liberal treatment" and that they should be allowed to move off the base unescorted. The image of Germans happily wandering around Dayton, Ohio, made Bissell blench.[28]

The news from Germany was equally disheartening. To the frustration of the American teams in Europe, while the British and French were promising the Germans that they could bring their families with them, the War Department ruled otherwise. Faced with the dilemma of abandoning their families to fend for themselves in the turmoil of Europe, the Germans were refusing to sign the contracts proffered by the United States. On September 3 Eisenhower appealed to the War Department to reexamine its policy. Only about one thousand people were involved, he argued, and their work "is about the only material dividend we are likely to get from the war. . . . It seems to me that the success of the whole project depends on having these scientists in a proper frame of mind." His appeal was rejected a week later. The only alternative was to extend temporary protection and privileges for the families in Germany. Eisenhower ordered a suitable housing area to be requisitioned, and Landshut, just northeast of Munich, was chosen as the ideal site.

Making Landshut habitable as a special enclave for the scientists' families was the responsibility of the Third Army. On the agreed day the first families arrived, but conditions in Landshut were — as Patton's headquarters later admitted — "extremely poor." Despite American promises, the houses lacked furniture, water, and sanitation, and there was no food, nor army personnel for protection. Amid complaints about the army's breach of trust, the families spent their first two nights in railway carriages. The chaos, the Third Army reported to Washington, had "undermined the confidence of the German scientists in the good faith of the American government."[29] As rumors about the bad conditions spread, other scientists refused to sign American contracts, while those who had already reached the States became restless. Ruthless requisitioning of furniture from nearby homes temporarily relieved the situation, but as Dr. Howard Robertson, the American scientific adviser, noted, the ban on research in Germany and the ban on families going to America were two good ways of encouraging the German scientists to migrate to other zones.[30] News of the shambles arrived in Washington at the same time as reports from Europe about the consequences of the double ban: Scientists were being successfully recruited by the Russians.

Since the three powers had found themselves allies through misfortune rather than design, throughout the war Anglo-American
cooperation with the Soviet Union had inevitably been circum-
spect, especially regarding intelligence. But at first there was no
suggestion of ferocious competition for German experts. As late as
August 26, 1944, the Combined Chiefs formally urged the Russians
to prevent the retreating German army from destroying important
intelligence objectives and offered to send a list of targets that the
Combined Chiefs wanted Allied officers to inspect. The Red Army
was in turn invited to send investigators to the British and American zones on similar missions. The Russians replied on November
3, simply asking to see the promised list. Meanwhile, the Anglo-
American team had visited the V2 site in Blizna, Poland, and returned with their suspicions about Russian intentions confirmed.
Distrustful, the Combined Chiefs sent Moscow the CIOS black-
target list but deliberately excluded the most important targets,
including the newly built chemical factories in Poland, which, according to British intelligence, were "of outstanding importance."[31]

It remains unclear whether the British and Americans naively
hoped that Soviet experts would fail to recognize the value of the
factories, but the British were clearly cautious when the first major
postwar scientific issue arose — the allocation of captured V2 rockets among the Allies. On May 15, London's attitude toward the
Soviets was still reluctantly benevolent: "Though it would be desirable to prevent information as to secret weapons falling into the
hands of European powers, no such policy could be carried out in
view of the rights of powers signatory to the Instrument of Surrender to share in all surrendered enemy equipment." The British
ruled out the option of destroying Nordhausen before the American
withdrawal in case of "unfortunate repercussions" and suggested
that the Russians and French should each be allocated 10 percent
of the rockets but that they "should not be handed over until a
specific request has been received for them."[32]

Still smarting at the humiliating treatment that the Russians
had dispensed to the team waiting to visit the torpedo research
center at Gdynia, the JIC in Washington stiffened the terms: "Al-
lotment to the USSR should always be subject to reciprocal action,
not necessarily in kind but in equitable exchange of information,
material or visits."[33] At much the same time, the American CIOS
team in London was told that the JIC "desires no exchange of

technical information with the Russians, inasmuch as such an exchange would benefit the latter completely and would be of almost no gain to CIOS."[34]

In effect, the military had declared unrestricted competition among all the Allies except for the United States and the United Kingdom. Relations quickly deteriorated, and on June 26, when Churchill told Truman that Britain would share information only with America,[35] the British Chiefs of Staff translated the message as meaning that wartime cooperation was at an end and no information should be given to the Russians except on a reciprocal basis.[36] By the eve of the Potsdam summit, both America and Britain had together decided to deny German science and technology to Stalin.

Watching impatiently in Germany, Roy Fedden, an engineer himself, did not believe policy statements would be enough. No one in London, he felt, seemed to understand that after the withdrawal of the western powers from the River Elbe under the Yalta agreement, Russia would inherit the bulk of Germany's precision engineering, its aircraft, car, and machine tool industries, together with its highly skilled engineers. The West was left with little more than coal mines and steel mills in the Ruhr. Bosch managers had complained to Fedden that their advanced fuel-injection research factory in Berlin had already been transported to Russia and they would have to start again from scratch. Other Germans told him that the Russians had seized whole factories — with thousands of machine tools and jigs — that could produce revolutionary jet aircraft and rockets, all substantially superior to anything ever seriously considered in the West. Subsequent intelligence assessments would report that Fedden was probably understating the Soviet windfall. The Russian zone contained thirty-one aircraft factories, twenty-six motor manufacturers, twenty-eight accessory plants, the heart of the Telefunken and Blaupunkt electronics research laboratories, and the Zeiss optical factories.[37] Frustrated and alarmed, Fedden arranged the evacuation of twenty engineers and their families and asked the ministry in London to care for them.[38]

Although politically Washington still rejected Britain's anti-Sovietism, American intelligence teams in Europe had exceeded even British antagonism toward the Russians. The evacuation in late June of the Peenemünde scientists and their families by the U.S. Ordnance unit, to prevent capture by the Russians, had not been an isolated operation. In anticipation of the handover in June to the Red Army of the Magdeburg bulge inside the future Soviet zone, both western Allied units ordered German scientists, often at gunpoint, to leave their homes and move west. It was a wholesale seizure. Colonel Richard Ranger of the Signals Corps removed sixty scientists and their families from Thuringia to a requisitioned schoolhouse in Heidelberg;[39] and the Seventh Army removed twenty-three aircraft engineers from Halle to Darmstadt and two hundred university professors to Zell am See, near Salzburg, although denial to the Russians was not yet officially approved policy.

The largest group transported, more than 1,300 people, were Zeiss and Schott scientists and technicians from Leipzig and Jena, who manufactured the finest optical instruments in the world. In a massive night swoop authorized by SHAEF headquarters, Allied units ordered the scientists and their families to leave their houses, in some cases at five minutes' notice and at gunpoint, and drove them in military convoys to the western zones. Those who protested about losing their homes, furniture, and clothes or at abandoning absent members of their family were assured, on Eisenhower's authority, that they would be properly compensated in the West.

In July 1945 SHAEF was dissolved, and most of the British and American intelligence officers were demobilized and returned home. In addition to the optical experts, many engineers, chemists, and professors drawn from the electronics, aviation, and weapons industries had been moved out of the Soviet zone. More than five thousand forcibly uprooted Germans, billeted in requisitioned homes in Heidenheim, Gandersheim, and Hillersleben, now gradually realized that they had been abandoned, often without their wives and children, penniless, without clothes, without their equipment, and without any prospect of employment. The earlier promises that their qualifications would entitle them to jobs in America or Britain were patently threadbare. Nor was their plight improved in the autumn by the impatience of recently arrived military government officers, for whom they were just one more irritating inheritance. Repeated requests to London and Washington for orders remained unanswered. In growing desperation, some of the older technicians began contemplating suicide, while others complained that even colleagues who had been ardent Nazis were receiving privileged treatment in both the Russian and French zones. "It is impossible," reported one frustrated intelligence officer, "to get anyone to indicate any interest in the matter."[40] His predicament reflected the fact that unlike the Russians, the West momentarily lacked any coherent policy for the employment of German scientists and technicians.

In early September, General Vassily Sokolovsky, commander of the Soviet zone, wrote to General Lucius Clay, the deputy military governor of the American zone, politely asking for the return of forty-nine kidnapped German specialists because the factories in which they had formerly worked were paralyzed in their absence.[41] Sokolovsky's message repeated a similar letter that Stalin had sent to Truman a few days earlier. Clay, keen to save the high cost of supporting unwanted Germans during the coming winter and still anxious to preserve decent relations with the Russians, replied that the Germans would be released by October 10. But by the beginning of that month, the mood at his Berlin headquarters had changed considerably. The distrust between the two powers, which would eventually divide Europe, was growing. Negotiations with Sokolovsky at the Allied Control Council in Berlin about industrial reparations and the economic management of Germany became tense, and the Allied foreign ministers' meeting in London ended inconclusively. Both the American and British military governors were warning their respective governments that unless a solution to the scientists' plight was produced quickly, they would be turned loose within four weeks. Both governors were alarmed by intelligence reports that, in the absence of western offers, top German scientists were being seduced by the attractions of high pay and excellent conditions in the Soviet Union.

Lieutenant Karl Olsen, head of FIAT's industrial branch in Berlin, was among the first to notice a growing swell of German scientists moving into the Russian sector. Many were Nobel Prize–winners who had worked at the world-famous Kaiser Wilhelm Institute in Berlin. After signing long-term contracts, dozens had already flown to Moscow, many of them accompanied by their staff and families. Among them were three leading nuclear physicists, Dr. G. Hertz, Dr. N. Riehl, and Baron Manfred von Ardenne, the inventor of the most powerful electron microscope of the time. They were joined by Professor Otto Warburg, a Nobel Prize–winner and director of one of the Kaiser Wilhelm institutes, who, on discovering that his laboratories were occupied by American soldiers, had accepted a Russian offer to bring his whole team to the East.

"The voluntary movement of German scientific personnel into the USSR or Russian-controlled territory," wrote Olsen, is not difficult of explanation. At present, according to reliable reports, the working and living conditions provided are satisfactory, food rations are generous and salaries are very high. The importance of these favourable conditions increase as the present winter progresses. Of at least equal importance is the consideration that only in the Russian zone of occupied Germany are there opportunities for German scientists to carry on research. . . . In contrast is the present negative policy as regards research in the American zone [where] there is no opportunity to continue scientific work.[42]

Unlike the western Allies, the Russians had established three occasionally rival research agencies in Berlin to employ Germans on professional terms in the former Kaiser Wilhelm institutes. The Soviet Technical Commission, a Red Army agency divided into fifty subcommittees, was busy investigating every German development from lacquers to lubricants, while the People's Commissariat, a Communist party agency, recruited specialists, mostly former Nazis, for research. The third group was a less concentrated network of Germans controlled by the Russian government.[43] In the autumn Olsen reported that the Russians were developing three different rockets in Berlin and Peenemünde. The Germans were paid extremely well according to a twenty-two-grade bonus system, which rewarded the most senior scientists with high wages, comfortable villas, and domestic staff, plus ample supplies of food, cigarettes, and clothes, while those on the lowest level received a weekly ration of five cigarettes.[44] But Russian wages were not the major lure.

"The leak into the Russian zone and into the USSR," reported T. M. Odarenko, an American agent, was not solely due to the favorable conditions offered by the Russians: "The present policy of the United States occupational authorities is the exact opposite to that of the USSR."[45] Odarenko pointed to the plight of 250 scientists who had been moved "hurriedly and without authorization" by U.S. Army Intelligence and Office of Strategic Services units from the Soviet zone to Austria. All of them, without exception, were destitute — abandoned by their erstwhile saviors.

The use made of scientists in the American zone was completely chaotic. Overnight, the scientific institutes were closed and thousands of first-class scientists became unemployable under Joint Chiefs of Staff directive 1067, an all-embracing punitive order that had been published in November 1944 in line with Henry Morgenthau's scheme to deindustrialize Germany and that imposed a complete ban on scientific research. As a result, the abandoned scientists were left to find a new career for themselves, on the grounds that if they were given research work, their discoveries would "contribute to Germany's future war potential."[46] Ironically, those punished were mainly scientists who had been involved with nonmilitary projects — and were therefore least likely to be Nazis. Early in September 1945, Gruhn attempted to mitigate the harsh effects of the ban by organizing work for a Telefunken research team in Heidelberg, but his enterprise was vetoed by FIAT's chief, Ralph Osborne, on the grounds that it infringed "the Bible" (JCS 1067) and Allied Law number 25, which ordered the dismantling and destruction of all German wartime research.[47] For the same reason, Osborne was powerless to protect the "unique" Zeiss teams and could only urge that they be kept together either in Germany or in America. Paradoxically, those Germans involved exclusively in military research were offered employment, by all three western military governments, in "illegal" research centers in Germany.

The Royal Navy opened four centers,[48] and the RAF at least five, which were code-named "Matchbox,"[49] while the French had established a scientific center at Ravensburg and would soon open several more. In October, Eisenhower authorized many "research centers" to be reopened, mostly engaged in weapons development and war studies, where former Nazis were employed so long as they had not held "leading administrative and policy-making positions." But since the same order contradictorily stipulated that none of the denazification directives was to be broken, all the conditions were ignored, and notorious former Nazis were employed to develop the West's military potential.[50]

The secret use of these Germans by the western powers undoubtedly influenced the Russian announcement issued on October 11 ordering all scientists to register with the Soviet military government. Karl Olsen interpreted the announcement as signaling the end of "voluntary" recruitment, although he hoped the scientists could recognize the Russians' poisoned chalice. Meanwhile, the French were undoubtedly offering better terms than the rest of the Allies, and their success was so embarrassing that it had to be concealed. Before the war French weapons development had proceeded at much the same pace as Britain's and had outstripped America's. During the occupation, the Germans exploited the best French skills and made full use of France's vast factories, though they carefully avoided entrusting the French with too many secrets. However, German fears of French duplicity were often unfounded. Collaboration with the Nazis proved highly profitable for French industrialists, and during the weeks after France's liberation, CIOS investigators were appalled at their ally's stubborn refusal to release wartime secrets.

When CIOS protests failed, Eisenhower wrote to the French government asking for its help. The reply from General Alphonse Juin, chief of the General Staff, underlined France's reluctance to cooperate. CIOS teams, Juin requested, should be "instructed to refrain from asking any questions or conducting any inquiries which might appear to be aimed at obtaining information of a confidential character on French industries." Yet in the same letter, Juin asked that the French army's newly created Scientific Coordination Committee be allowed to operate with CIOS teams in Germany.[51] British and American ambivalence, distrust of de Gaulle, and the fear of a Communist coup forestalled any chance of approval: Cooperation with France was just as distasteful as cooperation with Russia. "Nothing," advised the American CIOS team, "is to be gained by French participation."[52] At the same time, the British decided that the French, like the Russians, should be denied access to the V2 rocket secrets; and Lieutenant Colonel Pash of the Alsos team supervised the complete destruction of the Haigerloch laboratories, hours before a French military unit arrived, to prevent France from inheriting Germany's nuclear secrets.

British and American suspicions of a French conspiracy were, in fact, well founded. During May, Brigadier General Eugene Harrison, a G2 officer in the US Sixth Army Group, operating with the French army in southwest Germany, discovered that intelligence agents working under cover of the Securité Militaire were systematically ordering, and sometimes threatening, Germans in the area not to cooperate with CIOS teams. At the Askania torpedo laboratories in Konstanz, Harrison reported, the director, Dr. Wilde, was told that if he revealed data to CIOS teams, he would be listed as a war criminal and arrested; attempts to reach forty cases of Messerschmitt documents hidden in the French zone were frustrated; Herman Maier, a German radio engineer, claimed that French industrialists had warned him not to discuss his radar research; German scientists were refusing American contracts, because they did not dare leave their families alone in Germany; and French agents were rumored to be arresting the wives of German experts and forcing them to blackmail their husbands into returning to the French zone. Angered by French obstruction, Harrison protested at the Securité Militaire headquarters but was rebuffed and pointedly denied access to the files and samples accumulated by French intelligence. Relations with the French, Osborne reported to Washington, were in "a hiatus. . . . Mutual, incipient distrust has appeared and will increase."[53]

France's success in scooping up German experts infuriated British and American intelligence. A G2 report to Washington urged cooperation with Juin, because by excluding the French, "the British and US authorities will in turn lose a great deal of valuable technical and economic intelligence uncovered by the French."[54] Belatedly and begrudgingly, the Combined Chiefs agreed. But the CIOS lists released to Juin were out of date, and on the chiefs' orders, the existence of the top-secret blacklists was concealed. For Juin, their behavior signaled unrestricted competition. By autumn 1945, the Scientific Coordination Committee under General Bloch-Dassault had become a highly effective intelligence group, and throughout Germany, agents of the DGER — the Direction Générale des Études et Recherches de Défense Nationale, equivalent to the OSS or MI6 — were successfully recruiting German scientists. It was some time before British and American intelligence agencies understood that French success was a legacy of wartime collaboration. For four years the French had been working closely with the Germans; one year's interruption caused little more than a hiccup in their relationship.

"The French knew what had happened in Germany during the war, and the Germans wanted to continue their work. Their partnership was natural," remembers Hans Munzberg, a pioneer jet-engine designer at BMW. Under Dr. Hermann Oestrich, Munzberg and two hundred senior technicians were developing the BMW 003A jet engine, featuring axial turbines two years ahead of the British radial design. The Allied bombing of Berlin in 1944 had forced their evacuation to a salt mine, one-quarter mile below ground, in Stassfurt, near Magdeburg. "Our work ended," recalls Munzberg, "just a day before the American army arrived." On April 12, when Stassfurt surrendered, Oestrich had already hidden his technical records in the town's cemetery. To his surprise, the following day a ten-man American technical team, mostly Pratt and Whitney engineers, arrived and asked for Oestrich by name. "The Americans," says Munzberg, "were tough and anonymous. They ordered us to restart production. Berlin had still not surrendered and we were already working for the Americans."

After four weeks, Oestrich and Munzberg were flown to Munich for intensive interrogation. During their absence, the salt mine was cleared and most of the design team evacuated, just hours before the arrival of the Red Army. By then, the questioning had been completed. Uncertain about the future, Oestrich and Munzberg moved to the bombed-out BMW headquarters and waited for work. "Fedden came in July and paid me to design a slow turbo-prop plane. Then we just waited. At the end of August, an American offered us both six-month contracts, but without our families. When we hesitated, he threatened us that failure to accept would leave us unemployed forever. We weren't impressed." By then Oestrich had been secretly approached by DGER agents, had flown to Paris, and was negotiating to take a hundred of his best engineers with their families to France. According to Munzberg, "Oestrich trusted the French because it was the same people with whom we had worked during the war. The Americans did not seem to have anything to offer." The French offer was undoubtedly the best deal available: The standard five-year contract contained a "gold clause" to protect earnings against devaluation, there were generally few restrictions on movement, scientists could travel with their families, and everyone was offered the possibility of French citizenship within two years.

With military precision, in *Nacht und Nebel* (darkness and fog) twenty French army trucks picked up forty of Oestrich's team and their families in total secrecy and ferried them to the old Dornier factory in Lindau, in the French zone. Over the following six months, eighty more BMW engineers arrived. United with their families, the German engineers, including former Nazis and SS officers, enjoyed a privileged life and comfortable working conditions. In July 1946 "Gruppe O" was sent by train to Decize, about twenty-five miles from Nevers, to design the ATAR jet engine for a high-altitude plane. "My great reward," says Munzberg, who later became director of development, "was the Australian government's decision in 1964 to buy a SNECMA jet engine designed by Gruppe O instead of the Rolls-Royce Avon as expected." Airbus Industrie in Toulouse also bought the SNECMA jet. The Airbus managing director, Felix Kracht, was an old friend of Munzberg's and had also been recruited by French agents in 1945.

French recruitment was carefully targeted and the scientists judiciously but tactfully isolated. In Decize, Gruppe O lived in the old police barracks and was only gradually allowed to mix with local Frenchmen, but early fears of hostility from the local French inhabitants soon proved groundless. Rocket scientists, also recruited from the American zone, were more strictly guarded. The "Sänger Gruppe" — the pioneer of the ram jet, Hannes Schneider, who developed liquid propulsion for the Mirage's high-altitude acceleration, and Wolfgang Pils, a Peenemünde scientist who developed the French army's Veronique rocket — were held in close but comfortable custody. But a larger group of rocket scientists, contracted to assemble V2s in St. Louis, were able to return to their homes in Germany each night. Many had been discreetly contacted by Lieutenant Colonel Henri Moureau while working for the British in Cuxhaven and had disappeared after the Backfire launchings. In the summer of 1946 three hundred were moved to Vernon, France's new rocket center.

Rolf Engel, an SS officer who during the war had supervised the production of solid-fuel rockets at a Skoda plant in Czechoslovakia, was recruited by French agents while hiding in the American zone, fearing arrest for his wartime activities. Over a period of three weeks, "a French air force captain attached to the DGER arrived in civilian clothes to negotiate." Like other Germans, Engel was attracted by the French promise that the scientists could work with their own team, unmolested by legal restrictions, and would be well paid. "The French just didn't hate us in the same way as the other Allies." Engel's Nazi record as a highly praised SS officer since 1936 was ignored. As a lieutenant in the Einsatzkommando in Muhlhausen and Strassburg in October 1940, he had been particularly commended for his "intelligence, hard work and competence" in suppressing the French Resistance, then abruptly disciplined for theft, black marketeering, and falsely stating that he had a doctorate from Munich University.[55] Transferred to SS headquarters in Danzig, he became a self-taught rocket expert as a result of regular visits to Peenemünde and Nordhausen before transfer to Czechoslovakia. Engel had learned enough to convince his French interrogators and a generation of experts that he was a fully trained member of the rocket team.

At the end of the war, formally hired by ONERA (L'Office National des Études et des Recherches Aéronautiques) to build a French rocket, Engel was driven secretly to Baden-Baden during a snowstorm, then flown to Paris. Incarcerated in a mansion in a Paris suburb, Engel spent most of the following six months directing DGER agents, each armed with handwritten letters from himself, to find other rocket experts in Germany. Masterminding the French search at the Château de la Muette was Captain Clement, who had spent the war with de Gaulle in London and, according to Engel, was "a cold man who disguised his dislike of the Germans because he realized France needed us." Most of the twenty who were eventually hired were found in American camps. At Châtillon-sur-Seine, the center of French aviation research, Engel met dozens of other German designers who had worked for Messerschmitt, Heinkel, and Dornier. "It was marvellous for us and also for the French. They soon knew everything." All of them agreed that working for the French had one overriding advantage: "It was easier to run back home than swim back."

Turning a blind eye to Engel's Nazi career was consistent with French policy. Not only did Bloch-Dassault sanction the employment of many Nazis in France, whether at the gun development institute in St. Louis, near Basel, or at the rocket center at Vernon, but, contrary to Germany's terms of surrender, Paris ordered armaments factories in the French zone to continue production of war materials for the French forces. Engel was particularly proud of the fact that Clement never censured him for his Nazi past; and his past was never mentioned when, during the 1960s, Engel led the German team to negotiate the construction of the European space rocket, ELDO.

The British were irritated but not surprised by what was condemned as disingenuous opportunism. Anyhow, British illusions of superiority were such that French successes were considered negligible compared with the British operation. By autumn 1945, more than 250 German civilian scientists and engineers had been flown to Britain for interrogation.[56] Through Inkpot passed the cream of German science and engineering, many of whom later went on to the United States, France, and the Soviet Union. All of them were properly treated but baffled by their reception. Rudiger Kosin, a jet designer at Rechlin, was among many at Göttingen who was "invited to come to London for fourteen days." Initially reluctant, he agreed because "I wanted to see the effects of our bombing." But having been whisked to London in such urgency, he was "left sitting around for six months among the most interesting people, playing cards, football and attending lectures given by the other experts." Kosin was unimpressed by his occasional interrogation: "They all thought that they knew more than us." Others returned to Germany disgruntled, complaining that they had been squeezed "like lemons," without any thanks or acclaim, which they felt was their due.

Among them was Kurt Tank, of Focke-Wulf, who had designed the Stuka dive-bomber. Tank and his team of aircraft designers were proud of their achievements and were aggrieved that the British, instead of instantly rewarding their talent with an offer of permanent employment, had unceremoniously flown them back to Germany. Handel Davies, one of many who spoke with Tank for hours, was not surprised that he failed to find employment in Britain. "He was such an important man, so 'big,' that it would have been very difficult for an aircraft manufacturer to have fitted him into their own design team."

Soon after their return to Germany, Tank sent an emissary to Berlin to contact the Russians. The Russians' first offer was rejected, but on November 15 a new offer was discussed by about twenty aircraft designers, who met in Tank's home. There was unanimous agreement that they would individually "disappear" into the Soviet zone two weeks later. Within days, British intelligence heard of the conspiracy from an informer at Göttingen. Despite Davies's misgivings, Walter Cawood, the amiable controller of research and development at the Ministry of Aircraft Production, felt it was time the British government made positive offers to the Germans.

The British had already listed 185 Germans whom they wanted. Nearly half were already held, sixty-three were being sought, thirty-five were held by Americans, and six by the Russians. The American list contained 113 names. Altogether, twenty were wanted by both of the Allies. Infuriatingly, recruitment was paralyzed by, as it seemed to London, the inexplicable failure of the U.S. Chiefs of Staff to approve the British proposals.[57] Unknown to the British, the American chiefs had delayed their decision partly out of uncertainty about how to reply to the British request that the results of research be shared. While the sentiment of the wartime alliance with Britain remained strong, the chiefs were unwilling to share America's atomic secrets with the new — and mistrusted — Socialist government in London. Perplexed by the silence from Washington and anxious to hamper the Russians, Cawood appealed to the British Deputy Chiefs: "Unless we take immediate action, it is likely that the services of these scientists may be lost both to us and to the Americans."[58] Cawood suggested that the Germans be given contracts equivalent to those offered to British scientists, with a salary of eight hundred pounds a year. His recommendation arrived amid a growing stream of intelligence reports from Germany about prolific Russian recruitment. To defeat the Soviet challenge, the Joint Intelligence Committee put forward three possible tactics that the Allies could adopt: place no restrictions on the German scientists, knowing that some of them would eventually go to the Russians; employ the Germans on sufficiently generous terms to make Russian offers uninteresting; and ruthlessly intern those who were too dangerous even to be allowed to work for the West.[59] The JIC urged that whichever strategy was adopted, the government should recognize that denying the scientists to the Russians was almost as important as their recruitment. As a sign of urgency, the British sent Gruhn a warning that Tank and Hans Multhopp, an important member of his team, were "being approached by the Russians" and might well "accept such an invitation." To lure the Germans away from the Russians, the British army in Germany was authorized to tell Tank that he would soon receive an offer from Britain. If he remained unamenable, he was to be arrested immediately.[60]

But there was still no reply from Washington. The Cabinet therefore unilaterally decided that German scientists could be "employed in the national interest, provided that they are servants of the state." Cawood was authorized to offer contracts to two Focke-Wulf aircraft designers in Tank's team — including Multhopp, a former Nazi party member and SS officer — but not to Tank himself. At Farnborough, Multhopp would eventually calculate the angle of lift-off along a wing span without a computer, an astonishing achievement that formed the basis of the design for the British Lightning fighter. After four years, Multhopp's arrogance was deemed intolerable, and he was sacked, later to become the chief scientist of the giant American aviation and space contractor, Martin Marietta.

Ernest Gruhn envied the British military's apparent ability to extract a policy decision from its government. To his chagrin, the State Department remained intransigent. Although there were now eighty-eight Germans in America, technically they were allowed to stay, under military custody, for only six months. Despite pressure from Toftoy, who had named 107 Germans as needed for the rocket team, the possibility of an agreed policy for their permanent employment in the United States seemed to be steadily receding. Between soldier and civilian there were irreconcilably conflicting visions. On behalf of Hap Arnold, Theodore von Karmen, and the others who had forged the wartime marriage between the military and the scientists, Robert Patterson (promoted in the fall of 1945 to secretary of war), told a congressional committee, "The laboratories of America have now become our first line of defense."[61] Gruhn would have added that the Germans were needed to staff those laboratories. If only the State Department, Gruhn thought, could understand the scientists' predicament and the military's aspirations. Writing to William Clayton, an assistant secretary of state, Gruhn emphasized the dangers of Russian recruitment and once again stressed the potential benefits to American industry: "We believe that the United States is sacrificing a potentially great addition to our scientific resources by not making immediate provision for the evacuation to the United States of a small number of the top technical brains of Germany. There is a widespread demand in science and industry that such personnel should be brought to this country."[62] Gruhn listed as desirable recruits the chemist Dr. Walter Reppe, the physicists Hellmuth Hertz and Georg Joos, autobahn specialist Otto Graff, and the nuclear chemist Otto Hahn. Gruhn showed no embarrassment either about the lack of any evidence that American industry needed theoretical scientists from Germany or that his promise of "careful screening to insure against the importation of anyone harboring anti-democratic principles" turned out to be hollow. But Clayton's officials, deluged with more complicated problems than they had ever faced in wartime, were adamant that there would be a public outcry if Hitler's scientists were admitted into America. Fortunately for Gruhn, no one noticed that Reppe was at that time incarcerated in Dustbin as an ardent Nazi and suspected war criminal.

Industry was Gruhn's only possible ally. At Gruhn's request, attorney John Green drafted a supportive letter for Secretary of Commerce Henry Wallace to send to the president[63] and another, requesting admission for the scientists, to be sent to James Byrnes, the secretary of state. At the behest of his officials, Byrnes immediately rejected Wallace's plea.[64] Next, Gruhn arranged for a "personal" letter from Patterson to Byrnes. Rival drafts circulated for some eight weeks, and the fulsome rhetoric of the final text, which spoke of the Germans as "leaders whose genius, driving force and imagination have led to [unique] achievements," attempted a

Churchillian evocation of historic destiny: "There rests upon the United States the obligation to transplant these increments of progress, fitting them into our own scientific, technological and industrial structure."[65] Hoping to draw support from industry, Gruhn also issued a detailed description of the procedure for the industrial employment of German scientists.[66] To his acute embarrassment, Green disowned the plan, accusing Gruhn of lack of realism.[67] American industry, said Green, certainly wanted to employ "selected top-flight German scientists," but before industry could offer the military outright support, it was essential that the government agree upon a policy for its use, and at that time, the military's conditions posed an insurmountable obstacle. Controlling the plunder of Germany had become the military's preserve, and any American or British civilian claims were subordinate to military interests.

8

The Irreconcilables:
Diplomats and Soldiers

ALBERT PATIN was among the first six aviation specialists who arrived at Wright Field in Ohio on November 17, 1945. For Colonel Donald Putt, who had investigated the research institute at Volkenrode, Patin symbolized the best and brightest of German expertise and innovation, and gratifyingly displayed an endearing commitment to using those skills to America's advantage. Fast-talking and persuasive, Patin would be used by Putt both to convince doubters about the benefits of Overcast and as an example of the misery caused by its implementation. During the Third Reich, Patin's factories and laboratories had employed six thousand people to produce his unique automatic control and navigation equipment for aircraft, the precursor of robotic takeoffs, landings, and in-flight steering. After visiting his factory, Captain Helenes Freiberger, an American technical investigator, reported that "the practicability of his projects is unquestionable, the soundness of his principles a revelation."[1] Nimbly, Patin also convinced Freiberger that he was an avowed opponent of Hitler's regime, eloquently describing how he placed his own life at risk to sabotage production. "Patin was never very much interested in helping the Nazi regime," reported Freiberger, "therefore trying all sorts of tricks and intrigues to hamper production or block the flow of raw materials to his factories and laboratories. It is interesting to note in this connection that Patin halted the development of a superior bomb-sight. . . . Without doubt, Patin was free of all Nazi politics." The American officer had been skillfully duped. Patin gratefully seized the offer of a contract and an escape route from the ruins of Europe.

But the American dream soured soon after his arrival. Already depressed about leaving his family in Germany and by the tedious journey from Europe, Patin found little consolation in the bleak plains of Ohio. Hilltop, his new home, was a Spartan set of barracks beside a noisy dirt track and was shared with a small group of other German aviation experts. European culture and sophistication seemed a distant memory in that alien environment. Although the Germans had been politely welcomed, the fierce anti-German antagonism of the servicemen who surrounded them deepened their homesickness and longing for news from their families. Contrary to the contracts they had signed in Germany, mail delivery was taking ten weeks, since, unknown to them, letters were being censored three times. The first letters from Germany intensified their gloom. Descriptions of desolation and chaos at Landshut (now unofficially code-named "Camp Overcast"), the lack of food, and the inexplicable refusal of the American army to pay their families as promised were shocks for men accustomed to status and comfort. Letters from Patin's wife asking him to return to Germany were harrowing. "I am terribly worried about you," she wrote. "Do not worry about me. Except for the mental suffering, I am well." Hunger, cold, and the loneliness of their families in Germany were being aggravated by word that American army officers at Landshut had callously dismissed any chance that the families would eventually travel to America, because their husbands would "return in a year." For Patin and his colleagues at Wright Field, the prospects seemed bleak. As he confided to Putt, they felt "a complete loss of hope here" and feared other scientists in Germany would be deterred from signing contracts.

Committed to Overcast's success, Putt wholeheartedly sympathized with the Germans' plight, especially their complaints that contrary to promises, their movements at Wright Field were excessively restricted. But when he protested to Major General Clayton Bissell of Army Intelligence that Overcast could succeed only if "a more liberal treatment of the German individuals"[2] was approved, Bissell ignored his suggestion, despite the very real danger that the scientists' work would suffer. The Germans were already allowed to travel under escort to the local town, Dayton, and to the Pentagon the notion of loosening the restrictions was inconceivable. In the midst of daily reports from Europe of new discoveries of Nazi atrocities, the public's sensitivities were still too raw. But Bissell's reaction provoked Putt to increase his demands for the Germans' welfare.

At Patin's behest, Putt tried to convince Bissell that the scientists needed assurances regarding the likelihood of reunion with their families, patent protection for their inventions, and the extension of their contracts for long-term work. Bissell passed the requests to other departments, but outside air force headquarters, sympathy for Putt's protests was at best cool. In Germany, U.S. Army headquarters emphatically rejected doing more for the 320 dependents at Landshut. The terms of the contracts, they told Putt, were being fulfilled; granting extra privileges would cause resentment among other Germans and "only encourage further requests."[3]

After Christmas, to Putt's dismay, morale at Wright worsened. Patin and his fellow scientists were becoming unwilling interrogees. The constant stream of air force officers always asked the same, laboriously translated questions, and the Germans feared that without their patent rights established, their ideas would be stolen and their importance diminished. Debriefing the Germans was also handicapped by the Pentagon's security restrictions, which forbade disclosing secret American data, dooming any possibility of intimate seminars with American industrialists. Again, Putt bombarded his headquarters with complaints that the conditions imposed were "critically affecting" the scientists' work.[4] They were suffering, he wrote, isolation not only from their families but also from their associates, who had agreed to wait in Germany for a summons to America. By February, Patin's best technicians were destitute and dispirited.[5] Letters from his staff in Germany, intercepted by Army Intelligence, reported lucrative offers from Russian and French agents that were too tempting to ignore. "They do not very much like to work for the Russians and would of course prefer co-operation with the U.S. authorities," wrote one of Patin's scientists on the verge of accepting a Russian offer.[6] Another letter warned in the absence of news from America that Patin's chief test pilot, Burgen, whose ability he judged to be truly exceptional, was being tempted by an excellent offer from the Russians.

In Ohio, to Germans and Americans alike, it seemed that officials in Washington were still blind to the race for German scientists in Europe. At Putt's urging, Patin counseled patience, since the U.S. Air Force would eventually offer contracts. To those in Germany, wondrously immune to the antagonism of their recent enemies, American obstruction and obstinacy appeared quite extraordinary. American officials, it seemed, believed that a scientist could develop his theories in the middle of the Ohio wilderness without his team. Putt now judged that only the creation of a sense of crisis would provoke change.

At air force headquarters in Washington there was greater sympathy for Putt's complaints, but the task of unraveling history was awesome. Overcast had been sanctioned as a short-term project purely for purposes of interrogation. Presidential and political approval had been won by assurances, which Putt chose to ignore, that the Germans would swiftly be returned to Europe. Circumstances had undoubtedly changed. The interrogations had revealed that the immaturity of American aviation design could be best solved by retaining the Germans for future weapons development. But technical details alone could not transform Overcast from a short- to a long-term operation. That needed a delicate balance of diplomacy and apprehension. Adroitly, Putt supplied material to feed the State Department's developing fear of Soviet military power. His source was Patin's alarmist reports.

At Putt's request, Patin delivered a formal complaint that summarized the depression and even suicidal tendencies of each scientist at Wright Field. With the report, which Putt sent to Brigadier John Samford at air force headquarters, was a plea to "improve the morale and save the existing situation."[7] Echoing Putt's plea, Samford immediately forwarded the report to the War Department, together with a clutch of intercepted letters describing the plight of German scientists and their families: "Immediate action in this situation," he wrote, "is imperative if we are to divert the services of valuable scientists from France and Russia to the United States."[8]

Coinciding with the arrival of Samford's memorandum, Putt's complaints, and similar intelligence reports from Europe was an alarming and seemingly authoritative JIC warning to the Joint Chiefs that the immediate development of Soviet military power was limited by only two shortages: industrial facilities and competent scientists. The second deficiency, the JIC reported, was rapidly disappearing because of the Russians' aggressive recruiting in Germany. Excellent offers to German scientists by the Soviets and the virtual "full operation of . . . every important German laboratory, research establishment and factory in the Soviet Zone . . . should enable them not only to duplicate many important German developments, but also to continue along the lines of German research." The JIC urged the chiefs to reconsider America's comparative restraint. Releasing the scientists after interrogation or pending shipment across the Atlantic, failure to provide security for their families, the denial of secret information to scientists already in America for purposes of discussion, and allowing Soviet intelligence teams into the American zone were, the JIC claimed, critically harming American interests.[9]

The JIC's summary was ominous and its recommendations decisive:

> Unless the migration of important German scientists and technicians into the Soviet zone is immediately stopped, we believe that the Soviet Union within a relatively short time may equal United States developments in the fields of atomic research and guided missiles and may be ahead of U.S. development in other fields of great military importance, including infra red, television and jet propulsion. In the field of atomic research for example, we estimate that German assistance already has cut substantially, probably by several years, the time needed for the USSR to achieve practical results.

The reader was left in no doubt about the American intelligence assessment: A few hundred German scientists could significantly tip the strategic balance between the two powers. The truth of that statement had still to be established, but its source was unassailable — the experience of the Allies during the war.

The JIC's three recommendations to the Joint Chiefs — tantamount to a major policy reversal — were, first, that German scientists and technicians should be prevented from falling into the hands of the U.S.S.R. or being interrogated by that nation; second, that the American army in Germany should give the scientists and their families all the provisions they needed; and third, that the commander in Germany should be ordered to urgently compile a list of one thousand scientists and technicians, describing their qualifications and families. In summary, the military wanted the Germans to be given immigration visas so that they and their families could eventually become American citizens. Approval would be a dramatic step.

While the Joint Chiefs pondered the report, attempts inside the State Department to mediate between conflicting officials had failed. Instead, the antagonism between those who were sympathetic to the military and those who were irreconcilably anti-German had deepened. During the five months of peace, the civilians' adulation of the military and the army's own autocracy had been eroded.

Very gradually, civilian officials expected their relationship with the armed services to resume its peacetime status. For State Department officials, this attitude implied that the military's interests were expected to become more compatible with the wider public interests than had been necessary in wartime. With more than one hundred Germans already in America and many more expected, the State Department needed to agree on a policy, even if the military still continued to import the Germans without visas under "military custody."

Seymour Rubin, who sensed that his own speedy promotion within the State Department was not completely unrelated to a sudden bias in favor of Jews, attempted to fashion a compromise in mid-January 1946. "I personally feel quite strongly," he wrote, "that encouraging the immigration from Germany of large numbers of young research or scientific people would be a mistake."[10] An inter-American agreement in Mexico City on repatriation of Germans, he wrote, had resolved to prevent the reconstruction of Axis "centers of influence." The declaration, part of the Safehaven Program aimed at eradicating Nazi influence and recovering Nazi Germany's billion-dollar plunder and assets, which had been secretly and methodically deposited in neutral countries, mirrored the four Allies' agreement at Potsdam. This policy demanded the return from neutral countries to Germany of "obnoxious Germans and their families whose presence abroad constitutes a danger in view of the possible future renewal of the German war effort." Rubin feared that for America to admit indoctrinated Nazis while publicly demanding that Argentina and other Latin American countries expel Nazis who had successfully sought refuge in the Southern Hemisphere would place the department in an indefensible position.

The intergovernmental agreement was in truth a smoke screen. The crux of Rubin's opposition was the weight of public opinion, which, he felt, could not be ignored:

> I think that the United States at the present time is in an extremely delicate position vis-à-vis the political and racial prejudices of large classes of the American public and that such a time as this is no time to introduce into this extremely complicated and potentially dangerous situation large numbers of Germans in order to reap scientific profits which no scientifically trained person has testified will actually accrue.[11]

To Rubin's surprise, he found himself violently rebuffed and his motives impugned by colleagues.

Reflecting the department's virulent animosities, Claire Wilcox, an economist who clearly sympathized with industry's interests, scathingly condemned Rubin as one who "sets up a straw man to be knocked down." They were not about to admit large numbers of young and dangerous scientists, insisted Wilcox, only a few older men. Personalizing the dispute by suggesting that Rubin's argument was emotionally motivated, Wilcox sardonically conceded that "Mr. Rubin is as disturbed, as I am, about the existence of anti-Semitism in the United States. In arguing that the admission into this country of any scientifically trained person who happens to have been a citizen of prewar Germany would necessarily strengthen anti-Semitism here, he becomes involved in the same sort of nonsense that the Nazis preached."

Rubin was understandably offended: "Mr. Wilcox . . . does not seem to me to raise the level of debate in the Department. . . . I should point out that anti-Semitism is not the sole or the chief evil of fascism." Referring to the original suggestion made in April 1945, which stressed the need to control the exodus of large numbers of young German scientists, Rubin insisted that it was up to Wilcox to prove a special case for the scientists coming to America. There was, Rubin argued, another class who were far more deserving of American hospitality than Hitler's scientists — namely, the remnants of persecuted minorities in displaced-persons camps scattered about Central Europe, many of whom were homeless, desolate, and sick. "If keeping Nazis out of the United States is a mistaken policy," Rubin acidly commented, "a good many people in the Department should be told that and instructed to reverse a course they have mistakenly been following for some time."[12]

But the War Department had no time for State Department bickering. The government needed a policy, and the War Department was irritated that, as so often, decisions were paralyzed by diplomats' squabbles. The latest demand for speedy recruitment of Germans was sent by Lieutenant Commander Snapp of the Joint Intelligence Staff. Warning that the Germans would be recruited by "nations who might attack the United States," like so many military officers, Snapp viewed scientists as pure idealists devoid of political opinions: "Germans eminent in such fields," commented Snapp about rocket and jet experts, "were not active or ardent Nazis."[13] It was a sweeping judgment that was patently untrue, but the Pentagon's pressure worried some in the State Department: "I have been needled by the army again . . . with reference to German technicians," wrote Assistant Secretary Willard Thorp to James Riddleberger, a senior European expert in the State Department. "If we are going to do anything about this, we ought to move soon. Apparently the Russians are now broadcasting invitations to German scientists, with rather attractive promises of special treatment."[14] Putt's objective seemed to be accomplished.

Tempers in the department quickly cooled. Rubin and Wilcox agreed that a limited number of scientists should be admitted on immigrant visas, provided they could make "the greatest possible contributions to science and industry" and none of them was guilty of holding "anti-democratic principles," defined as "past voluntary and active participation in the activities of the Nazi party." On the surface it seemed that the State Department had hammered out an agreement, but in the all-important visa controls department, one official was simmering with fury about the military's distortions and demands.

Samuel Klaus, a highly intelligent forty-two-year-old lawyer, was quietly but critically watching events unfold. Born in Brooklyn and educated at Columbia Law School, Klaus was acknowledged by fellow lawyers to possess "one of the finest investigative minds in or out of government." A multilingual bachelor with a passion for collecting rugs, Klaus had spent the war establishing the Safehaven Program and arrived in Europe in early 1945 to set in motion the investigatory network that would try to trace and extract the ill-gotten Nazi funds. As a Jew and Hebrew scholar traveling in war-stricken Europe, Klaus was naturally affected by the overwhelming evidence of Nazi atrocities. Passing through Nuremberg, he had discussed the Nazis' crimes with the American war-crimes prosecution team and had been both intrigued and amazed by the documentary evidence already collected, which damningly exposed the close relationship between notorious party activists and the whole spectrum of German society. On his return to Washington, Klaus felt that he understood better than most the reality of the Nazi state and, especially, how many Germans had profited both financially and professionally, regardless of the morality of Hitler's policies. The German scientists were, he felt, an example of that calculated opportunism.

Before adopting any public position, Klaus characteristically decided to investigate whether the German scientists were as outstanding as the military claimed. Good planning and careful assessment of others' motives were, Klaus appreciated, a vital part of thorough investigation. With Herbert Cummings, a close friend in the visa section, Klaus sent James Conant — Bush's deputy — the War Department's list of favored Germans and asked whether they indeed possessed unique skills that made their presence in America imperative. To their surprise, Conant commented that none of the Germans was so vital that his knowledge could not be extracted within six months. "We were both amazed and excited," remembers Cummings. "The military had been won over by phoney propaganda that the Germans were the greatest scientists." For the moment, neither said a word.

Ostensibly, the State Department's position was that non-Nazi scientists could be admitted for a short period after selection by the military, subject to a final security check by the Department of Justice. Strict entry procedures had been drafted, including the proviso that direct employment for industry "will be discouraged."[15]

But the intelligence reports from Europe and the JIC's recommendations were causing politicians to change their policy. At a cabinet meeting toward the end of February, with President Truman's consent, Secretary of State Byrnes and Secretary of War Patterson informally agreed on a new policy regarding the German scientists. It was acknowledged that allowing the scientists to return to Europe was compounding the danger; that short-term interrogations needed to be replaced by long-term employment and eventual citizenship; and that to deny the scientists to other countries was possible only if they were admitted to the United States, with their families as potential immigrants. The agreement, called "To facilitate entry in the U.S.," was ratified by the all-important State-War-Navy Coordinating Committee on March 4, 1946, and enshrined as SWNCC paper number 257/5. The policy statement emphasized that while limited cooperation with Britain should continue, Soviet and even French recruitment of scientists, sometimes by force, had "serious military implications to future United States national security." Moreover, it decreed that outstanding scientists were to be admitted to America in the "national interest" for both military and civilian exploitation. Everyone concerned, as Klaus silently noted, had decided to ignore the American immigration laws, which expressly prohibited the admission of "enemy aliens" or citizens of countries with which America was at war. Nevertheless, SWNCC 257/5 did not ignore the Germans' wartime activities. Entry to America was explicitly denied to any specialists or members of their families who were "active Nazis or otherwise objectionable." Each German's record was to be examined to establish that there was no evidence of support or sympathy for the Nazi regime. Anyone who had been more than a nominal member of the party, had been a member of the SS or the SA, or had received unusual recognition for his services to the regime would be deemed to have supported the Nazis.

The burden of implementing the new policy fell on the commander of the U.S. forces in Germany, General Joseph McNarney. The order from Washington was to start aggressively recruiting scientists and to generously succor their families. McNarney and Colonel R. D. Wentworth, his G2 officer who was delegated as responsible for Overcast, were skeptical about its feasibility. Wentworth had already found the Joint Chiefs' order to "prevent" German scientists from leaving the American zone impossible to carry out. Officials in the Pentagon seemed to believe that because Germany was "occupied," it was possible for the American military to exercise tight control. The reality was strikingly different. The government of Germany was at best in a state of controlled chaos. Talented officers were fast disappearing home across the Atlantic, and those who remained, many of them second-class people unable to find satisfactory civilian work, were responsible for so much and their resources so overstretched that General Lucius Clay's military government seemed forever poised on the edge of a perilous precipice. In those conditions, it was practically impossible to prevent foreign agents from moving around the American zone or scientists from leaving.

Nevertheless, Wentworth's new orders were to list one thousand top scientists of paramount interest to America, to provide extra rations for their families, and to prevent the French and the Russians from interrogating any scientist unless America was offered reciprocal facilities. Wentworth responded with a laconic cable to Washington: "Not clear here as to what constitutes an important German scientist or technician for your purposes. . . . The number of top German scientists in this zone can be estimated as not exceeding 300 persons, but the number of key technicians is impossible to estimate." As for extra rations, McNarney was similarly discouraging, complaining that "preferential treatment" would "impose serious burdens." Their complaints got a frosty reception in Washington.

How to judge an "important scientist" was no problem for Colonel Ernest Gruhn, in the JIOA office, who quickly jotted down likely candidates: Nobel Prize–winners, the thirty top-level chemists and physicists, and the leading experts on missiles, fuels, atomic energy, military and chemical gases, electronics, and biological warfare, plus a long list of experts who could apply "pure science to war purposes." The directive that he sent to Wentworth was substantially less specific: "Scientists of outstanding prominence or ability in any field [and] persons who possess distinguished or unusual intellectual attainments of a scientific or technical nature" were all to be listed. If there were any further problems of identification, Wentworth was advised to consult the ubiquitous Dr. Werner Osenberg at Dustbin, who was still clutching his list of fifteen thousand scientists.[16] Unenthusiastically, Wentworth began systematically to divide technology into twenty-six areas and list the top sixty-five men in each field.

In America, however, Gruhn was displaying signs of political maladroitness. Keeping the operation totally secret was impossible, since the Germans were scattered around the country and were mingling with American citizens. Because the government's first announcement had, deliberately, never been contradicted, the public believed the Germans were just temporary visitors. Yet the rest of the operation was top-secret, and it fell to the army to deflect attention from the secret long-term immigration and denial policies. This deliberate deception would soon be extended to the State Department and the White House. In spring 1946, however, it simply amounted to emphasizing the harmlessness of the Germans and their potential benefit to America. Gruhn hoped to control potential criticism by arranging a visit for journalists to Wright Field to meet "representative German scientists." In a lengthy press release, he described the recruits as "comparable to Prof Einstein" and cited the new denial policy as evidence that the government was "using vacuum cleaner methods to acquire all the technical and scientific information that the Germans have."[17] Had the press been more alert, Gruhn could have been seriously embarrassed. Albert Einstein had vigorously protested to President Truman about allowing any German scientists into America, and apparently no one realized that there was a possibility of large numbers of Germans arriving in the United States.

Fortunately for Gruhn, the newspapers placidly followed the line offered by their army escorts, concentrating on Soviet and French successes and on complaints that America was "missing many bets." All the articles featured photographs of gray-haired Dr. Alexander Lippisch, the designer of the Me 163, standing beside drawings of his rocket plane. The benign-looking German was described as a collector of rare butterflies, a painter, and an enthusiastic cyclist. The image of an educated and innocuous German was perfectly captured. Lippisch was at that moment designing arrow-shaped airfoils for Boeing's 500-mile-per-hour Stratojet. No one revealed to the press that the air force was already rightly skeptical about his ideas. Instead, together with descriptions of German development of artificial limbs that would help America's own war-wounded, the army's gentle persuasion seemed to have accomplished its objective. However, not everyone was so easily placated. After reading the articles, the Federation of American Scientists protested to the president: "Any favor extended to such individuals represents an affront to the people of all countries who so recently fought beside the United States."[18] Surprised by the vehemence and the origin of the protest, Military Intelligence officers confirmed that Overcast should retain its high-grade "secret" classification, not only to protect their activities from interested foreign powers but more in the hope of preventing an embarrassing public debate in America. But the question of security classification was a symptom of a more fundamental dilemma.

By April 1946 an unmistakable urgency surrounded discussions concerning Overcast. Employing German scientists had become an important strategic objective approved at the very highest level. Yet there seemed to be little progress. Reports from Europe suggested that French and Russian recruitment was more intense than ever, while those few scientists recruited by Wentworth had not been granted visas. Clayton Bissell of Army Intelligence felt that the whole operation needed urgent review. In the developing anti-Soviet mood, recruiting German scientists had become a matter of vital importance, not only as a symbol of American virility but as a decisive element in a future war. A new era was dawning that required different policies.

Throughout April, JIOA arranged a series of special all-day conferences for the Military Intelligence officers involved, and Wentworth was summoned from Europe. Others present were representatives from the three armed services and a member of the Alsos team, Sam Goudsmit. Supported, apparently without question, by an unassailable triumvirate — the president, the Joint Chiefs, and the powerful SWNCC — the officers sought to reorganize and reinvigorate the operation. Gradually they began to realize that while selecting the scientists would not be difficult, the problem was arranging their admission under America's very precise immigration laws. Clearly, a new strategy was needed.

One hundred and seventy-five scientists were already in America. Technically and practically, in order to remain in the United States they needed to leave the country, apply for visas, and then reenter. But for the bulk of the scientists still in Europe, the legal problems were considerably more awkward. Although denying them to "potential enemies"[19] was considered vital for America's security, many were either not strictly volunteers or indisputably had been active Nazis. Under the terms of SWNCC 257/5, both categories were expressly prohibited from entering America. Throughout April the intelligence officers at the Pentagon conference searched for a solution. Finally they agreed that, despite the State Department's known views, the visa problem should be temporarily ignored and the scientists brought to America on special contracts, without their families.[20] Reassuringly, Gruhn asserted that this was permissible within the framework of SWNCC 257/5, and at the end of April Wentworth returned to Europe expecting to speedily contract hundreds of scientists while G2 officers in Washington were finally agreeing on the legal mechanics for entry with the State Department.

Appropriately, with the new era the operation was given a new name: Overcast was replaced by Paperclip.[21] The old code name had been compromised because letters from the scientists in America to their families at Landshut had been diligently addressed to Camp Overcast. Attempts by the military censors to prevent delivery of the letters were forbidden in case their activities were explicitly exposed. The new code name was selected because recruiting officers had identified scientists to be offered contracts by slipping an ordinary paperclip onto their files.

Equally appropriately, the new era began with the arrival of a new deputy director of JIOA. Captain Bousquet Wev, a conspicuously zealous naval officer, treated his responsibilities at the newly reconstituted JIOA with chauvinistic passion, unwavering obedience, and obsessive secrecy. His first task was rigorously to enforce the "minimum publicity" policy to prevent the recurrence of risks similar to the one that Gruhn had fortunately survived. The need for secrecy in order to protect the army from its critics was expounded by Colonel L. R. Forney, the chief of G2's policy staff: "Publicity may lead to erroneous interpretations on the part of scientific, labor, Zionist or left-wing political elements which might exert sufficient pressure upon Congress, and the departments concerned in evolving the policies, to defeat the ultimate objectives desired in long-range exploitation." It was a tone that Wev perfectly understood.[22]

Lieutenant Colonel Monroe Hagood was the chief of G2's special exploitation branch in the War Department directly responsible for Project Paperclip. On May 2 Hagood was summoned to the State Department for what he believed would be a routine meeting to discuss Paperclip; to his surprise, Sam Klaus was there waiting for him. Over the previous weeks, Klaus had circulated within the visa section a series of intricate legalistic assessments setting out and examining the obstacles to the smooth implementation of SWNCC 257/5. Adroitly, he had successfully braked the State Department's hitherto freewheeling acquiescence. The department, he showed, through its consular officials, was entrusted by Congress with policing the immigration laws, and neither the military nor the politicians could circumvent them simply by waving a policy document.

For his first meeting with the military, Klaus decided to fire a small warning shot. With little formality, he recited a description of the international agreements for controlling German scientists, especially in the American hemisphere, and his department's approval of those policies. After all, he said, the American government would violently resist the settlement of a German atomic scientist in Argentina with intent to develop a bomb; the agreements were essential for the world's long-term security, and Paperclip seemed to be incompatible with them. Hagood could not hide his surprise but was sufficiently familiar with Washington's political maneuvers to understand that, despite Klaus's disarming description of their meeting as "informal," the visa section was challenging the very validity of Paperclip. On his return to the War Department, Hagood considered the several bureaucratic routes he could use to confront Klaus, eventually deciding that the best would be through Patterson, the secretary of war. Since Byrnes, Secretary of State Dean Acheson, and Secretary of Commerce Wallace were continuing to discuss Paperclip's implementation unaware of a small clique's determined opposition, Hagood felt that only Patterson's intervention at the highest level could suffocate Klaus's ploy.[23] It was the beginning of a bitter argument between the military, for which the sole consideration was expediency, and those who considered themselves the public guardians of the nation's morality.

While Hagood's grim news was digested, JIOA's naval representative, Commander J. Horan, was delegated to discuss entry procedure with Howard Travers, the chief of the State Department's visa division. Travers had just returned from a fact-finding mission to Europe and was stunned by the prospect of admitting hundreds of thousands of destitute refugees, known as displaced persons. Shortly after his return, he had appeared before the House of Representatives' Immigration and Naturalization Committee, which was considering the legislation proposed by Congressman Ed Gossett that sought to bar anyone who had served in an army fighting against the United States, or who had been even a nominal member of any Nazi organization, from entering America. Indeed, the net was so wide that nearly all German scientists would be excluded from the States by mere membership in their professional societies. Nevertheless, knowing that the president had personally endorsed Paperclip, Travers was initially sympathetic to Horan's inquiries. But his mood changed dramatically when Horan mentioned that, although Truman had agreed to a "limited few," the War Department had on its own initiative expanded the number to one thousand. In the light of the Gossett Bill the scientists — or "agents of death," as Travers's assistant described them to Horan — were definitely not "deserving" and did not have the visa division's sympathy.[24] Horan reported the meeting to Hagood and Gruhn, and awaited further instructions.

On reflection, Travers soon realized the imprudence of creating an impression that he was acting in isolation. To prove that he was motivated not by prejudice but by the law, shortly after Horan's visit he sent JIOA a seven-page description of the exhaustive inquiries that the visa division was legally bound to undertake on receipt of each scientist's application. Such inquiries, he explained, were "the basic ones confronting the Department of State prior to granting visa facilities." Not only would each of the scientist's statements need scrupulous checking, but the scientist's contacts and his status with other scientists and organizations both before and during the Third Reich would have to be investigated. Membership in organizations, especially Nazi groups, and the receipt of any honorary awards would also need to be convincingly explained. Finally, to avoid the risk of embarrassing incidents, those who were eventually admitted would have to be widely dispersed, away from "areas having large German minorities yet unassimilated."[25] It needed little reflection for the JIOA officers to understand the time-consuming implications.

Travers's motives were not prompted by any political prejudices. Fearful of hostile "press scrutiny," Travers naturally wanted to avoid potential and, he believed, inevitable embarrassment. "If criticism is to be avoided, a serious attempt will have to be made to justify the stand the United States government has taken in a Safehaven Program, a Repatriation Program and the Potsdam Declaration." Travers's solution was to admit the Germans on temporary visitors' visas, on probation, or as prisoners of war without their families: "Otherwise the United States government has traded all of its trinkets and cannot force compliance with any demand. . . . Why give them everything before they deliver anything?"

Together, Travers and Klaus had succeeded in reopening the State Department's internal divisions. Even Acheson was puzzled, since he remembered the president approving Paperclip, and during recent discussions the Latin American problem had never been mentioned.[26] Yet inexplicable contradictions constantly arose, created, it seemed, not only by his own staff but also by the military. Only recently, when the civil government departments agreed to declassify and publicize the future admission of German scientists for industry, Army Intelligence had blocked the initiative.[27] Alarmed by the drain of scientists to the French and Russians, the Joint Chiefs had initiated an adjunct scheme within Paperclip to list German scientists whose sole importance was their denial to "any potential enemy." This new and more aggressive denial policy was automatically classified as secret. Fearing that publicity about the civil program would provoke public protest and abruptly curtail the whole operation, the Joint Chiefs demanded that Paperclip remain classified.[28] Their argument was irrefutable: Since similar names would appear on both the civil and military lists, the "secret" operation would be compromised. Paperclip had not yet started, but it was already suffocating amid bureaucratic conflicts.

Putt's fury was almost beyond control. More than a year had passed since he had marveled at Volkenrode and argued the importance of using German skills in America. After a great deal of effort, Overcast had been finally approved by the State-War-Navy Coordinating Committee, yet the chances of recruiting the Germans seemed to be deteriorating daily. Putt was reportedly also threatened with an ultimatum from the Germans: Their contracts would expire in two months, and they had unanimously pledged to refuse renewal unless their status was changed. "According to continuous and increasingly alarming reports reaching this Command from extremely reliable sources," wrote Putt in one of his ever more frantic letters to the commanding general of the army air force in Washington, "the American zone is literally crawling with French and Russian agents whose work has become rather fruitful and facilitated by the sorry fact that German scientists have received no clearcut, positive offers from this country." Letters to Wright Field from scientists who had been waiting for a year to join their associates described what Putt called the "fabulous contracts" offered by France and Russia that guaranteed the scientists generous financial and professional security and the company of their families. "Restrictions imposed on German scientists now in the United States must create the impression in Europe and among their former colleagues that the scientists here are prisoners for all practical purposes. This impression is likely to have a very detrimental effect upon any attempt by the United States authorities to make contracts with the scientists still in Germany."[29]

The information arriving at Wright, on which Putt's report was based, was indeed alarming. Among the many scientists successfully recruited by the French were Oestrich's Gruppe O, already "500 strong" and destined to double; Dr. Siegfried Decher, a Junkers jet pioneer, who was about to leave for Turbomeca in the Pyrenees with a large team; and Dr. Hans Gessner, a designer of the Kochel wind tunnel, who had been offered a salary double the amount he formerly earned in Germany and the promise that he could take twenty assistants and their families to France. Meanwhile, the Russians had finally succeeded in luring Patin's test pilot, Burgen, and Moller, the head of Patin's autopilot section, to Moscow; and an axial compressor specialist, Friedrich, and a jet specialist, Waldmann, both needed in America, had left for the Soviet zone. Once again, Putt's complaints were listed and forwarded to the War Department's director of intelligence, including a warning that many Germans in America now feared Russian agents would kidnap their wives, especially in Berlin, and blackmail them into returning to Europe.

To ill-informed intelligence officers like Monroe Hagood, Putt's strictures seemed genuinely frightening. Hagood was already studying another report, less emotional but equally disquieting, from Arthur Price, a junior intelligence officer who had just returned from Europe to compile the first denial list. The French, Price discovered, were employing as many Germans as the Russians and were deliberately ignoring the wartime activities of even the most ardent Nazis. Confirming Hagood's conclusion, Price reported that the British were also "highly alarmed" and supported the urgency of America's denial policy. Yet Price's list of 116 scientists who should be admitted to America reflected the forgive-and-forget mood spreading among newly arrived American officers in Europe ignorant of the true nature of Nazi Germany and included several I.G. Farben directors who had been charged with war crimes and were about to be prosecuted in American military courts at Nuremberg.[30]

The paradox of considering the admission of murderers but excluding the families of scientists at Wright Field did not escape Putt, who by then knew that his earliest prize, Albert Patin, had concealed his own Nazi activities. Information from other Germans revealed that Patin had been a colonel in the Brown Shirts, had enjoyed very close associations with Nazi leaders, including Goering's nephew, and during the war had amassed a huge fortune, which had soared by an astonishing two million marks a year. Contrary to his assertions to American interrogators in July 1945 that he had hindered production, in reality Patin had been showered with Nazi honors as a reward for the high output that he achieved by expropriating French factories and employing eight hundred slave workers. To Putt's relief, Patin refuted the allegations — and Putt willingly accepted his word. The past, he felt, was irrelevant, and State Department officials had no right to question military necessity.

In June, Putt chose General Curtis LeMay, a deputy chief of the Air Staff, as his next target for complaint: "It would appear that the lower echelons of the State Department are ignoring the fact that policy has been established by the State Department representatives and it is their duty to expedite implementation, rather than resist the program."[31] Putt clearly had Klaus in mind. On

June 10 Wev had sent Wentworth in Frankfurt a list of twenty-two scientists who were to immigrate with their families to America.[32] Klaus had been sent a copy of the message and immediately saw that it contained only a very brief descripion of the State Department's requirements for a visa. Now was the moment, he felt, to make a stand. Klaus sent Hagood and Gruhn an eleven-page analysis of the "basic information" the State Department required. Under American law, Klaus explained, the American military could not duplicate the French and Russian practice of simply driving their prized Germans across the frontier. The immigration laws, he reminded them, stipulated that each scientist's beliefs would have to be tested not only by counterintelligence but also by State Department officials; moreover, the State Department needed to be convinced of each German's flawless past and good faith, and that his entry was not "prejudicial to the interests of the United States" and was in the "national interest."[33] As Wev discovered with growing exasperation as he pored over Klaus's requirements, in theory there were no fewer than forty separate conditions that had to be satisfied before any scientist could enter the United States.[34] After brief discussion, Wev decided to take the offensive against Klaus's high-minded sabotage.

Herbert Cummings, Klaus's colleague and friend, felt the first hint of the army's offensive. Walking along New York Avenue in Washington, Cummings was accosted by a JIOA staffer, Major Simpson. With little introduction, Simpson hissed at Cummings, "Get that little Jew off the committee." Taken aback, Cummings replied, "Do you realize that Bill Douglas of the Supreme Court called Sam [Klaus] one of the greatest investigators in America?" Simpson was contemptuously persistent: "Get him off. He's a menace."[35] Cummings returned to his office shaken but more convinced than ever that the military's motives were not creditable. Many of the Germans, he suspected, were opportunists, not geniuses, and many of them were hiding dubious backgrounds. Klaus was right; each German had to be critically investigated as required by law. But telephone calls suggested that the chance encounter with Simpson was the curtain raiser to a grim war of nerves: "The military just didn't want any interference."

Wev quickly drafted a protest for the Joint Chiefs to present to the State-War-Navy Coordinating Committee deploring Klaus's visa procedures. "Experience to date," argued Wev, "has made it clearly apparent that little, if anything, of value in the way of exploitation or denial is likely to be accomplished."[36] Wev's anger at the State Department's sabotage was shared by Patterson, who condemned as "most unsatisfactory" Klaus's insistence that administrative regulations should be construed as inflexible laws: "More than a year has elapsed since the German surrender, and the obstacles placed in the way of carrying out this program are for practical purposes insuperable."[37]

The bureaucrats' disagreements were only part of Patterson's dilemma. On July 17, 1946, a priority message arrived from the commander of the U.S. forces in Europe voicing his irritation at the confused and impracticable orders that the Joint Chiefs were dispatching. Tersely, McNarney warned that the relaxation of controls in Europe had made movement between the zones effectively unrestricted; the denial program was therefore "exceedingly difficult" to execute. Since many of the 869 scientists by then listed were of no military importance, he recommended that the denial program be abandoned and the few important scientists immediately evacuated with their families to the United States or Britain. McNarney was clearly trying to force Washington to cease interdepartmental squabbles, confront reality, and relieve him of an impossible burden. But his message included a second, more ominous warning: "There is a large number of former Nazis and mandatory unemployables among those shown on the lists. These cannot now or later be employed in the United States zone of Germany except in the common labor category."[38] Alarmed War Department officials realized that they had to overcome two obstacles: how to bring the scientists to America and how to subtly amend the high moral principles that had been established in May 1945.

Since July 3, when the Gossett Bill was passed by the House of Representatives, Wev had been seeking to neutralize its effect on Paperclip. Like many Americans who had not served in Europe, Wev was not only ignorant about life and survival in Nazi Germany but could not understand Gossett's intense emotion regarding membership in the Nazi party. For Wev, it was easy to sympathize with General Patton's unfortunate public comparison of Nazi party membership to being "like a Democratic and Republican election fight," a tasteless quip that cost Patton his job. To defeat Gossett's bill in the Senate, the War Department needed to exercise its muscle among its supporters in Congress. In alerting the War Department's lobbyists to campaign for a legislative waiver for the scientists, Wev distortively explained that "membership in the Nazi party . . . [was] a prerequisite to healthy existence in Germany."[39] It was this kind of attitude that made State Department officials despise and suspect the military.

Within the State Department, Klaus had been under attack from above since late June. Dean Acheson had overruled Klaus's objections, deciding that in order to thwart likely South American protests State Department officials would have to deny that Paperclip contravened any international agreements. Regarding visa applications, Klaus's attempt to enforce rigorous entry requirements was firmly stamped on. "I hope this isn't being loused up again by fuzzy distinctions," scribbled a State Department official.[40] Mindful, however, that Klaus's stance was supported by law, Patterson secured an undertaking from the Cabinet that the president would issue a new directive ordering the admission of the scientists.

Acheson fully supported Patterson's criticisms of his own staff. State Department officials were still interpreting the president's "limited few" scientists as only fifty — but for the War Department, in the light of McNarney's reports about the disappearance of scientists into the Russian and French zones and a recent announcement that Argentina intended to recruit German scientists, fifty was clearly derisory. Impatient with the internal disputes, Acheson handed over all management within the State Department to General John Hilldring, the assistant secretary of state for occupied areas and chairman of the SWNCC, who supervised the visa section and sat on the department's coordinating committee. Acheson's brief to the forceful general with a booming voice was explicit. Klaus was to be neutralized. Naturally sympathetic to the military — "like a Trojan horse," some would mutter — Hilldring was staunchly pro-Paperclip, and his influence was immediately felt. The numbers to be admitted were expeditiously increased to one hundred and then one thousand. The blunt ban on "active Nazis" specified in SWNCC 257/5 was altered to a vague formula aimed at those who might "plan for the resurgence of German military potential." By the time he met Howard Petersen, the assistant secretary of war, on July 24, Hilldring had also resolved to "bypass the visa people" and authorize the immediate transport of one thousand scientists and their families under "limited military custody." Their visas, Hilldring decided, could be granted retrospectively after their arrival. "This represents a real but tardy forward step," Petersen told the secretary of war.[41]

At the end of the month, Hilldring's plan for the "expeditious" contracting of the scientists was put separately to the State-War-Navy Coordinating Committee by both the Joint Chiefs and the army. Visas would not be issued for at least twelve months after arrival; then the State Department would be ordered simply to accept the military's certificate of eligibility. Implicitly, the State Department was excluded from exercising any control over the scientists' entry. Even the "Nazi clause" was redefined, with the military retaining complete discretion: "No specialist or member of his family will be brought to the United States under this program if placed in an automatic arrest category through the denazification program of the United States military government, until such time as the Commanding General USFET [United States Forces European Theater] has certified the removal of the individual from such category."[42] When Dean Acheson presented the president with the finalized draft of the directive, Wev believed JIOA had finally won complete control and congratulated himself that Klaus was roundly defeated. The naval officer had not, however, reckoned with the determination and skill of a lawyer who, in Rubin's view, "had conspiracy on his brain, whether they were Nazi or army conspiracies." Like a hound, Klaus would never give up once he had the scent of wrongdoing in his nostrils. Klaus's riposte was swift but passed momentarily unnoticed by the legally unqualified military officials.

The new, top-secret directive on Paperclip, approved by the president, was circulated on September 3. According to SWNCC 257/22, a maximum of one thousand scientists "at any time" could be brought to the United States by the military, and their families would follow later.[43] Their salaries, at a maximum of $40 per day or $10,000 per annum, would be similar to that of American employees. Security restrictions would be relaxed but not removed. If a scientist was unsatisfactory, he would be repatriated to Germany; if he stayed, the military would, after investigation, deliver the "best information available" to the Justice and State departments with an application for a visa. However, regarding the crucial Nazi clause, where the War Department thought it had won a victory, the high moral principle seemed intact. Within the space of a week, the innocuous determining phrase that appeared in the old directive had been replaced by a stipulation that was considerably stricter: "No person found by the Commanding General USFET to have been a member of the Nazi Party and more than a nominal participant in its activities, or an active supporter of Nazism or militarism shall be brought to the United States hereunder." Klaus's phrase had been ingeniously restored. Inattentive, the army failed to notice the change and believed that it had retained the definitive and final word.

With the directive approved, Hagood suggested that Paperclip would be "enhanced rather than compromised" by a strictly limited public statement. Ten days later an unusually forceful press release extolled the potential benefits that the military and industry would derive from the two hundred* Germans who had been admitted to America and reaffirmed the army's resolute discrimination against Nazis. The release noticeably omitted to mention that more than a thousand scientists and their families were now expected. Hagood felt exhausted but exhilarated. Paperclip, he believed, could at last get under way, and a "tentative operating procedure" was issued outlining how, within four months, the additional 767 scientists would be contracted, transported, and housed with their families in America.[44] Yet four weeks later Hagood was on the verge of nervous collapse and had threatened resignation.

In anticipation of the major policy change, in July 1946 Major George Collins of JIOA had arrived in Europe to estimate how long the nominal security checks — now a mere sop to satisfy the State Department — would take. Both Colonel Eugene Kolb and Lieutenant Colonel Daniel Garvey, in charge of the military's Counterintelligence Corps, he discovered, were depressingly pessimistic, pleading that because of gross undermanning, it would take between sixty and ninety days to check just forty Germans.[45] To investigate one thousand and their families, Hagood realized, would literally take years. Worse still, on the same day that Hagood requested the dispatch of extra investigators to Germany, the army's director of services protested about the "immorality" of spending $2.5 million to house German civilians while dependents of American servicemen lacked decent homes.[46] The director was unmoved by the argument that compared to the $14 million per day the army had spent on ammunition, the Paperclip budget was a pittance to pay in return for years of knowledge about missiles and jets. The Germans, he declared, would have to remain homeless.

Another abrupt disruption to Hagood's timetable was a curt

*There were in fact 233 Germans already in America.

message from Frankfurt informing him that shipping shortages prevented more than fifty families from leaving Europe until the following year, and thereafter the future was uncertain. Hagood realized that he needed unchallengeable directives from the highest level in order to compel the other divisions to cooperate. In late September, that possibility suddenly seemed very bleak. With congressional elections imminent, the president ordered major cuts in public spending — which for Paperclip meant the closing of Fort Hunt, Virginia, as a reception center and a 60 percent reduction in personnel.

Hagood's protest to General Stephen J. Chamberlin, the director of Military Intelligence, unquestionably came from the heart:

> With my small staff in Washington, I have given eight months of my best physical and mental effort to this scientific program. . . . I am personally responsible for at least 50% of what progress has been made. Unless the War Department General and Specific Staffs give genuine and immediate support to this program, I can no longer voluntarily accept responsibility either professionally or from the standpoint of my own physical well-being.[47]

For Hagood the last straw was the news that the visa division was still dissatisfied and had reopened discussions regarding entry requirements.

On October 8 Klaus sat in Acheson's office with Hilldring's deputy, Ernie Gross. By the end of the meeting Acheson reluctantly made three concessions: that the inter-American commitments would not be sacrificed, that JIOA could not alter international treaties, and that the State Department would retain full control over the issue of visas in accordance with the law.[48] Gross also agreed that the army would be compelled to thoroughly investigate each scientist's background. But Klaus was still dissatisfied. SWNCC 257/22 had minimized the State Department's powers, and during the following days evidence had reached Klaus confirming his worst suspicions that the army believed it could impose its wishes on his department.

After discussions with George Haering, the new chief of the State Department's visa section, Colonel Thomas Ford, JIOA's director, had written to the Commerce Department that "the Department of State would accept as final, the investigations and security reports prepared by JIOA, for insuring final clearance of the individuals concerned."[49] Outraged by that interpretation, Klaus also heard that Ford's briefing to senior military officers regarding the scientists' immigration procedure had emphasized that the long list of formalities — the pre-examination procedures — would be completed in America by the commissioner of Immigration and Naturalization, and merely rubber-stamped by the State Department's compliant consul at the Niagara Falls border post in Canada.[50] Ford, it seemed, was implying that the consul would be denied his statutory powers. Klaus protested to Hilldring. Fearful of the growing anti-immigration lobby in Congress, Hilldring grudgingly bowed to Klaus's suggestion that the State Department demand an amendment to SWNCC 257/22, restoring to the department an absolute power to vet all the documents before a visa was issued; and with that right, also restoring a veto.[51] But what Hilldring granted with one hand, he withdrew with the other. Secretly, after the meeting, Hilldring agreed that the military's certification that a scientist was "acceptable from the standpoint of security" would be "deemed presumptive." The denial program would be interpreted as being in the "interests of national security" and therefore not subject, or so he believed, to America's immigration laws. The Joint Chiefs felt satisfied that they had recovered control of Paperclip: The Germans could be admitted unhindered. Once again, Klaus and his supporters seemed to be defeated.[52]

Reports from Europe underlined the urgency of a policy agreement. Relations with the French had been deteriorating since April, and a British proposal to Washington that Britain and America should refuse to divulge their joint lists of wanted German scientists to the French had been unhesitatingly approved by the Joint Chiefs, who condemned any exchange as "very detrimental."[53] Both Allies feared that unreliable Communist and Socialist politicians in France would leak the information, embarrassing them and benefiting the Russians. The very sensitivity of the Joint Chiefs' decision was marked by an unusual directive some days later asking for the return or destruction of all copies of the top-secret document that recorded the anti-French decision.[54]

The irritating evidence of French success in the American zone was compounded by intelligence reports that the Germans already in France were working independently of their French controllers and maintaining secret contact with other scientists in Germany.[55] In June, General Clay had protested to General Roger Noiret about French poaching and enclosed a list of ten scientists who had been smuggled out of the American zone. A second complaint four weeks later described in detail how a number of Germans employed by the American military had disappeared overnight. Dr. Karl Rawer, director of the ionospheric station at Kochel, had resorted to forgery and theft in order to deliver equipment to the French before leaving permanently for Freiberg, in the French zone; Dr. Andreas Schilling and his team of color film experts had fled Munich and were working for the French army in Baden-Baden; Dr. Bruno Eckert and a large group of air reduction experts had agreed to sign American contracts, then suddenly reneged in favor of the French; and the French were still housing and protecting Dr. Otto Ambros, although he had been charged with war crimes, including murder, at Nuremberg and his trial was imminent.[56] Ambros was eventually handed over to the Americans, but the vigorous contracting of Germans continued unabated.

French success was vexing not only the Americans but also the Russians. Stalin's government recognized the urgency of modernizing Russian industry and its military equipment. Western intelligence had noted vast shipments of machinery being transported eastward since May 1945, but the amounts were obviously insufficient, and Stalin needed the Germans who had designed and built the new technology. Despite Russia's apparent success in recruiting scientists and technicians, most of them remained in eastern Germany, and only a few hundred were actually working in Russia. Stalin's remedy was quite simple.

Serge Tokaev was the senior scientific adviser to Colonel General I. A. Serov, the Russian commandant in Berlin. Tokaev claims that Serov ordered him to contact Kurt Tank and Eugen Saenger, a jet propulsion expert. If Saenger refused a contract, he was to be kidnapped: " 'Nobody will interfere with you,' he [Serov] told me acidly, 'but remember, Comrade Stalin relies on you to produce results.' "[57] Tokaev was unable to recruit either German, but since Stalin's rearmament plans needed German expertise, Serov was ordered to deliver as many German scientists as possible to Moscow, regardless of their wishes. To implement Stalin's order, Serov organized the most peculiar kidnap operation in Europe's postwar history — and one that would have a dramatic effect on Paperclip.

"Operation Osvakim" began at 4 A.M. on October 22. Battalions of Russian soldiers sealed off whole areas of East Berlin while hundreds of arrest squads systematically combed apartment blocks, bursting through doors and ordering husbands and sons onto waiting trucks, which were driven to the Kaulsdorf and Friedrichshagen railway stations. The targets were scientists and technicians, and within twenty-four hours about fifteen thousand had been rounded up. Their destination, they were told, was Russia, and they would be returning in about five years. Most were allowed to pack their belongings, but those who protested violently were hustled out of their homes without even a change of clothing. Neighbors saw Russian soldiers loading complete households onto lorries, including china, chairs, pianos, bird cages, and even stovepipes. Some arrived at the station with their wives and children. Others, amid much sobbing and crying, had made the hasty and fateful decision to leave their families behind. In other cities there were similar roundups, for the targets were the same as the ones the Americans had chosen in July 1945: the optical experts at Zeiss in Jena, Junkers aircraft technicians, and ship designers from Rosslau.

Among the captives were 250 specialists from the division of the German electronic giant AEG known as Oberspreewerk, which manufactured signal equipment. Their arrest was particularly poignant. The Russians had made great efforts to attract scientists, many with international reputations, to work at AEG. High salaries, ample food rations, two hundred cigarettes per day, and beautiful houses in the Hirschgarten, a prosperous residential area, were an irresistible magnet, especially for former Nazi party members, who in the western zones could officially be employed only as laborers. A few days before Operation Osvakim, AEG's senior technicians were flown to Moscow to demonstrate a range of new models. They never returned. Rounding up their staff was easy, since most lived on the same Hirschgarten housing estate. All of them, it seemed, had been deliberately collected in one area in anticipation of a mass kidnapping.

Walter Ahrens, an AEG engineer, was among those visited by a Russian officer who, after a polite explanation, presented a document that Ahrens assumed was a contract for signature. But Ahrens was mistaken. The document was an order for his deportation. Realizing that with two soldiers standing in the entrance there was no chance of resistance, Ahrens and his sobbing wife slowly began packing. Furtively peeping out of the windows, Ahrens noticed that the house was not surrounded. On the pretext that they wanted to change their clothes for the journey, both went down into the cellar while the Russians continued packing. Without delay and without any possessions, they slipped out of the house and escaped in a tram to the American sector.[58]

Before the first of dozens of trains steamed out of the tightly guarded stations in Berlin early on October 23, all the scientists had been offered a choice: either undertake the four-week journey to Russia and sign a five-year contract guaranteeing high wages and comfortable living conditions, or sign a document that read, "The undersigned herewith declares his unwillingness to assist in the reconstruction of the Soviet Union." There was, the survivors recollected some years later, little choice. Life for the families in Russia was comfortable only for the first few weeks. Food, clothes, and income were no better than those allotted Russian engineers, and few were given special privileges other than a self-contained home.

Operation Osvakim was seized upon by the War Department. Not only, JIOA officers hoped, would many Germans be persuaded to wait patiently for American contracts, but both the American public and politicians — who, according to a Gallup poll, were opposed to "importing Nazi scientists" — might be converted after all.[59] Three months later the army had still not solved the dilemma of public hostility. A survey revealed that university professors were indignant at the prospect of Germans who had helped prepare the "Hitler war machine that nearly wrecked civilization" being offered American citizenship. Significantly, their opposition was based on the assumption that absolutely no Nazis had already been recruited and transported to America. Hagood realized that knowledge of the Germans' presence would have to be rigorously contained; pressure from Wright Field and the Navy Department to relax security for the sake of the Germans' morale had to be resisted or the project would explode. Unlimited freedom, he feared, would encourage loud social parties for colleagues or friends, and American servicemen would be offended by the sight of Germans enjoying themselves, so even their existing freedom needed to be "circumscribed" to avoid unfavorable publicity.[60] Unfortunately, Hagood conceded, it was "either useless or provocative" to explain American sensitivity and the army's problems in Congress to the Germans; nevertheless, only by presenting the advantages positively would the public be convinced of the army's case. Having successfully persuaded the Joint Chiefs to lower the classification of Paperclip to "restricted," Hagood arranged for a new press release to be issued.

In glowing terms the press release described how a handful of experts who were developing diesel engines, light metals, ribbon parachutes, supersonic wind tunnels, jet helicopters, and aerial photography had saved between two and ten years of American research and a "minimum of $750 million in basic rocket research alone." Aware of the public's suspicions, it went on to describe how these "world famous" and low-paid German experts, who were handing over "their knowledge without reluctance," were learning English and eagerly looked forward to becoming American citizens. The release particularly emphasized their impeccable moral virtues: "No scientist began work on any research and development project until he was carefully examined as to political background."[61] With deft timing, the press release was issued on December 4, the day the first twelve German families arrived in New York Harbor. On the orders of General Chamberlin, the director of intelligence, they were kept on board overnight to "prevent embarrassment and undue questioning by newspaper reporters."[62]

Chamberlin knew that the favorable newspaper stories that the army had successfully manipulated concealed a myriad of new problems. Having won the right to admit one thousand scientists, the armed services had failed to name more than six hundred and had not located or screened most of those who were named. An Army Intelligence screening committee established in May had compiled a register on five-by-eight-inch cards — but after reviewing it, Ford told Hagood it was worthless: "None of the individuals listed has ever before been recommended for exploitation in the US."[63] By now dozens of different lists existed, compiled by every agency, service, and headquarters. JIOA's alone contained 3,400 names.

The most important list was of the first forty-three scientists recommended for immigration. Yet there were some remarkable omissions. None of von Braun's rocket team were listed, nor was Dr. Georg Rickhey, the overall director of production at Nordhausen, who was working at Wright Field. It was a clear confession of the army's awareness that investigation of their Nazi backgrounds would be catastrophic. Albert Patin was included in the list, however — which, Putt suddenly realized in mid-November, could cause some alarming problems.

A recent arrival at Wright, Hermann Nehlsen, had been appalled to discover that not only were Patin and Rickhey in America, but they had been trusted with special privileges. Arguments between

Nehlsen, a committed anti-Nazi, and the two others resulted in a scuffle, and one of them was injured. A formal investigation could not be avoided. Putt's interrogation of Nehlsen elicited a detailed denunciation of Patin and Rickhey as committed Nazis. Nehlsen claimed that Patin had been an early member of the party, a member of the SA, a senior and much-decorated party industrialist, and a war profiteer; and that Rickhey had participated in the hanging of twelve foreign workers in Nordhausen in front of other slave workers. Putt had no doubt that if Nehlsen's information was true and came to be published, Paperclip would be doomed. To deflect the anticipated public outcry, Putt asked headquarters in Washington for an immediate investigation in Germany and suggested that future controls should be tighter.[64] It was purely a political maneuver. Patin had already been exposed, yet with Putt's connivance he had embellished his defense with a fanciful account of how he had "committed high-level industrial sabotage against Nazi production by slowing down production in his plants, firing plant supervisors when they had just worked long enough to become efficient, refusing to accept numerous government contracts by claiming inability to produce more, or by fictitious and unnecessary evacuation and misrouting of equipment."

As Putt knew only too well, during the past months many highly incriminated Germans had arrived at Wright Field. Rudolf Hermann, the aerodynamicist at Kochel, had held roll calls dressed in a brown uniform and won notoriety as a result of his frequent speeches stressing the importance of fidelity to Hitler. Friedrich Wazelt, a research engineer, had been an SS officer and was condemned by officers at Wright for being a "deceitful and sly character." Emil Salmon, an expert in high-altitude equipment, had been convicted by a denazification tribunal in Germany as a senior member of the SA for supporting, and possibly participating in, the sacking of a synagogue in Ludwigshafen. The evidence against Salmon was particularly strong. An eyewitness who was rated as "credible" by American investigators swore that Salmon had commented after the attack on the synagogue: "That was a good piece of work we have done." All three and many other former Nazis were Patin's colleagues and Putt's protégés.

The trial of major war criminals at Nuremberg had just been completed, ten Nazi leaders had been executed, and the Third Reich's atrocities once again widely publicized. If Patin's presence in America became known, it would cause highly unwelcome embarrassment; the risk of chance exposure simply had to be avoided. As soon as Hagood was told about Patin's background, he secretly wrote to JIOA to drop Walter Reppe from the list, since he was "presently in Nuremberg jail awaiting trial as a war criminal."[65] Cover-up was now vital, and with Putt's help even Patin was classed as a "non-ardent Nazi." The conspiracy's success depended, however, on removing the "obstacle" — Sam Klaus — in the State Department.

9

The Conspiracy

SEETHING WITH ANGER, in the spring of 1947 Thomas Ford, JIOA's director, and his deputy, Bousquet Wev, resolved to remove Sam Klaus not only as the State Department's representative on JIOA but from the visa section itself. Both fumed that his obstructionism was outrightly unpatriotic. Twelve months earlier, when Ford challenged Klaus about his obstructionism, Klaus had boasted that he would ensure that "less than a dozen scientists would ever be permitted to enter the US." His tactics had been completely successful.[1] During the year since SWNCC 257/5 was approved, not one of the 338 scientists and fifty-one families now in the United States had been granted a visa. Insecure about their future, the scientists complained that their work was suffering, while the military feared that until the Germans were given visas, Congress or any government hostile to Paperclip could abruptly deport all of them. Ford and the army were convinced that Klaus alone was to blame. During those months Klaus had successfully impeded the implementation of no fewer than sixteen of JIOA's seventeen policy papers. The seventeenth was about declassifying Paperclip, which he had no desire to block. Klaus's arguments — that the army did not have the authority to contravene American immigration laws or recent international agreements — seemed constitutionally unassailable. But for Ford, whose hatred of Klaus was aggravated by undisguised anti-Semitism, those objections were "intended to confuse the issue and delay the program." In writing to General Stephen Chamberlin, the chief of Military Intelligence, to demand his opponent's removal from JIOA, Ford characterized Klaus as "obnoxiously difficult . . . and insulting in his conversation."

Until 1947, despite the bitterness of their differences, the bureaucrats had managed to keep their row from the public. But on February 11 a well-informed and cogently argued article about Paperclip appeared in the *New York Herald Tribune*.[2] Ford at once suspected that the journalist's source was Klaus. Without sensationalism, the article accused the army of conspiracy and deliberate deception in telling the public that screening had prevented any active Nazi from arriving in America. Yet, the *Herald Tribune* pointed out with incontrovertible logic, the same scientists screened by the army to prove they were untainted had earlier been meticulously screened in Germany to establish their loyalty to Hitler; only after positive vetting by the Nazis were they permitted to research and develop weapons to kill Americans. It became difficult, the article argued, to decide "which of the two screenings failed to catch the dissidents." This simple logic effortlessly penetrated the heart of the military's deception, since the public had been repeatedly assured that the "limited number" of Germans in America had not been Nazis; yet in truth, many of them were highly incriminated and, if the military's plan succeeded, would become American citizens.

Two of the scientists were already controversial, although both were relatively innocent compared with many others sheltered on military bases. Nevertheless, their exposure unleashed an explosive wave of public anger. Dr. Claus Aschenbrenner, an optics expert described in his U.S. security report as a former Luftwaffe colonel, was working on an army contract at Boston University to perfect photogrammetric mapping. The uproar was caused by a newspaper's exposure of Aschenbrenner's presence on the campus. Outside the military, no one knew that Aschenbrenner had been an SS officer, had been classified by Army Intelligence as an "ardent Nazi," and had lied about his record.[3]

The second scientist exposed was Dr. Heinz Fischer, an expert on infrared spectroscopy. Soon after being seconded to Syracuse University in January, he had been revealed to be a former Nazi party member. Fischer was banned from the campus. "Why insult American scientists by asking them to work side by side with participants in the Nazi plan to rule the world?"[4] was the refrain of outraged American scientists. The army's "unbalanced sense of ethical values" also enraged veterans living near Wright Field who, seeing the scientists on the streets of Dayton, complained to the local newspaper that they had fought to defeat the "master race," not to provide them with board, lodging, and ten thousand dollars a year.[5] Terrified of further undesirable publicity, the air force temporarily suspended shipment of more scientists from Landshut[6] and ordered the commander at Wright that "the scientists be warned that their remaining in this country depends to a large degree upon the temper of the people, and especially upon the good-will of the leaders of public opinion, the members of Congress, [and] the press."[7]

Of greater concern to Ford was a protest to President Truman from the prestigious Federation of American Scientists, which complained that the employment of ex-Nazis was immoral. Extracting information from the scientists was understandable, wrote William Higinbotham, president of the federation, but granting preferential treatment and citizenship to Germans who at the very least had acquiesced to Nazi rule was an affront to those who fought against and suffered under Hitler. "It is not fitting that those who abetted tyranny should find a haven in free America . . . while barring those who were and are our allies."[8]

Discussions of morality were alien to Ford and others in JIOA. Suspicious that the complaints were politically motivated, even Communist-inspired, Army Intelligence organized a discreet investigation into the background of Higinbotham, the federation, and other protest groups. Unfortunately for the army, the results were not incriminating. Higinbotham was reported as "unquestionably a satisfactory citizen" despite "some association with known and suspected communists"; and the worst that could be unearthed about the organizations was that they were "nebulous" and "widely liberal."

In Ford's opinion, deflecting public prying and criticism was essential for the survival of Paperclip. But in their ardor he and others in the War Department, ignoring a suggestion that the army adopt a "frank and factual public relations policy,"[9] gradually became infected by the half-truths and self-serving justifications of the Nazi scientists themselves. Consequently, in his reply to Higinbotham, Ford misleadingly wrote that the military was not promising the Germans citizenship, and most of them would eventually return to Germany; and in reply to a series of questions from UPI, the news agency was told that any scientist discovered to be a Nazi was "returned to Germany."[10] To another inquiry, Ford wishfully replied that if the scientists had not joined the party, the SA, or the SS, "they wouldn't be alive today." Even Robert Patterson, the secretary of war, found himself entangled in his department's web of half-truths and distortions on Capitol Hill.

Congress was the focus for the more serious and immediate threat to Paperclip. To politicians in Washington, it seemed as though half of Europe's population wanted to immigrate to America. The descriptions of shattered and miserable refugees, the victims of Nazism, aroused much sympathy but also provoked fear. For each of the thousands of dispossessed families in camps in Europe there were two or more immigrant families in America, many of whom were lobbying their local politicians to repeal the tough immigration controls so their relations marooned in Europe could start life afresh. Although the proposed displaced-persons legislation limited immigration to 200,000 people, in America it was feared that even a slight lowering of the barriers would lead to a flood. Opening the gates to the dispossessed was therefore not universally popular, and whether former Nazis should be included among the privileged few was controversial. Admitting Nazis endangered America's security, and draining Germany of scientific talent would retard her economic recovery — an important consideration, since American subsidies and Marshall aid to the western zones had already been increased to $6.8 billion and were set to increase by another $5.4 billion. Nevertheless, some politicians did not disguise their preference for Nazis over Jews.

Although the Gossett Bill had not passed the Senate, in the new 1947 session three new bills had been introduced[11] aiming either to completely halt immigration or "prohibit the use by the US of Nazi scientists and other Nazi experts." It was Patterson's task to persuade leading congressmen to oppose the legislation for the sake of military research and denial to the Russians. The standard letter that he sent, drafted by JIOA, was flagrantly mendacious. The Germans, he insisted, were innocent victims: "Many of the scientists employed in the US were forced to join the Nazi party to survive or to be free to pursue their scientific studies. They were not in sympathy with Nazi doctrine, but because of their outstanding abilities and the responsible positions they held, they were given honors they could not refuse."[12]

Patterson hoped the public would understand that, in saving billions of dollars and years of effort, a possibly uneasy compromise was justifiable. But while there might be public sympathy for extracting information, no one had satisfactorily explained why the Germans, especially former Nazis, should also become citizens. Not surprisingly, Patterson was unprepared to admit publicly, or even privately, that by their mere presence in America and their growing knowledge of U.S. technical secrets the Germans were successfully blackmailing the American government. Even Dean Rusk, then Patterson's special assistant, failed to acknowledge the enormity of the conspiracy to deceive the public. In an internal memorandum commenting on a protest petition signed by Albert Einstein, among others, he tartly observed: "There seems to be a fairly general misunderstanding of the situation."[13] In truth, the "misunderstanding" was worse than the protestors imagined. Quietly operating behind a screen of misinformation, JIOA officers were plotting the perfect solution: to rewrite and sanitize the Nazis' wartime activities by falsifying the security reports that were a vital preliminary for the scientists' visas and their eventual citizenship.

Probing into the scientists' activities during the Third Reich was time-consuming but not difficult. With Teutonic efficiency, the regime had maintained detailed records of the eleven million members of the party and also of the hordes of affiliated organizations, including the SS. Many Germans had joined the party in 1933 because of threats that the alternative was instant dismissal. But the validity of such threats has always been questionable, especially among the professions. For the investigator, quick perusal of the records certainly indicated, albeit not conclusively, whether the individual was merely a nominal member of the party or had joined out of conviction and was an active participant. Circumstantial proof of a committed Nazi was membership in the party starting before Hitler became chancellor in 1933, promotion within the party hierarchy, or membership in the Brown Shirts (the SA) or the SS. Testimonials in the records by senior officials about a member's attitude and performance were often incriminating. On the other hand, many Nazi sympathizers did not join the party on religious grounds.

As part of the process of denazification, the western powers compelled every adult German to complete a 137-point questionnaire, or *Fragebogen*, setting out his or her record during the Third Reich. Despite the threat of penalties, those who were seriously incriminated usually lied. However, the Paperclip scientists realized that only a year after the war, falsehoods were still easily exposed, since nearly 90 percent of the highly revealing party records had survived. An attempt was made by the SS in May 1945 to pulverize them in a paper mill in the American zone, only to be foiled by American troops. Millions of files were returned to Berlin, where they were housed in the Gestapo's subterranean telephone-tapping headquarters. The Berlin Document Center was the first call for every JIOA inquiry about each scientist.

Ford depended upon Army Intelligence in Europe to sift through the records to complete the "security report" that would crucially determine whether a scientist was acceptable. The procedure was straightforward. A standard military form was completed and submitted to General Clay, who, if satisfied, would sign an agreed formula: "Based on available records, there is no indication that subject is a war criminal or an ardent Nazi. In my opinion he is not likely to become a security threat to the US." Yet, in Ford's view, the intelligence service in Europe seemed to be staffed by complacent, mediocre officers, unwilling or unable subtly to steer the operation in the right direction. Army Intelligence had sent Colonel Sherman to Europe to emphasize that "next to the security of our forces, Paperclip was their most important mission" — but to little effect. No one seemed to understand how vital it was to make sure the scientists received their visas.[14] In the wake of Sherman's visit, two messages were sent to G2 in Frankfurt to test whether his briefing had been fully understood. The first concerned Theodore Zobel, snatched from the British at Volkenrode, who was alleged to have conducted human experiments in wind tunnels at Chalais Meudon, in France. The second related to Ernst Eckert, a self-confessed SS officer denounced for having conducted tests on humans of how much cold they could withstand. Both were now working in America and had applied for visas. In January 1947, Ford asked G2 to investigate their history, hoping the officers would understand the need to "fail" to discover confirmatory evidence.[15] Satisfactorily, by March there was still no reply. But by then a series of other, more disturbing incidents had occurred.

First, a security report on Hermann Kurzweg, working for the navy at White Oak, Maryland, revealed that he was a former member of four Nazi organizations, including the SS. In Peenemünde, Kurzweg had pioneered the aerodynamic design of missiles and was later the deputy head of the Kochel supersonic wind tunnel. Under interrogation by J. H. Alberti in Maryland, Kurzweg had inevitably insisted that his professional position made membership "indispensable" but that he had remained a purely nominal Nazi. Alberti had not believed Kurzweg. Ford's dilemma was simple. If the State Department read the military government's report, Kurzweg would not receive a visa, even though his services were judged indispensable. The solution, a labyrinth into which Ford entered carefully, was to ask G2 in Frankfurt to provide mitigating reasons for Kurzweg's membership in the SS.[16]

Ford's motives were explained in a second cable sent on the same day, concerning Werner von Braun. The security report on the rocket expert showed that he had been a member of many Nazi organizations, including the SS, in which he had been promoted three times after 1940. Von Braun was too important for his past to interfere with his future status. Indeed, while other German scientists longed for reunions with their family, at that very moment von Braun was getting married to his eighteen-year-old second cousin at Landshut, having sailed to Europe at the army's expense. Ford did not conceal his real intent. Since von Braun would "undoubtedly remain in the U.S. indefinitely," it was necessary to make a "detailed report including any extenuating circumstances" to show that these were honorary appointments and that von Braun was no more than a nominal party member. Ford could only wait to see whether Army Intelligence in Europe understood what was expected: namely, to rewrite and falsify the two security reports. For the moment, a third cable — about Ernst Winkler, another wind tunnel expert from Peenemünde, condemned in the military government's report as an "ardent Nazi" — was not sent.[17]

Ford's cables had barely reached Europe when the army's precarious screen of secrecy was shattered. On March 9, during the course of one of his regular broadcasts, Drew Pearson revealed that Karl Krauch — a senior I. G. Farben director who, at Goering's request, had organized the mobilization of German industry for war — had been offered a Paperclip contract to work in America, with the assurance that his family could travel with him. Krauch never received the invitation; it was intercepted at Nuremberg prison, where he was awaiting trial as a war criminal, together with the other I. G. Farben directors. In Washington, Pearson's denunciation, which was broadcast to a large audience and carried great influence, swept like a typhoon through the corridors of power. Pathetically, G2 in Frankfurt cabled the Pentagon and urged it to issue an official denial; Ford and his superiors did not bother to reply. For eighteen months they had feared scandal. Arousing the indignation of such a well-known and highly respected commentator was the worst trauma imaginable. There was now a real danger that all the Germans would be returned to Europe.

Two days later, at 2:35 P.M. on March 11, General Chamberlin, the chief of Military Intelligence, was admitted to the office of General Eisenhower, the U.S. Army chief of staff, who had decided to hold a personal inquiry into the army's embarrassment. Significantly, Ford was not invited to attend. Instead, Monroe Hagood, the chief of G2's exploitation branch, who knew nothing of the plan to rewrite security reports, was recalled from the very eve of retirement to brief Eisenhower. Within twenty minutes, the briefing was completed. Eisenhower had been convinced that Paperclip was a legal and valuable operation, and he was apprised of the State Department's sabotage and the army's frustration that only sixty-eight families had arrived and all of them lacked visas. There was apparently no discussion about the presence of notorious Nazis in America. Eisenhower's tune had changed since the days when he demanded the strict enforcement of the nonfraternization policy in postwar Germany and dismissed Patton for underrating Nazi crimes.

Yet, despite Eisenhower's reaction, politically the balance was tipping against Paperclip. Sensing the tide of criticism, Rusk urged Howard Petersen, the assistant secretary of war responsible for JIOA, to be cautious:

> The public relations people are feeling mounting pressure on this German scientist business. . . . Our position is inherently weak because the State Department finds this whole program difficult to support. G2 should be told that the program should be restricted to genuine security matters and not expanded into borderline cases, in order that the President and the Secretaries of State, War and Navy can give the program full backing and absorb such criticism as will inevitably develop.[18]

After Eisenhower's briefing, special arrangements were made to postpone Hagood's retirement by a further forty-eight hours so that he was available to brief both Patterson and Petersen the following day. Again, there was no discussion about the use of Nazis, only agreement that the scientists were vital for American defense and that State Department opposition had to be finally crushed. Interrupting the meeting, Petersen telephoned General John Hilldring, who, among other duties, supervised the visa section, demanding to know why Klaus had still not been "plowed under" as agreed in August 1946.[19] Hilldring bellowed his promise that his obstructive official would be removed and the remaining three hundred scientists brought immediately to America. Despite Hilldring's assurances, Petersen remained distrustful and ordered his officials to draft a new directive that would bring the State Department into line. But he realized that Paperclip could no longer continue as before. Certain that a cataclysmic tide of embarrassing disclosures was about to engulf the War Department, Petersen told Chamberlin that Paperclip would have to end six weeks later, on June 30.

Despite the agonizing previous forty-eight hours, Ford was granted some consolation. Within the same week Klaus was removed from the visa section. Grimly satisfied, Ford resubmitted the visa applications for the twenty-four scientists at Wright Field, which had originally been forwarded in January. The names of six scientists had been quietly withdrawn because of their "doubtful" record, but with Klaus's removal Ford was optimistic that even those six Nazis would receive visas.

The twenty-four files were handed to Klaus's colleague Herbert Cummings. Cummings assumed the responsibility, intent on rebuilding an amicable relationship with the army. One of his concerns was to protect the State Department from the justifiable accusation that it had knowingly issued visas to notorious Nazis. The possibility was real, since over the past two years Army Intelligence had earned a dubious reputation for refusing to undertake even cursory background checks at the Berlin Document Center.[20] Each file contained the agreed formula signed by General Clay certifying that the applicant was not a security risk. Yet looking through the twenty-four cases, Cummings exploded when he noticed the undisguised contradictions between the OMGUS (Office of Military Government, United States) security reports and the actual party records.[21] Colleagues in adjacent offices vividly recall how "Herb hit the roof when he saw what the military was trying to pull."

When Ford heard that all the visa applications had been rejected despite Klaus's removal, he was perplexed. Cummings was neither Jewish nor known to be antimilitary. Surely, he suggested to Hilldring, since Clay had signed the agreed formula, there could be no doubt that the SWNCC terms were satisfied.[22] Briefed by his irate State Department staff, Hilldring had little option but to disagree. G2's checks in Europe, he told Ford, were unsatisfactory, and despite the formula agreed on in December 1946,[23] which apparently gave the Joint Chiefs the discretion to decide whether a scientist was acceptable as a security risk, the department wanted a detailed report on each scientist, including a complete set of photocopies of Nazi records sent from Berlin[24] and a full explanation of the national interest or national security reasons for each scientist's admission.[25]

Ford now finally fathomed that Klaus's opposition and total distrust of the military had not been the unfettered obstinacy of one man: Klaus's feelings were shared by virtually the whole department. It was the end of June, the date Petersen had stipulated for the end of Paperclip; and although termination of the operation had been postponed to September, he had accomplished nothing. Embittered and frustrated, Ford handed over control to his deputy, Bousquet Wev, who took over the helm in the aggressive style in which he intended to continue.

Wev's opening shot, a few days after his appointment, was to send General Chamberlin a long and blustering memorandum. "The complete stalemate which the program . . . has reached," he wrote by way of introduction, "makes it imperative, in my opinion, that the most positive and drastic action possible be taken in order to break the impasse which presently exists."[26] Wev, whose indefatigable dedication to Paperclip would over the next months lead him to engage in questionable practices, did not conceal his sympathy with the Germans and his anger about the undisciplined and unpatriotic casualness of Klaus and all the State Department officials. "The nebulous and noncommital manner in which most of the action has been taken," he thundered, ". . . [is] sabotage by delay." Wev claimed that the department's officials had subordinated American interests to "beating a dead Nazi horse" — an unfortunate phrase, considering the millions of innocent people who still bore the scars of Nazi brutality. But Wev's vision was sadly blinded by prejudice. "It is a known fact," he continued, "that any German who lived in Germany during the war and who possessed any capabilities whatsoever, was a member of some affiliation of the Nazi Party. Otherwise he was placed in a concentration camp." That a senior officer should harbor such ignorance so soon after the war was a shocking indictment. Surprisingly, Chamberlin, who was to receive several similar messages from Wev, never corrected his subordinate.

Wev's motives were undoubtedly patriotic. One thousand scientists, even if they were all former Nazis, could not, he felt, endanger America's security. Their past loyalty to Hitler was irrelevant compared to the danger of their returning to Europe and rewarding Russia with their own expertise and specific details of America's military vulnerability. Granted visas, they would, it was repeatedly asserted, contribute enormously to the nation's defense industry. "The German personnel now engaged," wrote Colonel H. M. McCoy from Wright Field to Air Force Intelligence in Washington, "are a necessary, vital and irreplaceable factor in the Air Force research and development program."[27] But there was another, more pressing reason for the military to retain the Germans besides their technical competence. As McCoy admitted, the Germans were cheap labor that the military could otherwise not afford. "It is also an incontestable fact that there is a crippling shortage of scientific and technical personnel within the US and more particularly within Government agencies. Hence these personnel now so employed by the Air Force are that many more bodies to accomplish a tremendous task which are not available to the Government from any other source." Sheer need and, some would argue, greed suffocated the "morality argument." JIOA naturally believed it represented the former of those views.

Wev's recommendation to Chamberlin accomplished its purpose. Over the telephone, Hilldring, who was indisputably biased because of his military background, yielded to pressure and agreed to relax his department's demand for exhaustive security reports. Hilldring also conceded that the secretary of war's decision on security would be final and unchallenged. The Army Intelligence department believed that processing the visas would henceforth be a mere revising and rubber-stamping operation.[28] Moreover, agreement had been reached not a moment too soon, since messages from General McNarney, the commander of the U.S. Army in Europe, suggested that competition between the superpowers for German scientists had noticeably intensified.

In February 1947, Werner Heisenberg, the brilliant nuclear scientist employed by the British at Göttingen, had told the *Washington Post* that his closest assistants were working for the Russians in the Urals and that he had also been made an offer.[29] Although Heisenberg's expertise was by then comparatively historical, the Pentagon feared that he and eleven other German nuclear scientists, including Otto Hahn, would be recruited by Moscow. McNarney had consistently stated that denial could only be effected by transporting the scientists to Britain or America and that the

U.S. Army in Germany should be relieved of the responsibility for enforcing the denial policy.[30] To protect American security, the JIC recommended that the nuclear scientists be brought to America but not employed. The British, annoyed that Truman would not share America's atomic secrets, rejected the proposal.[31]

Frustrated by the British veto, the Joint Chiefs of Staff suggested to McNarney and Clay that in the interests of national security, a few important scientists should be arrested and detained at the Dustbin internment camp to prevent their departure to Russia. Clay was outraged that the fledgling democracy he was trying to cultivate in Germany would be jeopardized before its birth: "I should like to point out," he retorted, "the illegality and impracticability of the detention of a scientist or any other individual solely because of his scientific knowledge, ability or preeminence in his field. The indefinite detention of all or any of the scientists on your denial list for these reasons is undemocratic and illegal under present laws."[32] In any event, Dustbin was full. Denial was only feasible, exclaimed Clay, if the Germans could be shipped to America. After this outburst, Clay partially retreated but insisted that to give their incarceration a semblance of legality, the suspect Germans should be placed on the denial list.[33] The first to suffer was Heinz Hintzen, a Paperclip scientist who had returned to Germany. Ostensibly he was jailed for theft, but the real reason was that he knew "too much about U.S. intelligence methods."[34]

Clay's reproach pressured Washington to find its own solution. One option was to get American commerce and industry to employ the Germans. At a crisis conference in April, Chamberlin had suggested to his beleaguered staff that the Department of Commerce should be compelled to support Paperclip by giving the denial policies a "wide interpretation." Wev had echoed that determination: "We must keep the State and Commerce tied up in this program." Chamberlin dispatched his staff with the order that everything was permissible under the banner of "national security," including transportation of Germans to America for industry at public expense, which was forbidden by law. Diligently, Wev compiled a long list of available German talent to be denied to other countries — including a geneticist whose hybridization process could increase yields of sugar beet and a hormone specialist who had developed effective immunization against foot-and-mouth disease. Industry was a natural silo for scientists whom the army was disinclined to lose. "If we [cannot] encourage civilian agencies to accept and exploit these scientists," wrote Wev, "they will be irrevocably lost to American science."[35] Nevertheless, the Department of Commerce remained steadfastly uncooperative — although American corporations had for months been attempting to employ German experts, especially in the steel, chemical, optical, and color-printing industries. Dissociating Commerce from Paperclip, Ray Hicks of the Department of Commerce wrote to a disbelieving Chamberlin that such an enterprise was "foreign to the normal activities of the department." But under intense pressure, Commerce reluctantly relented and agreed to farm out any scientists whom the army admitted to the States as a "denial" or "security" case. It was, however, only a partial remedy, since it was primarily the military that wanted the Germans, and those who were most needed were barred by their Nazi activities.

Nevertheless, with the "very stubborn, arrogant and unreasonable" Klaus (in the Pentagon's words) out of the way, the scientists' complete files containing visa applications and security reports that had been accumulating in JIOA's offices could now in theory be processed through the State Department without delay. One of those files belonged to Arthur Rudolph, the former Nordhausen production manager. By 1947 he and 117 other rocket team scientists had settled down in the parched desert of southern Texas. Slowly, they were reassembling a few V2 rockets from the hundreds of crates transported from Germany. Life was dull except for the disquieting frissons between von Braun's closest court admirers and others on the team. Most of von Braun's confidants were not scientists. Karl Fleisher, who was in charge of providing food in Peenemünde, had been masquerading as a top scientist since their arrest in Germany but in fact only managed the club in Fort Bliss; Magnus von Braun, the scientist's brother, acted as a messenger in Germany and performed the same function in America; Herbert Axster, the former patent lawyer and accountant, had become a "fixer"; while Walter Wiesemann, an ordinary accountant, had been described by von Braun as an eminent scientist but was in fact little more than a spokesman. On von Braun's insistence, members of the favored circle earned higher salaries than the real scientists, and their way of life made a mockery of the army's pronouncement that they were under "limited custody." As early as the summer of 1946, some owned cars, drove unescorted with local girls into Mexico, and were fussed over like heroes.

Early in June 1947 the tranquillity of the group's existence was slightly ruffled when two air force investigators arrived at Fort Bliss to question those scientists who had worked at Nordhausen. The exact reason for their sudden visit stemmed from a chance incident in the former concentration camp at Dachau, which had become the center for the American army's war-crimes investigations and trials. Among the team investigating those responsible for the brutal treatment of inmates at Nordhausen was William Aalmans, the Dutch interpreter who had been attached to the first war-crimes investigation team to visit Nordhausen. Aalmans, by then well known for his terrierlike tenacity, was drafted to Dachau to find more SS officers who could be brought to trial. "My greatest problem," he remembers, "was the wall of silence whenever I questioned the Germans." Among the fourteen thousand Germans imprisoned in the "beehive" at Dachau were a number of high-ranking SS and SD (Sicherheitsdienst, intelligence and counterespionage) officers who understood only too well that under American law the burden of proof lay on the prosecution. These officers regularly briefed SS noncommissioned officers, explaining that their salvation rested in bluntly denying everything and pleading ignorance.

An additional obstacle for Aalmans was that the Americans had managed to arrest only eleven of the three thousand SS personnel who ran Nordhausen and Dora; and even after solitary confinement in airless cells where their diet was bread and water, all eleven either feigned amnesia or placed all the blame on those known to be dead. One of them, Rudolf Jacobi, a heavy beer drinker, told Aalmans he could "only remember prisoners beating each other"; and Kurt Heinrich, the wiry Camp Dora adjutant, denied ever seeing a single dead person at Dora and, when asked whether there were crematoria at the camp, flatly replied "No."[36] The investigators, concedes Aalmans, were trounced: "My only hope to break down the silence was to find inmates who were eyewitnesses to actual crimes, but they were all dead, murdered by SS. The survivors we had interviewed two years earlier had disappeared, around the world. It was an impossible situation." On the telephone list salvaged from Nordhausen in April 1945 there were two names, Rickhey and Rudolph, that attracted the investigators' attention. "Frankly, I had no idea who they were and whenever I questioned the SS officers, they pleaded ignorance." Even two years after the war, the war-crimes investigators were puzzled about who actually managed the underground factory. "We didn't know," explains

Aalmans, "because we couldn't find anyone who would tell us."

The clue that led to Aalmans's breakthrough appeared out of the blue in *Stars and Stripes*, the American army magazine. "I was sitting just reading the paper in the sunshine when I just saw a tiny headline: 'German scientist applies for American citizenship.' The name mentioned was George Rickhey. I screamed for joy and rushed into the head office shouting, 'We've found him.' Within three days, Rickhey had been flown out from America." Aalmans fondly believed that Rickhey's deportation was due to his own demand from Dachau and knew nothing about what had transpired at Wright Field. Unknown to Aalmans and the American army command in Germany, Rickhey had been chosen as a sacrificial lamb. Within hours of his arrival, Aalmans's hopes were shattered. Rickhey bluntly denied all knowledge of events at Nordhausen. Instead of opening the lid on information that Aalmans desperately wanted, Rickhey hammered down the nails even farther. "He always told us that he was somewhere else and saw nothing," says Aalmans. "It was hopeless." Rickhey correctly sensed that his interrogators had failed to understand Mittelbau's management structure and the role of the scientists. Moreover, the investigators not only lacked any incriminating documentary evidence but also seemed to be unaware that Rudolph was alive and living in Texas. Yet, unknown to Aalmans, military investigators had already been sent to White Sands, New Mexico, where most of the Germans were by then living and working.

On June 2 Major Eugene Smith sat in the office of Holgar "Turtle" Toftoy, head of the Ordnance Department's rocket branch, opposite Arthur Rudolph. Smith explained that he wanted to establish Rickhey's responsibility for conditions in Nordhausen and especially whether Rickhey had ordered the regular hangings of inmates. For Rudolph, it was a difficult moment: Rickhey's conviction would clearly have serious consequences both for himself and for other members of the Peenemünde team. To his relief, Rudolph soon realized that Smith knew very little about Nordhausen, so he could safely feign uncertainty or ignorance about most details and carefully gloss over the remainder, including his own responsibility. With a practiced air, Rudolph told Smith that until the last few months, conditions underground in Nordhausen had been humane: "It was not dusty and the air was good. Humidity was normal. Working conditions appeared good. Some of the Haefelinge [prisoners] looked well-fed, others haggard."[37] Without batting an eyelash, Rudolph assured Smith that he ate the same food as the workers — "For breakfast, bread and butter [called margarine] sausage or canned meat or cheese" — and that he "did not see" any workers being physically punished. When asked "Did you ever see anybody die in the tunnel?" Rudolph emphatically replied "No." But with his next answer, he contradicted himself by confessing that he had watched the last stages of the protracted deaths of six to twelve prisoners hanged from a crane. "I do know that one lifted his knees, after I got there," admitted Rudolph, and unintentionally conceded that he had gone quite voluntarily to see the executions. Smith apparently failed to notice Rudolph's gaffe.

The following day Smith interrogated Werner Voss and Erich Ball, two other Peenemünde specialists who had worked at Nordhausen. Both admitted watching two mass hangings and, unlike Rudolph, testified that everyone had been present throughout the gruesome event. At that stage Smith gave up. At least six other Germans at Fort Bliss had worked in Nordhausen, including Magnus von Braun, but Smith was defeated by their carefully planned conspiracy of silence. To his superiors Smith reported: "Mr. Rudolph impressed the undersigned as a very clever, shrewd individual. He did not wish to become involved in any investigations that might involve him in any way with any illegal actions in the underground factory and as a result was cautious of his answers." The major had failed even to identify who was in overall command of Nordhausen. After each German had signed his own statement, Smith departed.

What followed was remarkable. Although the statements were apparently sent to the army's war-crimes prosecutors at Dachau, their significance was ignored or completely misunderstood. Forty years later, Aalmans is adamant that he and his colleagues "never knew that Rudolph had been interrogated." The implication of Aalmans's allegation is clear. Had the statements been properly processed at Dachau, the war-crimes detachment would have insisted on Rudolph's deportation from America so that Rickhey and Rudolph could have been played off one against the other. To prevent such a request being made and to avoid public embarrassment, the Pentagon efficiently minimized the importance of Smith's interrogations, ignoring the interests of justice. The alternative is that the American prosecutors simply did not understand the rocket team's pivotal role in the factory.

In July, a cable from Dachau requested von Braun's return to

Germany to act as a defense witness for Rickhey. On Toftoy's instructions the request was rebuffed, but as compensation the defense was offered General Walter Dornberger, who was still under arrest in Britain, or Karl Fleisher, the restaurant manager at Peenemünde, who was visiting Germany and certainly knew nothing about Nordhausen. Neither offer was accepted.

The Nordhausen trial started on August 7, 1947. By chance seven more SS guards had been discovered by Aalmans in a British prison, bringing the total accused to nineteen. The charges were limited to brutality and murder, ignoring the wider issue of responsibility for the inhuman conditions at the plant. Still confused about the relationship between the German civilians and the SS, the American prosecutors by chance extracted damning evidence against Rudolph without realizing its significance. In particular, Rudolph's former secretary, Hannelore Bannasch, later described as "honourable" by Rudolph himself, told the court that her boss had passed "sabotage reports" to the SS and that, despite an SS request, he had pointedly failed to order his subordinates to stop hitting prisoners. Bannasch's disclosure that Rudolph wielded responsibility for Nordhausen's conditions passed unnoticed both in the courtroom and in America. The four-month trial ended in fifteen convictions but only one death penalty. Aalmans was disappointed with and angry at the verdict. He also recalls that "there were many Americans going round asking why we were punishing Germans for murdering Russians when we would need the Germans to fight the Russians soon. The writing was on the wall."

Nevertheless, Rudolph's file in JIOA's office contained sufficient information to bar him from American citizenship, including a sworn affadavit explaining why he joined the Nazis in 1931. His early party membership automatically classified him as an ardent Nazi. Surprisingly, Rudolph made only a halfhearted attempt to conceal his belief in Nazism: "I joined . . . in order to help in the preservation of the western culture [sic]. In the years immediately following it did not turn out that my decision had been wrong from a business standpoint. Most that happened seemed reasonable. . . . During the last few years political developments became more and more serious, but I could not foresee this result when I entered the party." In other words, Rudolph admitted his enthusiasm for Nazism and believed that Hitler's advent to power heralded the dawn of a thousand-year Reich. His was only one of many files that, Wev realized, contained explosive material. Von Braun's security report declared that as a former SS officer he was a "security risk"; Kurt Debus's stated that "during the Nazi period, Debus was a staunch supporter of the Nazi deals"; while Dr. Hubertus Strughold's declared that "his successful career under Hitler would seem to indicate he must be in full accord with Nazism." Hilldring's retreat from insisting on the State Department's power of veto had been a welcome victory, but it coincided with an untimely exposure of the sensitivity of the army's position.

Rabbi Stephen Wise, president of the American Jewish Congress, had written to Patterson, the secretary of war, protesting about the presence of Ilse Axster, the wife of one of the Peenemünde team at Fort Bliss. Wise alleged that as a former official of the Nazi Party *Fräuenschaft*, or women's league, Ilse Axster should have been classified as a major offender under the denazification laws. Her presence in America, claimed Wise, proved that "screening was a farce and . . . the War Department 'screeners' are entirely incapable of performing this important task."[38] Wise knew very little about her husband, Herbert Axster, erroneously believing that he had been an innocent senior Luftwaffe officer. Wise demanded that Paperclip be terminated and that war victims rather than their oppressors be admitted to America. Patterson's officials were not inclined to concede anything to Wise, who, during the war, had forlornly battled against the State Department's reluctance to acknowledge the existence of Hitler's Final Solution. Patterson's first reply, which was at best equivocal, verging on the deceptive, explained that he was awaiting the outcome of an investigation already under way.[39] In fact, a routine security report from G2 in Germany about Ilse Axster, delivered to Ford in April, had portrayed her as a fanatic Nazi and a sadist.

During the war the Axsters lived on their large farm, Loddin, on the island of Rügen, not far from Peenemünde. Ilse, who had joined the party in 1937, was known to everyone as a convinced Nazi and had made impassioned speeches at party meetings urging followers to support the Führer and shoot Allied parachutists. Passion became practice, and Ilse, as befitted a member of the master race, strutted around her farm armed with pistol and whip. Numerous eyewitness accounts collected by Army Intelligence confirmed that she regularly horsewhipped the forty Poles and Russians working on her farm. These acts would have been sufficient to trigger her immediate return to Germany to stand trial had the army not been influenced by the importance of her husband as a member of von Braun's team.

Herbert Axster had joined the party on March 1, 1940, a gesture he later dismissed as merely an attempt to please the island's stalwarts, but this claim was belied by his conspicuously rapid rise to fame and fortune during the war. By training Axster was not a scientist but a patent lawyer and accountant. As such he was very useful to von Braun, whom he served as aide and confidant. At Peenemünde, Axster was General Dornberger's chief of staff, and as a lieutenant colonel in the army high command he basked in the privileges and glory reaped by the party faithful. Until 1940 Axster had been earning an average of ten thousand Reichsmarks a year. By 1943 his salary had quadrupled. The facts were irrefutable, and Ford's staff had concluded that Axster was "a notorious supporter and profiteer of the Nazi regime from 1933 to 1945."

At the time that the Axster file, together with Wise's protest, had passed up through the channels to Petersen, the politician was understandably keen to put himself at a distance from yet another potential scandal. Having read the Axsters' files, Petersen suggested that it would be better if Rusk took charge in view of "his close association" with the subject. Amid telegrams to the president and resolutions at public meetings condemning the import of German scientists, Rusk was too astute to touch the poisoned chalice: "This is one business I'm getting out of," he replied. "I'd suggest it be sent to G2 for action . . . in case this guy was a hot Nazi."[40] In April, although JIOA had decided that the Axsters' application for a visa could not be processed unless amended, Patterson told Rabbi Wise that their case was still under review. Pressure had been exerted on both JIOA and Patterson by the Ordnance Department's rocket branch.

Until Wise's protest, Axster had denied outright that he had ever been a member of the party, while his wife explained that she "was a supervisor of a kindergarten within a district with only a very minor rank in the party."[41] This rank, she claimed, had been given to her "because of her kindergarten experience." When in May Toftoy's emissary confronted the Axsters with the incriminating report from Europe, both only partially confessed. Relieved, Toftoy insisted that both must be protected and must remain in Texas.

Three months later Rabbi Wise wrote to Kenneth Royall — who as part of sweeping government changes had been appointed the new secretary of war — asking whether the Axster investigation had been completed and for a report of its findings. His letter ended with a discomfiting stricture: "As long as we reward former servants of Hitler while leaving his victims in DP camps, we cannot even pretend that we are making any real effort to achieve the aims we fought for."[42] By then Army Intelligence had received a further security report from Germany, which described Ilse as a "potential security threat" and an "ardent believer in and propagandist for National Socialism," while Herbert was condemned as a sympathizer.[43] Clay had nevertheless signed the agreed formula that Axster "is not likely to become a security threat to the US," thus relieving the immediate pressure for a decision, since under the new agreement between Petersen and Hilldring the army's decision on matters of security was supposedly final and could not be challenged. Ordnance's dilemma, however, remained. Although granting visas to the Axsters was legally impossible, allowing them to return to Europe would be sheer folly, given Herbert Axster's intimate knowledge of America's rocket program. Axster had become a denial case who had to be protected.

While Chamberlin was pondering the draft reply to Wise, the Pentagon's press office was on the verge of announcing the end of Paperclip. The proposed press release included a list of twenty-three Wright Field scientists who were applying for visas and gave the customary assurance that no active Nazis had been admitted to America. Yet, as Chamberlin knew, twelve of the named Germans had been members of the party. At the last moment the release was withdrawn. "If any of these individuals are spotted by sharp observers as having been associated with Nazi activities," commented Major General F. L. Park, chief of the public information division, "I think we are going to have a hard time reconciling that fact with the . . . statement."[44]

Influenced by that warning, Chamberlin's reply to Wise was deceptive: "The records and facts now available do not warrant deporting the Axsters. Mr. Axster's war service, administrative in character with the rank of lieutenant-colonel, does not disqualify him for exploitation in the US. Likewise, Mrs. Axster's participation as a minor official [kindergarten mistress] in the Frauenschaft, does not prevent her presence here with her husband." In his own reply to Wise, Kenneth Royall implicitly justified the deception: "I feel deeply that the program is for the best interests of the United States, and I can assure you that it is being administered within the War Department solely from the basis of national security and for the well-being of the American people."[45] Ten days later, on September 19, 1947, another security report was cabled from Europe. Ilse Axster was described as "an ardent Nazi and fanatical representative of Nazi ideology"; Herbert was accused of denouncing "a few members of his profession who were of Jewish parentage" to the Gestapo; and both of them were classified as "a potential security threat."[46]

In the new mood prevailing at the Department of War, the cable was ignored. Denial of the scientists to any other power surpassed interest in mere exploitation, and any thoughts of legality or morality were banished. Wise's group was condemned as the foolish tool of "foreign sources which desire to delay the development of new weapons in the US and weaken national security." To the military, it seemed as if the victims of Nazism could not understand national security and with "a few half truths" were, in effect, endorsing a Communist group whose objective was to discredit and deport the Germans. Again, the way seemed clear for the issue of visas.

Wev was optimistic that, at Hilldring's suggestion, the new secretary of state, General George Marshall, would effortlessly obtain the formal agreement of Attorney General Thomas Clark for the new procedures exempting aliens from immigration regulations "in the national interest." But to the surprise of all three, Clark and his officials were unwilling to assume legal or political responsibility for admitting anyone who was not certified by the State Department's visa section as "not a security risk." Deflated, Wev felt he was back at square one.

When news of the latest impasse arrived, a general panic seemed to envelop the Pentagon. Reports about the Red revolution in China and the machinations of the Communist parties in both Eastern and Western Europe acted as powerful incentives to those who feared the contagion of unrest and believed that America ought to be preparing for a new war. Consequently, no one in the Pentagon commented when a spokesman seriously estimated that the number of German scientists in Russia "may reach 150,000."[47] This wild exaggeration was seized upon by many, including Senator Styles Bridges, as proof that "America hasn't secured her share of the German scientists, while Russia has picked up a large number and is utilizing them to the full extent."[48] Chamberlin's staff did not care that many of the Germans on the denial lists were "not particularly desirable or eligible for shipment";[49] what really mattered was to prevent them from falling into Russian hands. JIOA had collected the names of 1,600 scientists who were to be denied to other powers, and even the British were no longer equal allies. Under the cooperation agreements made in 1945, Britain had released 250 scientists to America for interrogation but had received only seventeen in return. In early 1947 Farnborough wanted to interrogate Dr. Alexander Lippisch, the designer of the Me 163, and Dr. Ernst Eckert, a jet-fuel expert. Ford conspired to block British access.[50] Fearing espionage, others wanted to remove British officers from American bases. The proposal was rejected because of the danger of retaliation and lingering wartime sentiment, but it was evidence of the military's new preoccupation: Nothing should be allowed to obstruct its hunger for technical advancement and superiority.

At the air force's request, the date for the termination of Paperclip had been extended to September 30 so that "Project Abstract," the recruitment of forty German navigation and autocontrol experts, could be completed. Among those the air force contracted was Hans Giesecke, who before the war had studied in Portland, Oregon. Giesecke's German records revealed that he was a former SS officer, and his FBI file noted that he had made a succession of pro-Nazi speeches in Portland in the early 1930s, showing him to be no opportunist but a committed follower of Hitler's. Despite his Nazi past, Giesecke arrived in America in 1948.[51] The brazenness of Project Paperclip had spiraled to such heights that no scheme or suggestion was too extreme to be discarded, especially by other intelligence agencies.

In July 1946 permission was given by the army chief of staff for Paperclip to be used by the Military Intelligence service as a cover for bringing a maximum of thirty intelligence agents and specialists to America.[52] The decision contradicted Major General Clayton Bissell's edict the previous September, but once the machinery was established, the opportunities for abuse were too tempting to ignore.[53] The known "beneficiaries" of this extracurricular activity were East Europeans who had allegedly worked for American intelligence in Soviet-occupied Europe. The first list of this kind submitted to the State Department, in August 1947, named twenty-five men and women from Eastern Europe and included fifteen Finnish General Staff officers.[54] Unconvinced of their importance, Hamilton Robinson in the State Department refused to certify that their admission was "in the national interest." The identity of the other beneficiaries remains unknown. What is certain, however, is that the CIA and other agencies used Paperclip as a cover for importing those whom they wished to reward but who were too flagrantly incriminated to be officially processed — a scheme that was easier to execute once Paperclip became a totally unofficial and truly secret operation.*

Officially, Paperclip was terminated on September 30, 1947. In a public statement, the army announced that during the "procurement phase" 457 scientists and 453 dependents had been brought to America.[55] But with so much unfinished business and so many demands from the military for more scientists, the pressure for continuation was overwhelming.

In order to ensure the secret continuation of Paperclip, the air force orchestrated a chorus of praise for the genius of the German scientists. Two hundred and nine scientists owned by the air force, it was claimed, had begun to open up new horizons in weapons technology hitherto undreamed-of. In the Air Staff's opinion they were "superlative specialists . . . the best available in the world today,"[56] and they were saving the air force millions of dollars and up to ten years' work. "These German engineers," the Air Staff asserted, "are industrious, have technical and scientific training second to none, have production and operational experience in all types of advanced aircraft power plants and have demonstrated initiative, invention and practicability of design."

The air force proceeded to inundate Washington with an endless series of top-secret reports that listed projects masterminded by the Germans. Already under way were trials and experiments designed to test the feasibility of a diesel engine, new fuels and lubricants, guided missile control, helicopters, high-temperature alloys, precision optics, infrared detectors, in-flight refueling, pilot's equipment for high-altitude flying, ribbon parachutes, and a gunsight for night fighers "of epoch-making importance." Most astounding of all were the advances in jet-aircraft development that the German scientists had allegedly achieved. Theodore Zobel, Bernard Goethert, and Walther Boccius had delivered amazing calculations regarding airplane structures, delta-wing configurations, and aerodynamics, which finally convinced the air force of the

---

*The personal files in the National Archives in Washington regarding those admitted to the United States at the request of the CIA were withdrawn at the CIA's request.

superiority of German over Allied designs. Other impressive achievements included pioneering work on engine test stands, optic developments for high-altitude reconnaissance, mapping, gunsights, and evapographs. In the revolution of air warfare, the German contribution seemed paramount.

From its ordnance laboratory in Maryland, the navy reported that the German mathematicians, aerodynamicists, and experts in heat transfer had proven that "their professional education and training" were "superior to that of any U.S. personnel available." The Kochel wind tunnel was running at Mach 8, three times the speed and ten years ahead of the best American tunnel. Other Germans had produced original research on acoustic weapons, counterdevices, and explosives, and the Signal Corps reported that the Germans had "made contributions of an unusual and fundamental nature" in the realms of equipment design and development, generators, microwave techniques, and crystal structure.

To critics, the general euphoria seemed suspect. Later analysis would, in fact, suggest that some of the research was little more than a year ahead of the field and that the Germans' true value was their availability as highly experienced technicians and engineers — cheap labor for the military, which could not afford to hire Americans with similar qualifications. Equally, the assertion that the Germans were more security-conscious than Americans and could consequently be trusted did not correspond to the alarm with which the news of German scientists' duplicity in France was received. Throughout 1947, British and American intelligence reported the fears of General Achille Libessart, the head of the French Ballistics and Aeronautics Research Center in St. Louis, about the Germans working for their own ends in a conspiracy with other German groups employed by both Britain and Russia. To Libessart's anger, the Germans were ignoring French interests. His suspicions and warnings were taken seriously in Washington.[57] Orders were issued to tighten surveillance of the Germans in America, and there were attempts to insert American agents into French research institutes to discover how information on German work in America was leaking into France. The principal suspects remained German scientists returning from visits to Europe.[58]

But of greater concern were frustratingly inconclusive intelligence estimates of Russian progress. The only source of information was, as before, the web of German scientists themselves — whose "underground" gossip and indiscretions among wives, friends, and former colleagues had crossed Europe and the Atlantic. Monitoring of their letters, though haphazard, had been revealing, but carefully selected scientists were now asked to undertake a more formal investigation. The results were worrying. There had been approximately 2,500 aeronautic experts in Germany in 1945. Of these, 25 percent were now working in Russia (although the quality of their work was unknown), 12 percent were resident in America, 8 percent lived in France, and a mere 1 percent were in Britain, but the majority were still working in Germany itself. The investigation also revealed that the Heinkel and Junkers teams in Russia were developing a similar range of jet engines and planes to those the Americans were working on, while Soviet rocket development was definitely superior. During the war, the Red Army employed a wide arsenal of solid-fuel rockets as part of its artillery offensive, and the air force had used rockets with devastating success against German armor. Russia had therefore not needed German help to the same degree as America, but German experience was undoubtedly remedying inaccuracies and imperfections.[59] "Our enemies will have weapons generally comparable to our own," concluded an intelligence report to the Joint Chiefs in October 1947, "but we have the capability of obtaining [parity by 1955] and retaining superiority of performance."[60]

Those involved in Paperclip were in no doubt as to what that capability implied. At Fort Bliss, the Germans were pioneering work on Hermes 11, a $4 million ramjet-propelled rocket with a range of 400 miles at 12 miles' altitude and Mach 3.3. Yet, according to a report by an independent team, progress was slow and was severely hampered by the group's "security and citizenship status."[61] Their feelings of insecurity, it was hoped, would be cured by a new Paperclip project.

Although Paperclip had been officially terminated, certain politicians and the military had decided that it would continue in secret. The president was apparently not informed. Euphemistically, those involved in the conspiracy talked among themselves about the "procurement phase" having ended to be replaced by a "denial program," which served the same purpose. In October 1947 a new secret formula was agreed upon by the War, State, and Justice departments, known as the "escape clause."[62] Visas were to be issued provided Royall, at the War Department, simply certified that a scientist's admission was "highly desirable in the national interest." National security or denial of their services to another country was deemed to be in the national interest, and responsibility for security checks was transferred from State to Justice. Once approved, the State Department would simply inform the relevant consul that the legal requirements had been obeyed; then a visa would be issued. Once the pact was agreed on, Marshall asked Royall, seemingly as a casual aside, to take "some precautions . . . to guarantee that so-called war criminals are not certified."[63]

As if to confirm the validity of their conspiracy, at the end of October, on the same day that Major General Leslie Groves publicly predicted that it would take the Russians fifteen to twenty years to develop an atomic bomb, Soviet agents tried to kidnap Werner Eisenberg from his home at Göttingen. A new intelligence report used Groves's estimate, warning that the Soviets would possess the bomb by 1952. Denying Russia that nuclear parity now became enmeshed in the conviction that the Germans possessed the vital key to victory in a future conflict.

Clay was sent a revised JIOA denial list of 325 names, accompanied by orders to maintain surveillance to find those listed "attractive employment."[64] Only fifteen scientists were placed in the potential arrest category — to be detained "if the threat to US security warrants" — namely, the nuclear scientists in Göttingen and a number of experts on chemical and biological warfare who were too highly incriminated to be transported to America.[65] Within a few months, even those who had committed the most barbaric murders would be deemed eligible for entry into the United States. Meanwhile, a group, some of whose members were closely involved with one of the most nauseating aspects of Nazi science, had already arrived.

10

The Doctors from Berlin

ALTHOUGH THEY had only recently arrived in the hot desert of southern Texas, the German doctors whose new home was the Randolph Air Force Base in San Antonio were gradually beginning to forget the horror of the war. Led by Hubertus "Strugi" Strughold, they were feted as "geniuses" when introduced to their new neighbors by the U.S. Air Force. It was only two years after the war, but the anti-German resentment that lingered was soon dispelled. With charm and tact, they eventually blended into their new environment as much as traditional Germans could be expected to. San Antonio was a fortunate location for this particular group of Paperclip scientists. Living four thousand miles from Berlin, most of the locals could not even remotely imagine what had happened in Europe. Slightly embarrassing questions could therefore be politely brushed aside by the former Berliners without revealing anything unpleasant. Even those Americans who knew their secret did not dare, either before or after the Germans became American citizens, to probe their involvement in the horrors of Nazism.

Strughold's secret arrival in America in 1947 had been a carefully planned operation masterminded by Colonel Harry Armstrong, the wartime surgeon of the US Eighth Air Force. At the end of his distinguished career, in 1976, he would boast that the thirty-four German aviation doctors he brought to America had saved "a great many millions of dollars."[1] Before the war Armstrong had been an enthusiastic admirer of Strughold's and the German aviation doctors. They had met at an aviation medicine convention in Washington in 1934, an encounter that would later save Strughold the discomfort of prosecution as a war criminal. Throughout the conflict, as the Flying Fortresses mercilessly transformed many of Germany's elegant, ancient cities into a moonscape of rubble, Armstrong had monitored with fascination German innovations and developments, examining equipment salvaged from crashed Luftwaffe planes and studying interrogations of captured aircrews. His conviction that the German aviation doctors were the outstanding masters of his infant science was continually reaffirmed. From his prewar meeting with Strughold, of which he retained fond memories, he recollects that "we became quite good friends for two or three days and we had some common bonds." Armstrong never asked about nor showed the slightest interest in the circumstances under which his prodigies had served the Nazi cause.

Born in 1899 on a farm in South Dakota, Armstrong was appointed a flight surgeon in 1931, when flying was still a spectacular and rudimentary art. Never rising above 18,000 feet in their biplanes, fighter pilots sat in drafty cockpits fearing frostbite, suffered temporary blindness as their goggles fogged up, and were occasionally overcome by blackouts or carbon monoxide poisoning. In those days few pilots, and none of the small senior air staff, imagined that flying could ever be different. At the end of World War I, the tiny cadre of aviation doctors in America, as in every other country, closed down their primitive laboratories, certain that most of the problems of flying had been solved. Their lack of foresight was shared by the aircrews but not by Armstrong, who in 1935 became the director of the Aeromedical Research Laboratory at Wright Field. In Dayton in 1935, Armstrong had been subjected to ridicule when he publicly predicted that planes would eventually fly faster than the speed of sound. In retrospect, it seems a remarkable insight, especially since in 1935 aeromedicine was still a crude service; Armstrong's department's method of protecting pilots from freezing temperatures was simply to clothe them in reindeer skins.

Armstrong's prewar achievements, despite an annual budget of only $100 for equipment and $600 for animals, were impressive by American standards but paltry compared with Strughold's. Aviation medicine was a German innovation, pioneered in 1912 by Nathan Zuntz, a Jew from Berlin. By the early 1920s, eminent doctors in two major research institutes in Berlin had begun to probe the limits of pilot endurance. Inside centrifuges and pressure chambers, as well as on actual flights, they dangerously experimented upon themselves in order to judge the effect of violent changes in speed and height and to calculate the optimum mixture of air and oxygen that would save pilots from unconsciousness and death at higher altitudes. In the small international world of aviation medicine, their courage, insight, and results had been regarded with awe and discussed at congresses with reverence. Even in the isolation of war, Armstrong felt that the German doctors were worthy friends who by misfortune had become temporary enemies.

In May 1945 the American air force's chief surgeon, Major General Malcolm Grow, was determined to restore that prewar relationship. The Germans' accumulated knowledge was to be part of America's booty of war. Armstrong, then aged forty-six, was dispatched to the ruins of Berlin to hunt for Strughold and to interrogate and debrief him. But his round of visits to the wartime addresses of Luftwaffe medical research centers proved fruitless, since practically every building was damaged or destroyed. In the chaos of divided Berlin, Armstrong's hunt depended upon initiative and intrigue. Days passed before he found Ulrich Luft, a high-altitude specialist, in the remnants of the former Air Ministry aeromedical research center. Luft, the son of a Scotswoman, had done his earliest research on the Jungfrau, in the Alps, and in the Himalayas. Although the two had never met, it was for both a spiritual reunion. "I had read Armstrong's work before 1939," recalls Luft, who now lives in New Mexico, "and I knew that he had copied our oxygen equipment during the war." For his part, Armstrong was relieved that he had finally found someone who "felt that I was not tracking down potential criminals; that I simply was a fellow research person who was interested in their wartime work."

Directed by Luft, Armstrong was soon reunited with Strughold, who was working at Göttingen University, in the British zone. The horrors of war temporarily forgotten, the two doctors began intense mutual cross-examination to establish their progress during the previous six years. In that short period their specialized craft had been revolutionized. Jets, pressurized cabins, G suits, and proper oxygen masks had transformed flying from a jolly pastime to a sophisticated science. Despite American and British advances, Armstrong was overwhelmed as they talked by Strughold's account of the results that the Luftwaffe doctors had obtained. Conscious that his prize could still elude him, Armstrong was gripped by a nagging fear that America's allies would suborn or even kidnap Strughold and his colleagues. Luft had already been interviewed by the Russians but, fortunately, had not yet been recruited, and the arrival of a British investigatory team — headed by Sir Bryan Matthews, the director of the Institute of Aviation Medicine at the Royal Aircraft Establishment at Farnborough — to interview Strughold only fueled Armstrong's anxiety. As in all other fields, the intense wartime cooperation between Britain and America had been replaced by bitter competition for German knowledge.

"The Americans were edgy about having us around. They were polite and hospitable with their enormous food supplies," Matthews remembers, "but totally uncommunicative." Armstrong had, in fact, little cause to be suspicious. Unlike the Americans, before 1939 the British had never taken aviation medicine seriously. But during the brief span of war Matthews, a young Fellow of the Royal Society, had been abruptly promoted from working in totally primitive conditions to the command of a substantial institute. "When I took over in 1939, nothing had changed since the end of the first war," he recalls.

No one understood the problems of night vision or the need for oxygen. Pilots during the Battle of Britain could be heard hallucinating over the radio, calling out that they were landing when they were hovering over banks of cloud. The air marshals were so backward, stubbornly denying that oxygen deficiency was a problem. To convince one air chief, I invited him into a pressure chamber and secretly increased the altitude. When he was unconscious, we removed his braces. He still had not realised that he had been unconscious when he stepped out and I handed them back to him. It silenced his arguments.

Thanks to Matthews, by 1945 the gap between British and American aviation medicine had narrowed considerably, but the British still lacked sufficient maturity to appreciate the vast vista opened up by the war. When Matthews flew around Germany interrogating German doctors, he convinced himself that "the Germans had little more to offer from their wartime experience; and we knew about their pre-war work from their publications." His reaction was totally different from Armstrong's. As for the Germans, they were amused by one particular British error. The British, it emerged, had misunderstood a fundamental wartime discovery: Blackouts were caused not by oxygen deficiency but by G forces and by blood draining out of the brain.

Shortly before returning to Britain in July, Matthews traveled to Schleswig-Holstein, at the northern tip of Germany, where he interrogated Dr. E. Holzloehner, a physiologist employed by the Luftwaffe research institute. Willingly, Holzloehner described the Luftwaffe's attempts to improve the chances of survival for the hundreds of airmen who crashed in the North Sea. Holzloehner told Matthews that he had tested pills that would neutralize the salt in seawater and had also tried to find a method for rapidly restoring the body temperature of pilots who had survived crashes into the sea. Some of his guinea pigs had alas died, confided the German, but overall the results were promising. The unsuspecting Englishman left Schleswig-Holstein satisfied that the Germans had failed to find a solution to either problem. To his amazement, shortly afterward, Holzloehner shot himself in the head. Matthews suddenly understood that his guinea pigs were not animals but human beings. Ironically, Holzloehner "wrongly thought that we had realised." Nevertheless, Matthews did not report his suspicions to war-crimes investigators, since it "wasn't our business." In silence, the British investigators returned home, leaving the field to Armstrong. "We never thought of bringing any of the German scientists back to Farnborough," Matthews ruefully recollects. The British could see "no advantage or reason" for doing so.

The discovery that German doctors had carried out criminal human experiments had been made soon after the liberation of France, in autumn 1944. But when Sam Goudsmit, director of the U.S. War Department's top-secret Alsos mission in Europe, passed on revelatory captured documents to other scientific investigators in February 1945, he recommended that circulation be limited to Allied scientists. "The ultimate purpose of this procedure," wrote Goudsmit, "is to acquaint American specialists with the activities of their German colleagues. This is expected to have a profound influence upon their attitude towards enemy scientists."[2] If Goudsmit had been expecting Allied scientists to feel revulsion for the Germans, he was mistaken.

While Armstrong and Matthews were in the north of Germany interviewing Strughold, Major Leo Alexander, a U.S. Army doctor, was investigating the Luftwaffe's experimental treatment of exposure to cold. On June 5 Alexander traveled to the center of the research, the Institute of Aviation in Munich, to question Professor Georg Weltz, whose well-equipped laboratories included an "excellent low pressure chamber."[3] Weltz proudly explained to Alexander his startling discovery. Contrary to established prewar assumptions about the perils of the so-called "death by rewarming," Weltz had revived frozen animals by plunging them into hot water. His results, Weltz told Alexander, had been delivered to the Luftwaffe and the navy and also to the only major wartime gathering of Germany's senior aviation doctors, at Nuremberg on October 26, 1942. It was a conference about which Alexander and other American doctors were to hear more in the months to come. "It cannot be denied," reported Alexander, "that the fundamental observation of Dr. Weltz was sound. . . . The fundamental new factual observation upon which the research was based was the discovery that rapid warming in hot water of 40–45C was life-saving in guinea pigs and large pigs that had been chilled to the threshold of death." Alexander asked Weltz to show him the place where the experiments on large pigs had been performed.

Alexander's visit to the site at Gut Hirschau was disappointing. None of the equipment that remained was big enough for pigs. "Dr. Weltz was then asked whether his ideas, theories, practices and recommendations were ever applied to human beings." Enthusiastically Weltz asserted that the navy had found his "methods were excellent" but could produce no confirmatory evidence from his files. Alexander became suspicious. At the Gut Hirschau laboratories, Weltz had meticulously preserved test equipment for small animals, such as mice and rabbits, but strangely not for pigs. Nor could Weltz produce data on the use of his methods on the people rescued by the navy. There seemed one obvious conclusion: It "suggested to me that they had been filed together with other material which he did not wish to show." With some trepidation Alexander asked Weltz whether any of his experiments had been conducted on human beings. Vehemently, Weltz denied the existence or any knowledge of such tests. To allay suspicions, Alexander left Weltz without making any comment but "with the distinct conviction that experimental studies on human beings . . . had been performed but were being concealed."

Eager to establish the truth, Alexander began the long drive north to Göttingen. Strughold, he felt, could provide an explanation. But before reaching the northern university, Alexander heard that the American army radio had broadcast interviews with survivors from the Dachau concentration camp, which revealed that in Experimental Block number 5, fellow inmates had been immersed in tubs of ice with instruments attached to their bodies to monitor their painful deaths. His suspicions seemed to be confirmed. Ten days after leaving Weltz, Alexander was seated opposite Strughold. To the American's grim satisfaction, the distinguished German professor volunteered that he had also heard the broadcast and confirmed that he had heard Dr. Sigmund Rascher, a Luftwaffe staff surgeon, discuss at the Nuremberg conference his use of "criminals" for the experiments at Dachau. No one else, Strughold asserted, was involved.

The following day, Alexander walked into the neighboring office of Dr. Friedrich Rein, Germany's most outstanding physiologist. After a preliminary discussion about Dr. Rein's own work, Alexander inquired whether he knew about the Dachau experiments. Rein readily confirmed that he too had heard Dr. Rascher boast about his experiments at Nuremberg, but Rascher was not only in the Luftwaffe: He had also been a member of the SS and was an "unpleasant person." After five days in Göttingen, Alexander believed that he had established the truth. All the eminent German aviation doctors and physiologists he spoke to confirmed that Rascher had conducted the cold experiments and that his results were dubious, but that no one else was involved. Alexander then left Göttingen for Berlin. Unknown to the Germans, Himmler's vast private archives had been discovered, hidden in a cave in Hallein, and had just been returned to the capital. Swiftly but methodically Alexander and five assistants sifted through the mass of files until, with a cry of success, they found "a wealth of most revealing material," the records of the Dachau experiments, all personally annotated in green pencil by the obsessive SS leader.

The first discovery was a bizarre letter from Rascher dated May 15, 1941, asking Himmler for permission to use Dachau inmates for experiments. Rascher began by thanking Himmler for sending flowers and congratulations on the birth of his second son. "I shall take the liberty," he wrote, "to send you a small picture of both children some time." The child's mother was Himmler's former secretary, and it was widely rumored that Rascher enjoyed Himmler's trust because of an earlier intimate relationship between the SS leader and his secretary. But to Alexander's surprise, Rascher's proposed experiments were not to test survival in cold water but to investigate human physiology at high altitudes.

In his letter Rascher reported that the Luftwaffe was suffering losses because the latest RAF fighters could fly higher than the German planes. Atmospheric tests were therefore needed to establish new limits for the German pilots' oxygen needs and pressure endurance. Rascher expressed "considerable regret that no experiments on human beings have so far been possible for us because the experiments are very dangerous and we cannot attract volunteers" and asked as a "serious proposition" whether "two or three professional criminals could be available for these experiments?"[4] Nine weeks later Himmler approved Rascher's request.

As Alexander read through Himmler's files, he realized that the impression given by Strughold and the other doctors in Göttingen was deliberately misleading. Rascher might have made the formal application to Himmler, but he was not the initiator of the idea, nor did he envision working alone. The idea had been originated by his overall commander, Lieutenant General Professor Erich Hippke, the renowned chief surgeon of the Luftwaffe, and Hippke had approved the experiments on condition that they would be supervised by Weltz, who invited Dr. Siegfried Ruff to assist him.

Ruff was and still is an eminent aviation doctor and was one of the pioneers of specialized altitude studies. He had investigated the human element in airplane accidents, as well as the effects of flying on pilots, and during the war had been the director of the Luftwaffe's prestigious Institute of Aviation Medicine, the Deutsche Luftfahrts Forschungs Institute, in Berlin-Adlershof. Although not directly answerable to Hippke, Ruff enjoyed similar rank and status to his close friend and colleague Hubertus Strughold — who was the director of a comparable research institute financed by the Air Ministry. Strughold was directly answerable to Hippke. Their triangular relationship is crucial and controversial, but certain, as witnessed by Dr. Erwin Lauschner, Hippke's assistant: "Strughold and Ruff were close associates who had co-authored a textbook and were both frequent visitors, delivering their reports to my chief."[5] There can be no doubt that Strughold knew about, and at least tacitly approved of, Hippke and Ruff's proposed experiments. In February 1942 Ruff arrived at Dachau with his personal assistant, Dr. Hans Romberg, and his institute's glistening low-pressure chamber. The two doctors at once began intensive discussions with Rascher, Weltz, and Dachau's commandant about their proposed human experiments.

For all of them the work was important and urgent. The experiments started in March, and four weeks later Rascher sent Himmler the "first interim report" on the low-pressure chamber experiments. Inmates had been subjected to a simulated altitude of 12 kilometers. "The extreme fatal experiments," wrote Rascher, "were carried out on specially selected people, otherwise it would not have been possible to exercise the strict controls which are vitally necessary for the experiment." The human guinea pig specially selected for the first "terminal experiment" was a "37-year-old Jew in good condition" who lasted just thirty minutes. His death was carefully noted as he began to perspire and wriggle his head, developed cramps, became breathless and, with foam collecting around his mouth, lost consciousness and died. With Weltz at his side, Rascher performed the autopsy, calling out his observations to his assistant, including peculiar collections of blood and air bubbles, or embolisms, in the heart valves and brain ventricles. The case was, he proudly boasted to Himmler, "the first one of this type ever observed on man. The above-described heart actions will merit particular scientific interest because they were recorded until the very last moment by an electrocardiogram." In later experiments, the victim, a Jew accused of "race pollution," was taken unconscious from the pressure chamber and drowned so that air embolisms could be accurately traced during the autopsy.

The experiments ended in May 1942. A conclusive twenty-four-page report, signed by Rascher, was submitted separately to Himmler and to Ruff. According to Rascher's report, careful monitoring of the heart, blood, and urine in two hundred experiments had shown that flying without pressure suits and oxygen was impossible above 12 kilometers. Crews bailing out at 13 kilometers and over would be helplessly crippled by oxygen deficiencies and would need automatic ejection devices. Inmates who had been subjected to a simulated altitude of 20 kilometers became unconscious, then paralytic, and suffered long and unpleasant aftereffects. An eyewitness later testified that about eighty inmates died in the experiments, but the official report submitted to the medical profession, signed by Ruff, Rascher, and Romberg, explicitly stated that no deaths had occurred. But no one was deceived by the denial. As Strughold later admitted to Alexander, all of the ninety-five senior officers in the audience when the report was discussed at the Nuremberg conference in October 1942, including himself, Ruff, Luft, and fifteen other doctors and scientists, knew that the guinea pigs were human and that many had died. By then, the pressure chamber had been returned to Ruff's institute in Berlin.

Both the Luftwaffe and the navy were impressed by the results and understood the experiments' significance much better than others at the Nuremberg meeting. Forty senior Luftwaffe officers were invited by Himmler to a private screening of a film that showed the inmates dying in the pressure chamber. Among the audience were Hippke and the Air Ministry representative, Theodor Benzinger, a world-renowned expert on explosive decompression. The Luftwaffe's complicity in the crime was indisputable. Hippke wrote thanking the SS leader for his "great assistance" — but, to Rascher and Himmler's fury, at Nuremberg both Holzloehner and Ruff claimed credit for the results, thus minimizing Rascher's own contribution. In the recriminations that followed, Hippke was angered by Rascher's vanity but feared that the Luftwaffe's access to the inmates of Dachau would be endangered because Rascher, with Himmler's support, wanted to leave the air force and continue his work as a full member of the SS. At first, Hippke prevaricated.

Reading further through Himmler's file, Alexander soon grasped that after the pressure experiments, Professor Hippke asked Rascher to carry out cold-treatment tests. Hippke's only condition was that Dr. Holzloehner and two other eminent medical professors should join Rascher in Dachau for the human experiments. Hippke's interest was understandable. Many valuable pilots were dying of cold after parachuting out of their stricken planes. Vast numbers of German soldiers would have to face freezing conditions during the coming winter in Russia. Like any other ambitious physician, Hippke was not averse to the discovery of a cure by doctors answerable to him. The cold experiments started in autumn 1942 and were presented to the Nuremberg conference under the title "The Effect of Freezing on Human Beings." As explicitly described, inmates had reportedly been immersed in freezing water with thermometers in their orifices. "The rapidity with which numbness set in," the assembled dignitaries (including Strughold and Luft) learned, "was remarkable." The objective was to discover the cause of "termination"; the experiments revealed that "death results from heart failure."

After the conference, Himmler insisted that Rascher should investigate his suggested method of resuscitation — "animal warmth" — by placing a frozen man between two women. Despite Rascher's skepticism about Himmler's fantasy, four women were delivered to him in Dachau, and he was able to report one success. On regaining consciousness, the victim immediately began to have intercourse, and the monitor showed his temperature rising quickly. Eager to please Himmler, Rascher suggested that the next series of tests be transferred to Auschwitz. "The climate," he explained, "is colder and the camp itself is so extensive that less attention will be attracted to the work. The subjects howl frightfully when they freeze." Himmler agreed on February 26, 1943, but Hippke and Ruff saw little scientific merit in sexual obscenities, and Hippke abruptly disowned his previous responsibility. Hippke's reason for a change of heart in just eight weeks was not scientific but political. The Wehrmacht had just been defeated at Stalingrad, and the writing was on the wall. The doctors were eager not to have their names reappear in Himmler's files. Later Strughold and the other aviation-medicine doctors told the Americans that the Dachau experiments were not only unimportant but also of dubious scientific value.

Alexander's next discovery was a number of documents describing saltwater experiments. Himmler had granted permission for the use of Dachau for further human experiments, after receiving a proposal from Dr. Hermann Becker-Freyseng, a medical consultant to both Hippke and his successor Oskar Schroeder. Becker-Freyseng wanted to test a desalination process devised by Dr. Konrad Schaefer in the hope of saving Luftwaffe pilots forced to parachute into the sea. The records showed that Schaefer had attended the meetings at which Becker-Freyseng proposed and planned the Dachau desalination experiments. All of them, it seemed to Alexander, were culpable, though he reported,

> It is interesting and revealing to realize that only Dr. Rascher was named by Dr. Strughold and Professor Rein while their colleagues Holzloehner, Ruff and Romberg, whose participation in the human experiments was then not yet known to us, were still being covered up by Strughold, as well as by Rein; although Strughold at least must have been familiar with the parts played by his friend and co-worker Ruff and his colleague Holzloehner.

As Alexander correctly surmised, Strughold was in an embarrassing position. All the scientists above and below him — Hippke,

Ruff, Schroeder, and Becker-Freyseng — were implicated in the experiments. Nevertheless, since (as he rightly assumed) all his colleagues had destroyed or concealed their incriminating files, Himmler's files would expose only the complicity of the SS. So the blame was heaped on Rascher — who, all of them knew, had been executed on Himmler's orders two weeks before Dachau was liberated.

Alexander completed his highly incriminating report in July 1945. Its detailed exposure of the doctors' crimes should have been a warning to Armstrong and other Americans considering the employment of German scientists. Yet in newly liberated Europe and America, the revelations of Nazi crimes were still barely understood. Few could believe that tens of thousands of Germans had coldly and deliberately planned and accomplished the production-line murder of millions of innocent civilians, and it would take months to collate and analyze the meticulous records of the Nazi extermination program. Professional men, especially doctors, were appalled at the inhuman experiments performed in the name of science — but amid sensational revelations about gas chambers, crematoria, mass graves, and the extensive use of slave labor, the aviation-medicine experiments were momentarily overshadowed. Those later accused of protecting the doctors cited Alexander's testimony on the value of the German discoveries: Weltz's recommendation of rewarming humans using hot water, he concluded, "should be immediately adopted as the treatment of choice by the Air-Sea Rescue Services of the United States Armed Services." Armstrong and other American aviation doctors today insist that Ruff's altitude experiments at Dachau were equally valuable, and use was made of them after the war by American scientists.

Just as Alexander was about to deliver his findings in London, Armstrong presented the results of his own investigation to Major General Grow. His suspicions, Armstrong reported, were confirmed. The German aviation doctors had continued their impressive prewar research, had produced nearly two thousand unique medical documents, mostly classified Luftwaffe reports, and were willing to be intensively debriefed by the American air force. Fortunately, confided Armstrong with evident relief, the British had returned home convinced that the Germans had accomplished nothing new during the war and had concealed nothing. Consequently, he recalls, "We had an opportunity of acquiring all that information which probably represented five or six years of effort by perhaps several hundred scientists . . . [and was] invaluable to us." He also asserts, contrary to Sir Bryan Matthews's belief, that the Germans were "rather secretive even before the war." But Armstrong did not question the German doctors about their possible involvement in any crimes. At the dawn of the jet age, he was very much aware of the value of the German doctors' work and was solely concerned with extracting information. In July 1945, he writes, "I was predicting that the Germans and not the Russians would be our future friends and allies. Why it took the State Department and the government ten years to find that out is beyond my imagination. . . . I discussed it rather forcibly to the extent that I was warned by my friends that I should be a little more careful or I might possibly be court-martialed." With Grow's support, Armstrong obtained Eisenhower's approval for an operation to "exploit certain uncompleted German aviation medicine research projects."

Responsibility for the exploitation was passed to the Third Central Medical Establishment. The location was the former Kaiser Wilhelm Institute for Medical Research in Heidelberg, the picturesque and undamaged university town on the Rhine. Armstrong returned to America, leaving Colonel Robert Benford as director of the project. Benford's task was "to bring back from Germany everything of aero-medical interest to the Army Air Forces and all information of importance to medical science in general." Within a few weeks Strughold, Ruff, Becker-Freyseng, Schaefer, Benzinger, and Schroeder had arrived in Heidelberg and were employed by the American army.

At Benford's suggestion, Strughold organized more than one hundred American and German doctors and technicians to work in the laboratories and write reports of their conclusions. Army teams were dispatched throughout Germany to seize the best equipment available from former Luftwaffe institutes: pressure chambers, oxygen compressors, machines to create G forces, a huge centrifuge, an electron microscope, and an awe-inspiring collection of the finest machinery in the world. Life at Heidelberg was very pleasant. Despite the nonfraternization rules, Benford ran a liberal establishment for the scientists and their families. Food and drink were relatively plentiful, and the building was well heated. Strughold, Ruff, and the others felt secure. Outside, their fellow countrymen were less comfortable. In the autumn the daily civilian ration was held at a minimal 1,200 calories and often fell below starvation level; there was no fuel; most houses were destroyed or damaged, and families were cramped together in desultory accommodations; the infant mortality rate was nearly 80 percent. After a brief respite at Christmas, conditions were poised to worsen. For the aviation doctors and their families, however, Christmas was a jolly affair. Benford organized a joint American-German party in the institute's library, with "refreshment, music and movies." Benford was delighted that the Americans and Germans had become a "happy community."

At the beginning of 1946 Armstrong was appointed director of research in Washington under Grow, chief surgeon of the air force. To his disappointment, his large wartime staff had evaporated and returned to civilian life. The only suitable replacements for his proposed new school of aviation medicine, he felt, were the Germans in Heidelberg. Although Sir Bryan Matthews condemns him for "empire building," Armstrong believed that without the Germans, American aviation medicine would be a subject of "concern for the immediate future." Critics later alleged that in order to justify using the Germans to build his empire, he claimed that the Germans were geniuses. The truth lies somewhere in between.

In June Armstrong asked the director of intelligence to arrange for the first twenty-two aviation doctors to be brought to Wright Field from Germany as soon as possible, as part of Paperclip. One of the principal conditions of Paperclip was that none of the German scientists arriving in America would be former members of the Nazi party or have committed war crimes. In naming the twenty-two, Armstrong either assumed that in the interests of science past unpleasantnesses could be forgotten or was genuinely unaware of some of their activities.

But in Heidelberg Strughold was outrightly effecting a cover-up. In the same month that Armstrong submitted his Paperclip requests, Strughold began reading the first drafts of his colleagues' work. At Benford's suggestion, their collected articles would eventually be published as a monument to their achievements in two huge volumes entitled *German Aviation Medicine*. But from the first drafts Strughold saw that there were problems. Some of his friends had disagreeably mentioned the results of their human experiments in a way that might raise awkward questions. Describing a seventy-hour oxygen test at 9,000 meters, Becker-Freyseng compared animal and human behavior: "This test," he wrote, "showed for the first time that there are also dangers for humans." Similarly, Ruff commented on the results of his tests concerning the perils of oxygen deficiency. To protect himself and his colleagues, Strughold struck out the incriminating disclosures with a blue pencil. As Luft charitably says, "Strughold decided to let sleeping dogs lie." But it was already too late.

In Nuremberg, while the international court conducted the major war-crimes trial against twenty-two Nazi leaders, a dedicated team of American lawyers was preparing a series of subsequent trials against lesser but nevertheless notorious luminaries of the Third Reich, including senior German medical officers. In addition to Alexander's report, American war-crimes investigators had uncovered evidence of the Nazis' euthanasia program and a series of other fatal human experiments involving chemical warfare gases, typhus vaccines, and bone transplants. Telford Taylor, the chief army prosecutor, believed there was an overwhelming argument for indicting the German medical profession for complicity in Hitler's crimes. His problem was to find more detailed evidence and arrest the offenders. In many of the other cases there was no shortage of witnesses, but in a medical trial the key witnesses would be the victims, most of whom were dead. For the case against the Luftwaffe, although Himmler's personal archives were vital, the equally crucial personal files belonging to Ruff and Strughold from the Luftwaffe and Air Ministry were missing and had probably been destroyed. The hunt for more detailed evidence depended upon Taylor's staff, but they were woefully inept at interrogation and investigation. According to Foster Adams, one of the prosecutors at Nuremberg, "We didn't know what we were looking for, so we grabbed at everything."[6] In the absence of satisfactory evidence, the only solution was to strictly limit the indictment.

On September 16, a platoon of soldiers from the 303 Detachment of the Counter Intelligence Corps arrived at the Heidelberg institute and solemnly handed Benford their orders. The director was flabbergasted. Taylor had ordered the arrest of Ruff, Becker-Freyseng, Benzinger, Schroeder, and Schaefer, despite the fact that all five had been named by Armstrong as Paperclip scientists and believed that they soon would be destined for Wright Field. Instead, in a state of shock, they were driven under escort to Nuremberg Prison. Benzinger, a thin and impassioned former Prussian, still unreasonably blames Strughold for his arrest. Strughold, he maintains, "had to put the blame on someone because he was so vulnerable. In 1942 he was working under Hippke, next to Ruff and above Becker-Freyseng. He was wedged in amongst all the criminals and his way out was to point the finger at me. He was a brilliant manipulator." Ruff and Schaefer were less anguished by their arrest. Both knew there was a case to answer and were prepared to fight.

Strughold was undoubtedly relieved that he had not been indicted. In deciding whom to prosecute, as in other cases, Taylor's staff reluctantly made concessions — either because there was insufficient evidence or because another branch of the army or military government argued that the national interest overrode the interests of justice. Afterward some speculated that Strughold had been spared because without his presence the Heidelberg project would have collapsed. The prosecutors were aghast at what appeared to be the cynical use of German experts regardless of their past. Benford and Armstrong, however, never believed the allegations against the Germans and were outraged at their treatment. Colonel Paul Campbell, M.D., who worked with Benford, insists that all the scientists were "very carefully studied and screened . . . I am convinced in my own mind that none of them were in any way blemished." Armstrong believed that it was now more urgent than ever to move the remaining scientists to America in case more of them were selected for prosecution or had to stand trial.[7]

James McHaney from Little Rock, Arkansas, was appointed to prosecute the medical case against twenty-three Germans, including the Luftwaffe doctors. McHaney readily admits that he lacked scientific expertise and had never presented an equally complicated case. As he was soon to discover, the aviation doctors had resolutely committed themselves to total denial and mutual corroboration. Benzinger's defense during the preliminary interrogation should have alerted McHaney to the legal minefield that lay ahead. Although he admitted knowing of the human experiments and being present at the secret screening of the film report, Benzinger denied that he had initiated any of the experiments or even used the results. Without a single document or eyewitnesses to disprove it, Benzinger's denial was irrefutable, and he was released unprosecuted. On his return to Heidelberg, he found Strughold still "correcting" his colleagues' drafts.

Despite Benzinger's release, McHaney remained confident of securing convictions against the remaining Luftwaffe defendants. The prosecution opened on December 9 and was completed just six weeks later, but to his surprise the defense lasted six months. Out of all the defendants, no one exploited McHaney's weaknesses more adroitly than Ruff. Emphasizing the absence of any document that proved he had initiated experiments, Ruff argued that there were two sets of experiments at Dachau: those conducted by Rascher on two hundred inmates, and those conducted by himself exclusively on volunteers. Ruff was unable to prove the distinction between his own experiments and Rascher's, but McHaney found it equally impossible to disprove, and since American investigators had failed to produce credible eyewitnesses, his cross-examination often collapsed. None of the defendants recognized those flaws better than Ruff, who insisted that any qualms he might have held were allayed by his "recognition of the importance and urgency of the research involved," and he even boasted of his legal punctiliousness: "I knew that the experiments were legally authorised by Himmler. . . . As for medical ethics, it was different. It was a very new experience for us to be offered prisoners for experiments."

McHaney was constantly confused by Ruff's fumbling and incoherent answers. Nor could he pinpoint the flaws in Ruff's medical explanations. Even McHaney's expert witness from America, Professor Andrew Conway Ivy, was unable to produce a link of culpability between the Dachau experiments and the report signed by Ruff based on that work. In the dock, wrote one observer, "The defendants scarcely ever showed sympathy with their victims even at this late date. They were more concerned with the safety of their own skins than with the misery and death they had inflicted on others. At moments, one's disgust with their pedantically solemn eloquence on the subject of their innocence became almost unbearable."

Ruff, Weltz (who had been arrested in Bavaria), and Schaefer were acquitted. In the court's judgment,

> The issue on the question of the guilt or innocence of these defendants is close; we would be less than fair were we not to concede this fact. It cannot be denied that there is much

in the record to create at least a grave suspicion that Ruff [was] implicated in criminal experiments at Dachau. However, virtually all of the evidence which points in this direction is circumstantial in nature.

Becker-Freyseng and Schroeder were less fortunate: They were convicted and sentenced to twenty years and life imprisonment respectively. Yet neither Armstrong nor Benford ever voiced any condemnation of those convicted and continued to praise those who were acquitted. Indeed, Benford blames their prosecution on "American liberals" and especially laments the embarrassment caused to "my friend Ruff."

By the time Ruff had left the courthouse, the Kaiser Wilhelm Institute had closed. Under Strughold's supervision, thirty-four Germans had accepted Paperclip contracts, and most of them were already working at Armstrong's new School of Aviation Medicine at the Randolph Air Force Base in San Antonio, Texas. Immediately after his arrival, Strughold, at Armstrong's suggestion, began to organize the investigation of space medicine in order to "find a solution for a disease which did not yet exist." As for Ruff, he became the highly respected director of Germany's new aviation medicine institute, and the two doctors kept in close touch. Like most of his colleagues, Strughold took care to blur the facts established at Nuremberg. Just as the rocket team blamed the SS for the crimes committed at Nordhausen, so the blame for the Dachau experiments was heaped upon the SS, though only silence greeted questions as to how scientifically illiterate SS officers could have participated in abstruse medical discussions about human physiology. But Strughold was and remained an enlightened opportunist, as his American security report testified: "His successful career under Hitler would seem to indicate he must be in full accord with Nazism."[8]

Among those who arrived in America with Strughold was Dr. Theodor Benzinger, whose U.S. Army security report recorded that he had been a member of Hitler's SA and an active member of the Nazi party, and described him as a "typical Prussian German who is motivated by his own convictions to pursue an end in which he has an interest and a belief." The following year Schaefer joined Strughold in America to continue his work on desalination. Schaefer says that when he received his Paperclip contract, he queried whether his prosecution at Nuremberg would cause any problems.

"The American officer told me 'Forget about it.' " Soon after his arrival, the U.S. Army sent its report on his past to the army's director of intelligence in Washington. It stated that the investigations "failed to disclose any records of previous arrests." Schaefer's trial at Nuremberg and his involvement in the Dachau experiments were deliberately concealed. It was just one more incident in the Paperclip conspiracy.

11

Rewriting the Past

IN EARLY 1948 Europe seemed on the verge of a new cataclysm. To many in Washington the constant Communist-inspired strikes toppling governments and rumors of Communist coups suggested that Moscow was either masterminding the early stages of a revolution or on the brink of launching an invasion. Alarmed by events in Europe, Congress approved a phenomenal $500 million budget for one year's scientific military research, and the Pentagon hastily set about rearming America for a new and, some believed, imminent war. Lofty principles and solemn promises, the Pentagon argued, must no longer be allowed to stand in the way of defending the nation. Innovation was at a premium, and any and every German with a modicum of scientific or technical expertise was a potential target of a new dragnet, regardless of his past. For the military, especially the air force, it was an ideal moment to fuel hysteria in order to win blanket authorization for the indiscriminate issue of visas to Germans, despite the infamy or notoriety of their crimes. A note of frantic urgency crept into the impatient messages from Washington to Frankfurt peremptorily demanding German scientists.

Four weeks after the sensational "suicide" of Jan Masaryk in Prague in March and the Communist coup in Czechoslovakia, Colonel Robert Taylor III, the chief of the Air Force Intelligence requirements division, wrote a long memorandum to support the air force's claim for more Germans. Taylor based his arguments on the patently false allegation that the Russians had grabbed the lion's share of German scientists. Seventeen percent of German scientists, he estimated, had gone to Moscow, while only 6 percent had gone to America, 11 percent to Britain, and a similar percentage to France.[1] The estimate for Britain was wildly exaggerated and the American figure much too low. Nevertheless, Taylor's assessment, which was supposedly based on "intelligence channels," produced the desired effect.

The air force's Colonel Donald Putt, an investigator at Volkenrode, as ever, was at the forefront of the new drive. The German scientists at Wright Field had convinced him that in any future war the air force would need to house its headquarters, factories, and planes in fortified concrete bunkers. At Albert Speer's initiative, by the end of the war Germany's armament industry had been sheltered from attack in underground complexes impervious to even the heaviest bombardment. The officer responsible for the construction of these triumphs of engineering was Walter Schieber, the former head of the Reich's armament supply office and described by Speer as "Himmler's confidential agent in my ministry," who had increased production during 1943 and was awarded, on Speer's recommendation, the prestigious War Merit Cross by Hitler.

During the autumn of 1947 Schieber was among the 160 Germans being debriefed by the American army in Germany in order to elicit information about underground factories. Putt wanted him shipped to Ohio immediately. There was, however, a problem that he needed urgently, somehow, to overcome. Although Schieber's technical qualifications were obviously outstanding, the factories had been built by slave labor under the most atrocious concentration camp conditions. Schieber had not only witnessed and connived at the suffering of thousands but had indisputably organized their predicament. As a passionate supporter of Hitler, a known confidant of the SS chief Ernst Kaltenbrunner, and a party member since 1931, he had felt no qualms. Indeed, success had propelled him to the top ranks of the SS as a highly decorated general. In 1945 many would have willingly punished Schieber as a war criminal. Yet in 1948 his future looked promising. If he was not contracted by the Americans, it was certain that the Russians would make a generous offer. So, in reply to Putt's request, Colonel Robert Schow, the deputy director of intelligence in Frankfurt, suggested that Schieber be sent to the United States by air, using an alias and being protected by an escort "in order to minimize the possibility [of] unfavorable publicity in the US."[2]

At air force headquarters in Washington, Schieber's record was not seen as an insuperable obstacle. Clearly, a normal Paperclip contract was out of the question, but the Joint Chiefs could still sanction his employment. Accordingly, the air force sent Bousquet Wev, then the director of JIOA, urgent instructions:

> It is requested that every effort be made to obtain the services of Walter Schieber as soon as possible, and to bring him to the US. It is believed that Dr. Schieber's talents are of so important a nature to the US that they go far to override any consideration of his past political background, provided that he is not suspected of criminal acts. It is further considered to be of the utmost importance that he not be allowed to fall into the hands of a possibly unfriendly power.[3]

Under the new, secret Paperclip agreement, that eventuality could be prevented. The escape clause permitted the air force to continue issuing Paperclip contracts despite the formal announcement of its termination on September 30, 1947. Moreover, because it was classified as a top-secret operation that excluded even limited publicity, Putt hoped that committed Nazis such as Schieber could quietly slip into the country.

Schieber's denazification trial was imminent. Schow confidently predicted that the German tribunal would place him in a low category and levy a small fine. His optimism arose from the engineer's insistence that Hitler had ordered his dismissal in late 1944 because of Schieber's defeatism — but the proof was at best very circumstantial, and according to Speer, the Führer's order was the result of jealous intrigues within the SS hierarchy. To Schow's disappointment, in early March the tribunal convicted Schieber as an important Nazi and sentenced him to two years' imprisonment. Reluctantly, Putt canceled his offer. Schow, however, was unwilling to let the matter rest, especially after Schieber slyly convinced him that the tribunal's president was a Communist who had suggested after the trial that Schieber accept a lucrative Russian offer. Schow's gullibility even extended to arranging an "investigation" to prove Schieber's allegation. "Cancellation of Schieber's contract after he has possibly jeopardized his safety and after he has co-operated so whole-heartedly with intelligence agencies here," cabled Schow to Washington, "is certain to have an adverse effect on the future contracting or exploitation of specialists and will only serve as another example of broken faith on the part of the US."[4]

Had they known about it, critics in Congress would have been outraged by the notion of treating the fate of a former SS general as a trial of America's honor, especially since Schow and other senior army officers openly sympathized with Schieber as the victim of a miscarriage of justice. But the German's fate had been consciously elevated to a litmus test of America's new perception of Nazi Germany. Schow credited Schieber with espousing Nazism "to combat communism" and "improve Germany's economic plight." And to prove the former SS officer's lack of anti-Semitism, he even offered by way of defense the classic and shameless fiction proffered by so many committed Nazis. Schieber was quoted by Schow as saying, "In 1938, in the uniform of an SS colonel, I assisted a Jewish merchant in escaping to New York." In the very same week that senior Counter Intelligence Corps officers secretly transformed the former Lyons Gestapo chief Klaus Barbie into a full-time American agent in Bavaria, the deputy director of intelligence wrote to Washington: "There is no evidence to indicate that Schieber believed in or fostered any Nazi principles which advocated or condoned atrocities or inhuman treatment of persons or armed aggression."[5] Despite Allied agreements prohibiting dealings with the Nazis, Schow felt Schieber should be brought to America, since the French would have no inhibitions about attempting to recruit him and "it is believed that the British here likewise exploited similar offenders."

Both Putt and Schow were puzzled that Schieber had not benefited from the secret October 1947 agreement under which a visa could have been issued on a simple certificate from the War Department stating that his entry was "in the national interest." The denazification tribunals were nominally under U.S. control, and they believed the results could have been manipulated. Wev shared their disappointment. Everyone concerned had blithely believed that it would be relatively easy to turn even ardent Nazis overnight into honest American citizens, since there was to be no investigation, and only the signature of Kenneth Royall, the secretary of war, on the certificate was required. It was now clear that there was a need for some semblance of legality before senior officers and politicians would ignore a German's past. Wev had already noticed with interest that a visa application from Hermann Kurzweg, the former Peenemünde SS officer now supervising the Kochel wind tunnel for the navy in Maryland, had been approved by the simple expedient of rewriting his past. G2 officers in Germany had skillfully discovered "understanding" eyewitnesses who could provide extenuating circumstances to explain the unfortunate blot on Kurzweg's otherwise immaculate record. Here, Wev believed, was a method that even types like Schieber could exploit. The device seemed infallible. When issuing "revised security reports," G2 simply needed to reverse any description that suggested the German was a Nazi.

On December 12, 1948, Wev sent the director of intelligence in Frankfurt the names of fourteen Germans whose OMGUS security reports classified them as "potential or actual threats to the US." Among the fourteen were Herbert Axster, Werner von Braun, Theodor Benzinger, Adolf Thiel, and Helmut Schelp. All were long-serving Nazi party members, and some had been in the SS or SA. Written at General Stephen Chamberlin's behest, Wev's letter giving the names of the fourteen Germans was a masterpiece of deception. Ignoring the worst offenders, such as Axster, Wev claimed that some of those listed were wrongly condemned because they were merely party members, not party officials. The security report on Werner Gengelbach, for example, Wev wrote, described him as "devoted to his family and profession, only a nominal Party member, and not politically active, always reliable and humane." Frankfurt was urged to reconsider its position on the potential threat of the German scientists to U.S. security on the grounds that "the evaluation of the Military Governor with regard to reference specialists is unrealistic and based on a misunderstanding as to the purpose of the OMGUS security report. Immigration of a specialist whose report is so worded is jeopardized."[6] The remedy, Wev suggested, was the insertion of a "saving clause" that would allow for reevaluation. "There is very little possibility that the State and Justice Departments will agree to immigrate any specialist who has been classified as a potential or actual security threat to the US. . . . Because of the far-reaching effect of the Military Governor's security evaluation, it should only be made on the most sound premises and only when full information is available."[7]

The initial reaction in Germany to Wev's plea on Gengelbach's behalf was outrightly cynical. "The extreme ease with which the most highly incriminated respondent can produce parades of favorable witnesses in his own behalf," wrote Robert Bruce, a military government officer, "and the correspondingly great difficulty encountered by public prosecutors in finding witnesses to present derogatory testimony" rendered the favorable testimonials about Germans worthless. Clearly irritated by JIOA's invitation to join an underhand conspiracy, Bruce pointed out that the American military government had refused to grant even temporary exit permits to a number of German girls engaged to American servicemen who were seeking medical treatment in Switzerland, merely on the grounds that they had been Nazi party members. Wev was asking for a lot more: "It is felt that if the State and Justice Departments do not see the necessity or value of immigrating subject specialists to the US, then this headquarters should not revise or change its opinion of subject scientists merely to circumvent the rules set forth by the State and Justice Departments."[8] Wev filed Bruce's protest, and it was quickly forgotten.

The task of smoothing the process of rewriting the Nazis' past fell to Lieutenant Colonel Walter Rozamus, JIOA's new deputy director. Rozamus, the son of Lithuanian immigrants, was a hardened and experienced intelligence officer who had courageously fought his way across Europe after landing on the Normandy beaches two days after D day. The supreme irony of Rozamus's appointment to JIOA was that in April 1945 he had been with the First Army's frontline platoons when they liberated Nordhausen. It was a sight that the battle-weary officer would never forget: "You're hardened by your feelings in war, but this time I just felt like breaking down and crying. It was just unbelievable and still haunts me at times." Vividly, Rozamus remembers with a shudder that the corpses stacked by the crematoria and others hanging from meat hooks were so emaciated that there was not even an odor of death. Rozamus had no doubts about who was to blame: "Hitler" and no one else — a simplistic but useful notion that neatly avoided any self-doubts about his duties in the Pentagon.

Two years later, Rozamus arrived at JIOA's office in order to help those responsible for the horrors at Nordhausen become American citizens. The irony completely escaped him both then and forty years later: "What they did during the war was irrelevant," explains Rozamus. "We didn't care about their background. We had to keep the scientists out of the Russians' hands because they were vital in any future war and they could do us some good." As a soldier, Rozamus simply accepted that "they were fighting their war like we were fighting ours. And they were obeying orders just like us. . . . What they had done didn't enter my mind. I was concerned about the security of my country." As a loyal officer, Rozamus found it quite understandable that the Nazis should excuse their crimes by pleading superior orders. Similarly, he was blind to the paradox that while the Pentagon staff accepted the Germans' excuse, U.S. Army prosecutors in Nuremberg were busy systematically demolishing the selfsame argument.

To Rozamus, seated behind his Pentagon desk, his new task seemed amazingly simple. The services sent him completed visa-application forms for each scientist, and JIOA asked G2 in Germany to investigate the Germans' wartime activities. If Rozamus noticed that the security report contained incriminating information, then the report was simply returned to Germany indicating what needed to be rewritten. In Rozamus's language, he was asking for "a different interpretation": "I felt that by changing a sentence or two, we could use these people. I've seen sentences changed many times and it makes the difference between black and white. It was a smart thing to do." The key phrases to be changed always referred to the Germans' Nazi activities. Whether Rozamus or Wev, as loyal officers, were aware that the rewriting breached a presidential directive remains unclear; but Rozamus is emphatic that "Paperclip was approved by the President and it was my job to obey his orders." Mechanically, as each incriminated scientist applied for a visa, Wev and Rozamus wrote to the director of intelligence at the army's command in Frankfurt, bluntly asking him to "re-evaluate" the scientist's security report since "ardent Nazis" were barred from immigration.[9] Nazis, Rozamus explained, were no longer classified as a "security threat." With the "very stubborn, arrogant and unreasonable" Sam Klaus out of the way, Rozamus was satisfied that the scientists' files, including the revised security reports, could now safely be processed through the State Department.

For the military, rapidly rearming against Communism, the old criterion that Nazism was a threat to internal security was now an anachronism. Like Wev, most believed that "beating a dead Nazi horse" served little purpose and was, in fact, self-defeating. Former Nazis were proving themselves willing and able allies against Communism, which was "jeopardising the entire world."[10] There was, they felt, a sharp distinction between political subversion (because Nazis believed in totalitarianism) and outright espionage. Both risks, the military believed, were negligible. With Wev's vigilant assistance, the Pentagon's press office was intent on projecting "the correct image" of the typical German scientist. Some described their efforts as the best of Madison Avenue; to others they smacked of the brainwashing and manipulation of Goebbels's propaganda. For his part, Wev was undoubtedly pleased with the result. Journalists were assured that no "active Nazis" were being admitted to America and, as a novelty, were offered a profile of a typical Paperclip scientist: He had never been a member of the Nazi party and had been "arrested by Gestapo in June 1943 for subversive political activities and sent to concentration camps of Sachsenhausen, Dachau, Gross Rosen, Mauthausen and Buchenwald."[11] In fact, none of the Paperclip scientists had ever been sent to concentration camps. The truth, of course, was that some of the scientists had cooperated with the Gestapo, and others had exploited the helpless inmates of the concentration camps as slave labor or for unethical experiments. Obligingly, some newspapers submitted their stories to the Pentagon for correction. In an article about the elimination of "big Nazis" in the *New York Times*, Robert Buckhardt followed the Pentagon's line that any scientists who were party members prior to 1933 or had been convicted by a denazification court were automatically eliminated from Paperclip. Unwittingly, he had relied on old Department of War press releases. Without a qualm, the Pentagon removed the "mistakes."[12]

At the same time, other "mistakes" were being removed from the scientists' security reports. Herbert Axster's "revised report" now read: "Subject was not a war criminal and was not an ardent Nazi. The record of Herbert Axster as an individual is reasonably clear and as such, it is believed that he constitutes no more of a security threat than do the other Germans who have come to the U.S. with clear records in entirety." Axster's Nazism was conveniently blamed upon his wife. Since Walter Dornberger, as an army general, would not have joined the party, passing him off as clear of any Nazi taint was uncomplicated; and Arthur Rudolph's file now affirmed that he "was not a war criminal" and "was not an ardent Nazi."

Von Braun's SS record was cleverly circumvented. His earlier security report stated that, according to the military governor, he was "regarded as a potential security threat." Wev requested that this earlier description be omitted from von Braun's revised report. Adroitly, the new report stated that investigation of subject is not feasible due to the fact that his former place of residence is in the Russian zone where US investigations are not possible. No derogatory information is available on the subject individual except NSDAP records which indicate that he was a member of the Party from 1 May 1937 and was also a major in the SS, which appears to have been an [honorary] commission. The extent of his Party participation cannot be determined in this Theater. Like the majority of members, he may have been a mere opportunist.

The report concluded that since von Braun had been in the United States for two years, he was judged not to be a security risk, provided his behavior over the past two years had been satisfactory.

The turbine engineer Hermann Schnieder, who in 1947 was described as "a convinced believer in National Socialism," was now declared to be "not an ardent Nazi." Theodor Benzinger, the aviation doctor, who in early 1947 was found to be "active politically" in the Nazi party, was months later partially exonerated by the suggestion that "he may only have been an opportunist." And the security report on Albert Patin, an aviation expert, blandly stated that he was "not an ardent Nazi."

Some "mistakes" could not be so easily removed. The investigations reported that Dr. Wilhelm Eitel, who was researching synthetic materials for the navy in Tennessee, had remained a passionate Nazi even after the war. In Germany Eitel was regularly to be seen wearing a brown uniform and had collaborated with Dr. Wilhelm Frick, the minister of interior, over the dismissal of all his Jewish colleagues at the Kaiser Wilhelm Institute in Berlin. Frick was later executed by the Allies for war crimes, and in 1948 Eitel was judged by G2 in Germany to be "a security threat." But in America, where Eitel was in the midst of developing materials judged by the navy to be of "strategic" importance, the real threat to security was the possibility of Eitel being returned to Europe. For the moment, however, even JIOA could not persuade G2 in Frankfurt to rewrite his past.

The case of Kurt Debus, a close associate of von Braun's, seemed equally intractable. In March 1947 General Lucius Clay's office had made a routine statement that, his record to the contrary, Debus was "not an ardent Nazi." Just weeks later, his 1942 denunciation to the Gestapo of one of his colleagues as an anti-Nazi came to light. After investigation, Clay's office changed its classification to "ardent Nazi" and "potential security risk." Despite the precedents established by the rehabilitation of Axster, Strughold, and Patin, JIOA could not obtain an immediate revision. Attempts were therefore made by American officers to provide an excuse for Debus's action. Their justification for his behavior shows how, just two years after the war, the military had wholeheartedly adapted for its own ends the Nazis' tortured excuses. "Debus had not," his new security report stated, "deliberately denounced him [i.e., his colleague], but had been compelled to report their conversation to the Gestapo under his oath as an SS man."

However, most of the cases were comparatively straightforward, and by February 1948 four hundred seventy-five scientists awaited approval for visas. In December, the first six scientists, all unincriminated, had been selected as a dry run to test the new agreement and establish a solid legal precedent.[13] Progress was now expected to be swift, but once again nothing happened. All three military secretaries remonstrated with General George Marshall, the secretary of state. Two years after the first approval of Paperclip, they complained, "not a single visa has been granted, and no apparent progress in this matter has been made."[14] Wev was convinced that the State Department's visa section was ignoring the secret agreement reached in October.

Once again Wev, his fury barely constrained within the parameters of an official letter, wrote to the "culprit," this time Hamilton Robinson in the visa section, demanding that he withdraw the unfulfillable list of documents and investigations that, despite the October agreement, Robinson insisted had to be supplied for each scientist. Progress, he complained, had been slowed to "a snail's pace," and moreover, the ban on Nazis should be dropped in the national interest. It was a confused letter. Indeed, Wev was unable to conceal the fact that, although he was ostensibly protesting about the "extremely tedious and laborious task which has been most time-consuming," his letter was in effect a barely disguised demand that even convicted Nazis like Schieber should be granted visas.[15] It was also cynical — for while Wev and JIOA were extolling the trustworthiness of the Germans, the intelligence division, fearing espionage, was ordering Fort Bliss to exercise tighter security and censorship controls over the mail, movements, and relationships of von Braun's team.[16]

Robinson realized that the pressure on the visa section was no longer confined to the secret outbursts of government officials.

Critics in the Senate had begun to attack both himself and Sam Klaus for creating "confusion, agitation and turmoil" and were openly questioning where their loyalties lay. It was a foreshadowing of McCarthyism and would lead to the investigation of Klaus as a Communist sympathizer. Robinson felt, however, that both legally and morally he was safe. The visa section had, as required, sent a new circular, under Marshall's name, to consuls that explicitly switched the criterion for granting admission from a past free of Nazi activities to an assurance that, in the future, a scientist was unlikely to "engage in activities prejudicial to the public interest."[17] The State Department's veto had been effectively neutralized — but, in the process, Robinson found a new ally.

As ordered, the six "clean" files were forwarded to William Underhill at the FBI. But unfortunately for Wev, Underhill shared Robinson's prejudice that Nazi party membership was a bar to American citizenship and a threat to internal security. Accordingly, Underhill insisted on meticulously checking FBI files on each scientist. Replying to Wev, Robinson gleefully placed the blame for the new delays on the Department of Justice and flippantly assured Wev that "this Department has taken a special interest in the cases of the German scientists in a spirit of helpfulness to the appropriate authorities, and will continue to do so."[18]

Infuriated, Wev politely probed Underhill's motives to discover why his department's earlier support had suddenly altered, only to be brusquely rebuffed: "Send the Generals and Admirals to me," Underhill retorted, "I'm not afraid to tell them about it." Wev confided to Chamberlin, the chief of Military Intelligence, that he was genuinely baffled: "It is difficult to understand why, in the face of the threat of communism to the security of the United States, such a concentration and delaying investigation must be instigated." Although seventy cases had been submitted to the Department of Justice, only one application, that of Heinz Schmitt, a Junkers jet-propulsion expert at Wright Field, had been cleared. Neither Wev nor Chamberlin appreciated that the civilian officials were not only nervous of current criticism, but they also feared the adverse judgment of future generations.

Two weeks later, on May 11, 1948, Chamberlin met J. Edgar Hoover, the autocratic director of the FBI. Hoover's solution was simple: "Cut out all the red-tape," he barked to one of his aides. Before the meeting Wev had provided Chamberlin with a persuasive brief in order to convince the FBI director of the importance of supporting the operation. Each argument suggested that the Germans had rescued American science from the Dark Ages: $500 million had been saved on guided-missile development alone. Now the military feared that if the Germans were not quickly granted visas, both their morale and their work would suffer. Hoover readily sympathized. Chamberlin moved on. There was, he said, another problem. Investigations had shown that a few of the Germans were more than nominal Nazis. No doubt they had done some unpleasant things, but that was war. Since their arrival, they had eagerly adopted the American way of life, and many of them were keen churchgoers. The choice, said the director of intelligence, was stark. Either we forget what happened during the war, or we allow the Germans to return to Europe. The second option had drawbacks. German scientists recently returning from Britain had been quickly contracted by the Russians, a generous and, from the U.S. point of view, damaging gift to Moscow. The same would happen if the Paperclip scientists were sent back. Hoover was impressed. Although he was not eager to admit ardent Nazis into America, his agency's prime targets were Communists, not Nazis. The Paperclip scientists were, in fact, not the only Nazis whom Hoover would illegally allow into America. A large group of Byelorussian Fascists, guilty of the murder of tens of thousands of Jews for the Nazis, had been recruited by the State Department in Europe as anti-Communist agents and after 1948 were admitted as immigrants with Hoover's connivance. At the end of the meeting, Hoover promised that Underhill's obstruction would be erased.[19]

The military now awaited approval of the revised security reports. The visas could be issued without further problems, and Wev's tenacity had been rewarded. Four weeks later, on June 24, 1948, his deep suspicions about Soviet intentions toward America were confirmed. All road and rail connections to Berlin were cut by Russian soldiers. The cold war had broken out.

So far, five hundred scientists and 644 dependents had arrived in America. Despite the scientists' contribution, the army wanted to stop recruitment. Too much political effort was being expended, the rewards seemed uncertain, and it was impossible to quantify the benefits accurately. A Pentagon proposal to "emphasize to the American public that Project Paperclip is proving its worth" floundered because the Pentagon could not produce precise figures for "the actual value of the knowledge contributed by the Germans . . . although authorities place it at hundreds of millions of dollars." Nevertheless, the Pentagon claimed that "the program promises to save two to ten years in American research, since the Germans' experience has shown many blind alleys to be avoided, and narrowed down the fields to be explored."[20] Even if the air force and navy believed that the benefits were considerable, the Pentagon disliked the high administrative costs and feared the harmful publicity that would inevitably ensue if the conspiracy was exposed.

"We are on the ragged edge of cancellation," wrote Major General C. P. Cabell, the director of Air Force Intelligence, to Harry Armstrong at the School of Aviation Medicine, at Randolph Air Force Base, Texas, urging him to moderate his demands for more Germans.[21] Armstrong had requested the recruitment of fourteen more aviation doctors in addition to another thirty-nine already contracted by the air force under the escape clause. Armstrong did not oblige. He, like every other senior commander, was eager to recruit as many technicians as possible. If suitable Americans were not available, then the Germans had proven ideal substitutes. The arms race was no longer a novelty; it was vital for military supremacy. Digesting the development of wartime inventions by the air force and navy was still incomplete or had spawned a pace of obsolescence that was only gradually being understood. For the victors of 1945, the euphoria that followed victory had now all but disappeared, to be replaced by a gnawing uncertainty. Somehow, the other powers, even those without America's overwhelming wealth, seemed to be at least keeping pace with America's military development. Reliable intelligence reports confirmed that Russia's air force and navy were being dramatically modernized. Senior German chemical and biological warfare experts were said to be working outside Moscow,[22] and Russian rocket development was feared to be superior to America's.[23] Indeed, the air force and navy believed there was a case for more Germans, not fewer.

The new demands on America's armory were enormous. Submarine warfare, which until 1945 had been a British sphere of supremacy, was now being actively developed in the United States. Yet it was only in 1948, three years after the Russians, that American naval designers began to master the advanced engineering and technology of German wartime design. German experts had developed the quietest submarines, and only German pathologists and physiologists had probed the problems of escape, emotional reaction under stress, and the behavior of gases underwater, especially oxygen toxicity.[24] Accordingly, the navy asked JIOA to secretly recruit a complete German submarine team on immigrants' visas.

Other Germans were needed to operate the three new wind tunnels that had now finally been assembled. Unknown to the air force, which prided itself on its 16-foot wind tunnel, the German team recruited by the French from Oetztal were about to complete a 26-foot tunnel at Modane and had already started to construct two other supersonic wind tunnels. The U.S. Air Force's backlog of tests, it was claimed, would take 7.9 years to clear and by then would have increased to 19.9 years. No American had either the necessary training or experience. Theodore Zobel, an aerodynamicist based at Wright Field, nominated five instrumentation experts in Germany. The air force asked for them to be recruited in the "national interest" so as to "deny" them to other powers.

At Wright, Putt's staff was conscious that the new jet fighters, flying at over 600 miles per hour at 50,000 feet, needed new weapons and also new tactics in order to place the guns in a lethal firing position. "Aviation armament in this country is seriously inadequate," asserted the air force in its bid to acquire "creative aviation armament designers" of a caliber that did not exist in America.[25] The only remedy, they concluded, was to recruit Dr. Richard Braun and his six-man team, who had developed a whole range of new weapons during the war at Rheinmetall-Borsig and were known to have recently returned to Germany from Britain. Arranging their entry into America was no longer a problem.

By 1948, rewriting security reports — especially those that encompassed German denazification tribunal decisions, which were crudely distorted — had become a routine skill. Friedrich Wazelt, a committed member of the SS described as "deceitful and sly," was granted his visa because, as JIOA reported, a denazification tribunal had classified him as a nonactive party member on the basis of favorable testimonials. Reliance on tribunal findings had been condemned by senior military government officers in Germany because of the lucrative trade in fraudulent testimonies — wittily nicknamed *Persilschein* (*Persil* being the name of a detergent and *Schein* meaning license), since the bogus certificates could wash off even the brownest stains. But Wazelt was admitted on the grounds that his group's expertise in enhancing the stability of heavy bombers "exceeds that of any group in this country."[26] Wazelt was set in motion on the immigrants' itinerary — which nearly two thousand Germans would follow with military precision and without deviation — and, after arrival in America, was employed at Wright Field.

Accompanied by a military officer dressed in civilian clothes, the scientists and their families traveled in unmarked vehicles to the American consulates in Ciudad Juarez or Tijuana, in Mexico, or Niagara Falls in Canada. Each German arrived with a medical report certifying that he did not have tuberculosis or syphilis, three portrait photographs, and eighteen dollars. His travel document was then stamped with an immigrant's visa. After signing the necessary forms, each German walked back to the border and reentered America legally, no longer under arrest. By September 1948 seven scientists had been processed in Canada, and by March 1949 more than one hundred had visas, including most of the rocket team. Both Debus and Axster had to wait. A personal recommendation for Axster's visa was sent to Marshall, signed by Royall. "Although the reputation of his family in Germany was unfavorable," wrote Royall, "surveillance in the US for a period of more than three years has indicated that he has a wholehearted and sincere appreciation of American ideals. His value to this country, because of his technical qualifications and knowledge of present and future plans, outweighs the considerations of his family's past behavior." Fearful of political uproar, the War Department decided to wait. Although the intense pressure for visas had now abated, the importance of Project Paperclip was undiminished. On the contrary, reflecting the tension in Europe, recruitment for Paperclip was becoming more aggressive and more covert.

By the time Wev left JIOA in July 1949, individual scientists in Germany were being systematically monitored and their importance assessed. Those of value had been secretly registered on an objectives list by the Anglo-American Combined Allocations Board. British intelligence, in particular, not only monitored their movements but scrutinized all applications for foreign travel and often rejected requests for passports. A watch list was compiled of those employed in the eastern zone, noting the names of those who might be attracted by a western offer. Seeking any route to deny their services to the Russians, the British offered the Germans attractive terms of employment in Commonwealth countries. Even Otto Ambros, Heinrich Butefisch, Karl Krauch, and Georg von Schnitzler — the major I. G. Farben scientists convicted as war criminals at Nuremberg and still imprisoned in Landsberg — were placed on the restricted-movements list. Clearly, someone was contemplating employing them after their release. Other incriminated Nazis who had not been jailed were among the 150 leading scientists "employed" on the "consultants program" managed by Carl Nordstrom, the chief scientific adviser to the new high commissioner in Germany, Clay's successor John McCloy. The salary was nearly two thousand marks per month for doing absolutely nothing, apart from staying in the western zone. "They were not asked to do much," admitted Nordstrom, "but made to feel that they are wanted — to tickle their egos."

Financing unemployment was only one aspect of the strategy to control German expertise. By 1949 the Anglo-American blockade to prevent scientists from leaving Germany had collapsed and a lucrative smuggling trade was flourishing, attracting those who were unemployed because of the manpower and economic restrictions. For the majority of German scientists not offered contracts by the Allies, South America was an attractive alternative. The State Department's strategy to check the flow of German scientists seeking sanctuary in Argentina had been thwarted with impunity by well-organized syndicates. Applicants had a choice of routes. "Inter-service," an Argentine "tourist" agency in Frankfurt, directed approved Germans to the Zurich airport, where they embarked on Swiss, Swedish, or Dutch airlines.

The alternative route was through Denmark. After the war, Lieutenant Colonel Guenther Toepfke, formerly a senior aide to the German commander in chief of the occupying forces, had remained in Denmark as liaison officer between the Allies and the surrendered Wehrmacht group, and also to supervise the removal of two million German land mines. For both tasks, Toepfke was entrusted with a pass for crossing the frontier. Exploiting the privilege, he escorted, by some estimates, more than one hundred German armament scientists to the Copenhagen airport before he was caught. By 1949 other routes were firmly established through Sweden and Italy. Robert Murphy, the political adviser in Germany, cabled the State Department saying he needed policy guidance, since the "deliberate large-scale official Argentine enticement of German military and civil technicians of every degree of ability and of Nazi affiliations . . . had become virtually an open scandal."[27] Every Argentine consulate in Europe had become a recruiting office. The State Department considered protesting but was persuaded by the U.S. Embassy in Buenos Aires that a protest would be futile. Anticipating that the State Department would attempt to stop the emigration, JIOA quickly inaugurated a counterpolicy, the Point Four Program, which encouraged Germans to leave Europe for South America, using Switzerland as a staging post.

In Argentina, Kurt Tank, the aircraft designer rejected by the British, had established an aircraft factory with the help of Hans Ulrich Rudel, the Luftwaffe ace who would become an important link between fugitive Nazi war criminals and their distant homeland. Other German scientists had founded Argentina's infant nuclear industry, biological warfare laboratories, and small-arms factories. Murphy's colleagues at the State Department realized that to dissuade Argentina from the very policies the Allies were pursuing would require a feat of political gymnastics. On British advice, Washington reversed its policy and began encouraging immigration to South America, and also to the Commonwealth countries, as an effective means of denying scientific expertise to the Communists.

Even scientists exploited in Britain whose competence was doubtful had to be diverted from Germany to America in the interests of denial. Among those whose arrival from Britain was not announced were the chemical and biological warfare experts Erich Traub, Theodor Raetz, Max Gruber, and Friedrich Wilhelm Hoffmann. Their names had been deliberately excluded from "any allocation list to date," and they would remain similarly anonymous in America. One of the announced arrivals was Helmuth Walter, the submarine and torpedo developer. By 1949 the Americans no longer regarded him as a great scientist but rather as an enterprising promoter whose energy and business acumen had created a huge albeit profligate organization. Although the U.S. Navy had long since abandoned peroxide as a submarine fuel in favor of nuclear power (a development that was concealed from the British), Walter was judged to be of "denial importance" and was employed by Westinghouse. Among the more reluctant arrivals was Theodor Rakula, a turbine expert who had been allowed to accept a Swiss contract by the British but was at the last moment secretly "persuaded" by American agents to accept a Paperclip contract with the U.S. Navy. It seemed as if the Dustbin internment camp had been reopened in America.

The growth of military expenditure during the Berlin blockade automatically stimulated demands for increased weapons development and for more German experts, especially those who could develop and test missile controls and propulsion.[28] Accordingly, the intelligence agencies, rapidly infected by the looming war psychology, began studying a series of new plans to move the cream of Germany's scientists to America, if need be by force. The first of these, the Esso Plan, conceived in Washington in 1949, provided for the forcible evacuation of 1,500 scientists, and a parallel plan, "Project Echo," was devised by Colonel Oscar Koch, the director of American Military Intelligence in Austria.[29] In Eastern Europe, a Cominform operation directed by General Popov had been recruiting western scientists and employing others for specific projects to be completed in the West. As a counterattack, Koch proposed recruiting scientists in Eastern Europe and creating a scientists' haven in Austria. Among those he was planning to smuggle out was a team developing incandescent engine plugs in Czechoslovakia, though others were more important. Koch was later appalled to discover that the telegrams relaying offers to the scientists in Austria were routed via Prague or Budapest, where they were read by Soviet censors before being transmitted onward.[30]

Both Esso and Echo were seriously considered by American intelligence officers whose power and influence over the fate of European scientists was truly remarkable. For those scientists in America whose military work was complete but whose denial value was still important, JIOA indiscreetly sought employment in industry or in laboratories and universities. Every potential employer was inundated with lists and dossiers, similar to small advertisements, describing each scientist who wanted a job as "preeminent in his field." Most were placed without difficulty, but for some the reaction was discouraging. Unreasonably, in the army's opinion, although American industrialists and university teachers regarded the Germans as being well qualified, they found many of them "excessively Prussian" — too authoritarian, too demanding, and rigidly unadaptable. But eventually, discreet appeals to their patriotism and the attraction of future government contracts persuaded reluctant employers to reconsider their rejections.

Leonard Alberts, a former I. G. Farben steel and synthetic fuel expert who had arrived in America in 1946, had been transferred in September 1947 to the Bechtel Corporation, although the army knew he was a fervent Nazi. Five months later, when his former SS membership was exposed, both Bechtel and the FBI declared

Alberts to be an undesirable alien and a security risk. Even the attorney general insisted that he be denied citizenship and returned to Europe. But instead, Alberts was transferred to Blaw Knox in Pittsburgh. In November 1948, Alberts's visa application was rejected by the FBI on the grounds that his "arrogant personality" made him "undesirable for citizenship and a poor security risk."[31] The army disagreed: In the midst of the Berlin blockade, his skills were too valuable to lose. Two months later, it was claimed that Alberts had been the victim of "a misunderstanding . . . and misinterpretation." Although the Department of Justice was not to be so easily fobbed off and insisted that he was "pro-Nazi in his outlook and unscrupulous in his activities," Blaw Knox executives declared themselves to be "proud" of the association. At the outbreak of the Korean War the firm dispatched Alberts, accompanied by one of its executives, on a research visit to Germany. Two years later, Alberts crossed Niagara Falls with an immigrant's visa; apparently no one any longer regarded a German's wartime record as an embarrassment.

But for those scientists who were no longer required by the military on the grounds that they were unproductive or irksome, the future was punitive. Despite earlier assurances, their Nazi background, no matter how insignificant, was not concealed by the saving formula in the "revised security report." As State Department officials had feared all along, the Pentagon exercised discretion according to its own brand of expediency. Arthur Tiller, a ship designer who arrived with the first batch in 1945, found it difficult to settle in America and was deported, after a bitter struggle, in 1955. Johann Frank, an insignificant noncommissioned officer in the SA for eleven years, was also returned, because "his undesirable characteristics outweigh his value to national security."[32]

For JIOA, the outbreak of the Korean War on June 25, 1950, retrospectively justified the conspiracy and the deceit. With new vigor Paperclip, whose operations had been running down, burst into action. The Communist invasion was not only the first set war between the two new superpowers but also between the Osvakim and Paperclip Germans. In America, the Germans were drawn into the fight against Communism. Both the Esso and the Echo plans became serious proposals. In the air, on the ground, and at sea, weapons developed by teams in Germany since the 1930s were pitted against each other; the combatants' planes, tanks, guns, and shells had all benefited from the expertise plundered over the previous five years. Strangely, only rockets were absent from both sides' arsenals.

The Russian forces could have been armed with the Taifun antiaircraft rocket, the precursor of the devastating Sam missile. Taifun had been developed by two hundred German designers recruited from Nordhausen, but the Soviets failed to realize their opportunity. Both American and British trials of the Taifun had been relatively unsuccessful. In 1945 German experts had criticized the Taifun as ambitiously large and as too uneconomic to be practical during a war. Yet the idea was masterful, and while the Americans later developed a similar rocket, the Loki, and the British the Highflier, neither in 1950 could equal the Taifun's mass fire power, high speed, and simple, low-cost adaptability. Realizing that the development of rockets for future conflicts was essential, the Pentagon turned for assistance to the remaining German experts.

Amid the unrelieved tension that followed shattering South Korean defeats, many in Washington instinctively looked to the Germans for help. The new American high commissioner in Bonn, John McCloy, began discussions with the new chancellor, Konrad Adenauer, about the possibility of rebuilding the German army — a proposal bitterly opposed both in London and Paris. Among Adenauer's conditions was his demand that America commute the death sentences and release many of the notorious mass murderers and war criminals held in Landsberg Prison. McCloy hesitated until February 1951, but in the meantime those who had something important to offer the American war effort, including such industrialists as Alfried Krupp and Friedrich Flick and the directors of I. G. Farben, were given privileged facilities and were allowed to mobilize their industries from jail. For those who had so recently been condemned as war criminals, the flagrant seduction was farcical. As Fritz Ter Meer, a convicted director of I. G. Farben, commented, "Now they have Korea on their hands, the Americans are a lot more friendly."[33]

Indeed, fear of defeat provoked a new mood at the Pentagon. Only the Germans, it was felt, could relieve the chronic deficiency of scientists still crippling defense projects. On July 14, 1950, the commander at Wright Field sent Putt an urgent cable:

Due to the threat of impending hostilities in Europe and the possibility that forces of the USSR may rapidly overrun the continent, this command is concerned with the problem of immediate implementation of an evacuation program for German and Austrian scientists whose fields of activity, knowledge and ability are such that, should they fall into enemy hands, they would constitute a threat to our national security. Request that a meeting be called in Washington soonest to implement all plans for immediate evacuation of those scientists.[34]

Days later, the air force recommended that the Joint Intelligence Staff investigate the immediate revitalization of Paperclip, since Russia could start a general war at any time.

On November 22 "Project 63" was approved by the Joint Chiefs, with an initial budget of $1 million.[35] Described as "an accelerated Paperclip program," it authorized the European commander to evacuate 150 scientists on the "K-critical list" together with their families, as quickly as possible in the event of a Russian invasion of Western Europe.[36] Denial was now so important that the most ardent Nazis were welcome, even if there was no prospect of employment; it also meant that the most incriminated Nazis already in America could not now be returned to Europe. A new generation of JIOA officers under Colonel Daniel Ellis scanned the old Paperclip lists and sent recruiting missions to Europe, expecting to be greeted with the same enthusiasm that they encountered five years earlier. Ostensibly, experts in ballistics, bomb fuses, electronics, missiles, and every aspect of naval design were all badly needed. But by the end of the year, although the "denial and evacuation list" boasted sixty-two names, not one scientist on the K-list had signed a contract. Two American officers, neither of whom were scientists and therefore not competent to describe the scope of the proposed work to the Germans, visited the K-listed scientists. To the Germans' surprise, the Americans pleaded that they were not allowed to divulge why the offer was only for an insecure six-month contract, nor why they were to be paid even if there would be no work.[37] The attraction of America for the Germans — which was already tarnished by reports from returning Paperclip scientists that the German scientists in America lived like prisoners, needing special permission to travel and receiving the rations equivalent to those of a unskilled Ford car worker — received another setback when Congress passed the Internal Security Act. The new legislation, quickly approved amid a panic to protect America from Communist agents, forbade entry into America to any alien who had ever been a member of a "totalitarian party." Since no one in the military had wanted to publicly admit that former Nazis were entering America, the provision had passed through Congress without amendment. The immediate effect of the legislation horrified the military. Paperclip scientists arriving at New York Harbor were arrested, and immigration officers refused to permit their release. The reports from America about the scientists' plight arrived in Germany at the same time that other German scientists returned to Berlin from Russia. Inevitably, they had been carefully selected to present favorable accounts about their treatment, dispelling doubts about the future threat of kidnapping by the Russians. Since West Germany was destined to become a sovereign state and currency reform had unleashed an economic boom, few German scientists could find a reason to sacrifice their pensions, homes, and status for a suspicious short-term Project 63 contract.

Ellis seemed serenely unconcerned about his apparent failures: "There is no indication that they could contribute anything to the Russians now that would be a detriment to us."[38] But for other military departments, Project 63 was more than an extension of Paperclip. Ellis, it was felt, harbored an unhelpful attitude. Without proper supervision, Project 63 could be exploited as an unobstructed conduit by Germans who might otherwise be judged undesirable. Both the Chemical Corps and the School of Aviation Medicine hoped to recruit experts whose criminal activities had formerly excluded them from Paperclip. Conveniently, their wartime records could not be checked at the Berlin Document Center because, in the expectation of war, the irreplaceable Nazi files had been evacuated to Kansas City. Instead, the army now had to rely on polygraphs in order to discover the scientists' activities before 1945 and their postwar relationship with the Communists. Among those contracted were Kurt Blome and Marianus Czerny.

A former SA general, Blome was a biological warfare expert and had joined the party in 1931. Hired by the U.S. Chemical Corps in August 1951, at a salary of $6,800 per annum, he was certified by McCloy as "not likely to become [a] security threat to the US."[39] Blome sold his general medical practice in Germany and contentedly awaited shipment. In completing his JIOA application form, the U.S. Army had deliberately omitted details of his career between 1945 and 1948. Nowhere in his JIOA file does it reveal that in July 1945, while being interrogated by an American scientist, he admitted that Himmler had ordered him in 1943 to use concentration camp inmates for experiments on plague vaccine. Clearly eager to experiment, Blome suggested to Himmler that the SS finance a special isolation institute in Poznan for his work. Throughout the 1945 interrogation, he openly admitted his "intention" to conduct human experiments and was subsequently charged with crimes against humanity.

Prosecuted at Nuremberg together with the aviation doctors, Blome was acquitted because the prosecution failed to prove that his "intention" to experiment with inmates had actually been realized. Shortly after his release from Nuremberg Prison in 1951, Blome was interviewed about his work by Dr. H. W. Batchelor and three other American biological warfare experts from Camp Detrick, Maryland. By way of introduction, Batchelor explained to Blome through an interpreter that "we have friends in Germany, scientific friends, and this is an opportunity to enjoy meeting him to discuss our various problems." For the Americans it was an ideal opportunity to discuss the whole area of German biological warfare, including Blome's own discoveries, and elicit his help in finding other German biological warfare experts. Batchelor was clearly delighted with his cooperation, and as a reward, he was offered a Project 63 contract.

Marianus Czerny, another Project 63 scientist, was an expert spectroscopist. He had already been employed as a Paperclip scientist in California but had been returned to Germany because of sensitivity over his high-level Nazi contacts and his Gestapo activities. In the midst of the Korean War, the Pentagon assumed it possessed unquestioned power to mastermind and manipulate the location, employment, and destiny of scientists such as Blome and Czerny, as if they were strategic pawns in a military operation.

One of the first to arrive at Randolph Air Force Base was Dr. Walter Schreiber, described as a hygiene expert. During the war, Schreiber was the head of the Department for Science and Health in the German High Command, with special responsibility for combating infectious diseases and epidemics. Under his authority, "doctors" in concentration camps conducted experiments on inmates that usually resulted in a slow and agonizing death. Some of those convicted and sentenced to death in postwar trials in Germany for their part in those experiments claimed that Schreiber had witnessed their activities. Schreiber successfully denied the allegations, and American lawyers were unable to prove that the results of the experiments had been passed to Schreiber — who rapidly translated them into the sanitized and authoritative reports that so impressed first the Russians and then the Americans. In October 1948 Schreiber arrived in the American zone after appearing as a prosecution witness for the Russians at the international Nuremberg war-crimes trial against his former colleagues and mysteriously claimed he had escaped from his captors. Subsequently, in 1950, he was appointed camp physician at the U.S. military subpost at Oberursel and then was evacuated to Texas as a denial case with his family in September 1951. Soon after his arrival in Texas, protests began, especially from Jewish groups.

As the protests escalated, Robert Lovett, the secretary of defense, ordered an immediate investigation into Project 63, revealing that the army had never received high-level authorization for the operation. Alarmed by the glare of publicity, the army immediately canceled Blome's and Czerny's contracts. But to avoid endangering other Project 63 contracts or annoying Blome, the former SA officer was given Schreiber's post as camp doctor at the army's European Command Intelligence Center in Oberursel. In Washington, after intensive discussion, Lovett publicly pledged that Schreiber would be returned to Germany for investigation. To the military, Lovett's assurance was astonishing. If Schreiber was returned to Germany, the fate of many other incriminated scientists in America would be perilously uncertain, and Schreiber himself would undoubtedly be tempted to expose Project 63 as well as the presence of the aviation doctors at Randolph.

At first, Colonel Benjamin Heckmeyer, JIOA's new director, trotted out the customary neutral response, which ignored everything except the most recent past: "Although it has been alleged that Dr. Schreiber was implicated in human experiments during the war, these allegations are not supported by available records. Dr. Schreiber's conduct has been exemplary in all respects and the School of Aviation Medicine reports that he has consistently shown a highly co-operative attitude, intense industry and application to his assigned duties." Cryptically, Heckmeyer suggested that Schreiber had "indicated a desire to go to Argentina, where his daughter now resides, and carry on his research in his chosen field."[40] Schreiber's sudden preference for Argentina was the ideal solution. South America was by then a well-established haven for

Nazi war criminals, many of them traveling from Europe at Washington's expense. Lovett's pledge to return Schreiber to Germany was conveniently forgotten.

Air force headquarters in Washington immediately asked the air attaché in Buenos Aires to arrange Schreiber's immigration, "as his return to Germany is not desirable from our viewpoint." To sweeten Schreiber's agreement to leave America quietly, his contract was amended to allow the air force to pay for his passage, which had already been booked for May 22, and he was given a generous travel allowance. Amid fears of a congressional inquiry, a complete publicity blackout was ordered, and officers in Bonn and Argentina were asked to lobby government contacts to provide the passports and visas needed to ensure the speedy evaporation of an embarrassment. "Schreiber's immediate departure U.S. extremely urgent," Washington cabled General Lewis in Wiesbaden on May 6, 1952. "For your info, if entry into Argentina cannot be effected in immediate future, strong possibility exists subject may be returned to Germany regardless of objections above agencies. EUCOM [the European army headquarters] and CIA being advised this possibility."

Three months after Schreiber's safe arrival at his daughter's home in Argentina, the American Jewish Congress passed a resolution condemning the employment of former Nazis and calling for their return to Germany, the war criminals among them to stand trial. Lovett asked for a historical brief on Paperclip. The military, somewhat tainted by the debacle in Korea, chose its words carefully. The first draft began with the assertion that their programs did not "violate the existing laws or policies of the US from a legal or moral standpoint" and stressed that no one known to have been guilty of war crimes was admitted to the United States:

> Doctor Walter Schreiber, mentioned in the resolution, was completely investigated by the CIC and the CIA prior to his arrival in the US, without any indication of conviction for, or participation in, the inhuman Nazi medical experiments, nor of membership of the Nazi party. These allegations were first made without foundation by a Dr. Alexander of Boston, Mass., who is closely allied with the American Jewish Congress.

The completed memorandum submitted to Lovett, and signed by Major General Clark Ruffner, was a disingenuous cocktail of evasions and ambiguities. As ever, the use of criminals was flatly denied, while the protestors were condemned as victims of Communist infiltration. Schreiber, Lovett was informed, was only "alleged" to be employed by the German air force and "was neither accused nor tried for war crimes." Since he was now in South America, Ruffner proposed that the issue be forgotten and presented a draft reply to the AJC that unashamedly repeated Royall's riposte to a similar protest in 1947: "No known war criminal, ardent Nazi, or profiteer or notorious supporter of Nazism or militarism is eligible under the project."[41]

12

The Final Irony

ON THE DAY CHOSEN for the mass swearing-in of German scientists as citizens of the United States, few realized that the crown-
ing glory of the Paperclip conspiracy had coincided with the
anniversary of the kaiser's ignominious surrender in 1918. In a
bizarre public ceremony, rich in irony, on November 11, 1954,
about one hundred Peenemünde scientists were crowded, amid
jocular confusion, onto a floodlit stage in Birmingham, Alabama.
As the heavily accented voices discordantly swore allegiance to the
American flag, even fewer realized that Sam Klaus, now fighting
on another front, was suffering his second humiliating defeat. The
victors this time were not a handful of officers in the Pentagon but
a battery of European industrialists and bankers who had tena-
ciously clung to the spoils of war earned during the heyday of Nazi
Germany.

Klaus, the supreme investigator, had originally become preoccupied with Paperclip because it violated the Safehaven Program — an operation he had created in 1943 to eliminate the financial
and commercial power of German banks and corporations in the
neutral countries of Europe and South America. There was an
unusual and confirmed certainty about his targets. In anticipation
of war, all the major German corporations had masked the ownership of their subsidiaries outside Germany, using a variety of
ingenious disguises to avoid seizure. To explode their legal cam-
ouflage and to prevent German industry and the German military
from repeating their brilliant post-1918 plot to maintain secret
research and development centers in friendly countries, at the end
of the war Klaus had corralled compliant South American governments into agreeing to the repatriation of all Germans in the

Southern Hemisphere. Originally, Klaus had described the policy to America's allies as a means of preventing the "resurgence of enemy activity at its inception."[1] But with the enthusiastic support of Treasury and Justice officials, Safehaven was soon transformed into a dogged hunt for Germany's vast wartime loot stashed away in the banks and vaults of Europe. Estimates of the hoard's value were upward of $1 billion at 1939 prices, and some responsible officials put Germany's total foreign assets at three times that amount. Safehaven, in their eyes, was synonymous with a crusade for justice. Their targets were the neutral countries — Portugal, Spain, Sweden, and especially Switzerland — who, in enviable contrast to the misery, despair, and destruction surrounding them in Occupied Europe, had enjoyed security, peace, and considerable profit at their neighbors' expense, while others were suffering the privations of war.

Throughout the war, Anglo-American policy toward the neutrals had been frustratingly ambivalent and difficult to reconcile. The British regretfully recognized the limitations of their own power to enforce a blockade and, within those constraints, did their best by means of diplomacy to lure the neutrals away from close relations with the Axis countries. The Foreign Office believed there was no alternative but to accept that the neutrals would continue trading with Germany and to try to extract some advantage from the situation. Officials at the Board of Economic Warfare in Washington were outraged by Britain's tolerant attitude and disdainful of her failure to destroy Germany and the neutrals by economic sanctions. Impatient and unwilling to be soothed by British explanations, the board's representatives in London demanded tough measures against Hitler's silent supporters.

Franco's Spain should have been Hitler's natural ally — but, preoccupied with ensuring his own survival, the new dictator had refused to openly declare any allegiance. Similarly, Portugal's dictator, Antonio Salazar, sympathized with Hitler but resisted exposing his impoverished country to the ravages of war. Both countries provided a welcome and welcoming haven for Nazi agents while tolerating an Allied presence. Historically, Sweden and Switzerland had remained politically and militarily neutral during all of Europe's fratricidal conflicts since the age of Napoleon. Emotionally and economically, however, despite the horrors committed in Occupied Europe, both sympathized with the Teutonic cause. Undoubtedly Switzerland, with her wealth, industries, and strategic location, was the most important "neutral" throughout the war, especially since 100,000 Germans were permanent residents. Moreover, the Swiss railway network was the hub of Central European trade, while Swiss banks had traditionally prospered by affording foreigners a discreet "Safehaven" for their fortunes.

The official British and American policy was to prevent all imports from reaching Switzerland except food and fodder. But unofficially, Washington and London recognized in exasperation that Switzerland's intimate peacetime links with Germany had hugely expanded since the outbreak of war. Blinded by their pro-German bias, many Swiss were convinced right up to 1945 that Germany would be victorious. Despite Allied protests, throughout the war Bern placed the Swiss railways and Alpine tunnels at Germany's disposal, to serve as a strategic link with the Wehrmacht armies in Italy. Every major German industry had either tentacles penetrating deep inside Swiss society or business associates across the border. Swiss executives naturally maintained close ties with their German parent companies, and Switzerland's exports to Germany of ammunition, aircraft parts, radio equipment, fuses, diesel engines, and chemicals ceaselessly grew. "These activities," Henry Stimson, the American secretary of war, was told, "were of substantial assistance to the Germans in waging war."[2]

Simultaneously, Swiss bankers, courteously and occasionally even enviously, provided an efficient and flexible service for their powerful German clients, often reaping huge profits in the process. Intercepts by Allied intelligence of messages between Switzerland and Germany proved to Washington's satisfaction that "Switzerland's aid to the enemy in the banking field was clearly beyond the obligations under which a neutral must continue trade with a belligerent."[3] In return, Germany supplied coal and steel — imports that were vital to Switzerland's survival — and thus provided the Swiss with an excuse for supping with the devil. The Allies, in their darkest hours, were impotent and had no alternative but to turn a blind eye. For the Allies to justify their inability to enforce their blockade, they had to deem Switzerland's infractions of her neutrality acceptable, since the country was a good intelligence center, a useful refuge for escaped Allied POWs, and a source of valuable materials.[4] Allied propaganda, however, claimed that the blockade had successfully isolated Germany and was fatally squeezing the nation's industrial life. In fact, the opposite was true. German scientists and technicians had astonishingly produced —

in place of the blockaded metals — rubber, textile, and petroleum products, a range of synthetic substitutes that were superior to the natural equivalents. American experts, wrote David Gordon of the blockade division, "woefully underestimated the extent and significance of these preparations." These and similar revelations of German ingenuity transformed the anger of many Allied officers into awe, but such feelings did not inhibit those officials whose objective was to strip Germany of its plunder. Their hopes of success improved following the Wehrmacht's collapse at Stalingrad and the Allied victory in North Africa.

On January 5, 1943, the State Department issued a warning that it would not recognize the legality of any sale of German looted gold. This warning was provoked by the discovery that during the previous twelve months Germany's gold payments to Switzerland far exceeded her prewar reserves;[5] the extra gold came from the reserves of the banks in the countries occupied by German armies. By the end of the war, 1.6 billion Swiss francs of gold had passed from Germany to Switzerland, ten times Germany's total prewar reserves. In protest at her close relations with the Nazis, the Allies sharply restricted Switzerland's food supplies for three months in 1943 and demanded a 40 percent reduction of Swiss exports. After the Swiss had given assurances that they would comply, Allied intelligence chiefs prided themselves that their pressure had been successful;[6] but in fact, Swiss supplies to Germany actually doubled during that period.[7] As payment, Germany used the stolen gold, thus creating a precious lifeline for foreign trade.

Nearly all the looted gold passed through Switzerland, but by September 1944 Swiss banks were embarrassed by the amount in their vaults and began negotiating secret sales. Postwar investigations revealed that while $161 million of Dutch gold was sold to Switzerland, a mere $30 million had been passed on to Sweden and Portugal. Not one of these three neutrals could have been in doubt as to the gold's true ownership, since the bars were carelessly delivered in their original Dutch wrapping paper. The officials of the Reichsbank took more precautions when they wished to dispose of $123 million of stolen Belgian gold. Before delivery, the bars were resmelted, impressed with prewar German markings, and only afterward sold to the Swiss National Bank. Admiring the finesse of the procedure, the Swiss National Bank followed suit, resmelting the looted gold in its vaults and converting it into Swiss coins. But this nonchalance was abruptly curtailed by the Normandy invasion. In some frenzy, at clandestine meetings through-out Germany, bankers, industrialists, and even senior Nazi officials established sophisticated schemes for the transfer of money and technical know-how to secret safe havens for use after the inevi-table defeat. The foreign destinations were obvious, but the meth-ods and the camouflage used were brilliant and had been artfully devised to be legally impenetrable. In their haste, however, elab-orate and costly deceptions were occasionally abandoned. On June 26, 1944, Allied agents noted a German plane landing at Lisbon. Two couriers carrying four bags, labeled diplomatic baggage, were met by a car from the German embassy; each bag contained twenty kilos of gold. The event inaugurated a pattern that would be re-peated throughout Europe over the following weeks.[8] "This ten-dency of the Germans," noted a member of the Foreign Office, "to transfer nest eggs to their Legations in neutral countries needs watching. But I do not see what more we could do to prevent it."[9]

The source of Germany's loot was not only the national banks of its defeated adversaries. During the twelve years of the Third Reich, German bankers, industrialists, and entrepreneurs ran-sacked the continent of Europe and amassed vast amounts of val-uables: precious stones, objets d'art, shares, minerals, machinery, and patents. Among their victims were governments, corpora-tions, and private citizens. The gigantic institutions of the Reich robbed and pillaged on a vast scale. The proceeds of plunder swelled the assets of the mighty Deutsche Bank five-fold to $5.5 billion. The scale of theft by individuals was also gigantic. Craftily, how-ever, most of their loot was not deposited with the prestigious Zurich headquarters of the Swiss banks. Instead, it was entrusted to compliant branch managers in unknown Alpine villages and small towns far beyond the suspicions and penetration of any Allied investigator.

Kurt Becher, a colonel in the SS, was typical of many furtive German visitors to Switzerland in the last year of the war. Born in 1909 in Hamburg, Becher ended his wartime career as Adolf Eichmann's superior officer in Budapest. While Eichmann super-vised the rounding-up of Hungary's 200,000 Jews and their trans-portation to immediate death at Auschwitz, according to at least one published report and various government documents in Berlin, Becher took charge of the doomed Jews' valuables, worth many millions of dollars. The "legitimate" destination of the loot was Himmler's headquarters, and thence to the Reichsbank in Berlin.

En route Becher siphoned off several sacks of precious stones and headed to St. Margarethen, in Switzerland, where he deposited a considerable fortune for safekeeping. After the war Becher was released unprosecuted from an American internment camp, and he used his nest egg to establish one of Europe's largest grain dealerships, based in Hamburg and still flourishing today. Over the years it has earned many millions of dollars in profits. It was to prevent the lasting enrichment of former Nazis like Becher that Klaus sought the support of America's allies for the Safehaven Program. Only a united front, he realized, would compel the neutrals to hand over the German deposits.

The British were, on all counts, very reluctant partners. Washington's declaration about looted gold in 1943 was, in Whitehall's opinion, too difficult to implement, and Klaus's scheme to seize German assets in all the neutral countries was sniffily criticized as a legal minefield.[10] Disconcertingly, there can be little doubt that British hesitancy to strip the Germans of their ill-gotten wealth was associated with a strain of anti-Semitism within the Foreign Office that had been only too evident ever since the first reports of the Nazi persecution policies in the early 1930s. After a deputation from the Board of Deputies of British Jews left the Foreign Office in April 1944, having sought support for the recovery of stolen Jewish property, one official wrote: "We shall be under very strong pressure (particularly in the U.S.) to allow the Jews not only to stamp on the Germans' faces — after *we* [emphasis in original] have knocked them down — but to strip them naked as well."[11] At the same time Con O'Neil, an enigmatic junior official in the Central Department, voiced Britain's unwillingness to offend the defeated Germans by "seeking to re-establish the position of the Jews in Germany, which no German is likely to want."[12] In a draft directive addressed to Eisenhower to guide his postwar policy in Germany, Foreign Office officials decided that the Germans should not be compelled to compensate the Jews. At best the Jews might expect to recover a small part of their losses; for the rest, they should be content with their liberation. Washington took a considerably more robust view.

In August 1944 the master plan for world economic recovery was agreed to by the Allies at Bretton Woods, a spa in New Hampshire. Resolution VI of the final statement called on the neutral governments to freeze all German assets in their countries and to hand them over to the Allies, who would represent the new government of Germany. Within days of publication, Sam Klaus and his close friend Herbert Cummings, of the visa section, were dispatched by Cordell Hull, the secretary of state, to London and to the neutral capitals to explain the Allies' hunt.[13] Cummings recalls that on their flight from northern Scotland to Sweden, "Sam spoke the whole time with some Soviet officers, in fluent Russian. They were as impressed as I was." The duo returned, having achieved little other than an agreement with the Foreign Office to collect and share intelligence about Germany's assets.[14] Only the course of the war would shake the neutrals' stance of noncooperation and indifference.

The change occurred in January 1945, as Germany's desperate attack through the Ardennes was repulsed and the remnants of Hitler's last army on the western front retreated dejectedly toward the Rhine. Apart from innumerable German "diplomatic bags" being shipped from Spain to South America,[15] and mysterious submarines sailing toward the South Atlantic, the obvious loopholes were fast disappearing. Argentina suspended her business links with Germany; Sweden reduced her massive exports; and Switzerland allowed her trade agreement with Germany to lapse and for the first time enforced controls. Less obvious loopholes, however, rapidly emerged. The Stockholm patent office was flooded by a massive number of applications from all the major German corporations, and Swedish industry purchased expensive German machinery at knockdown prices in a series of covert deals to allow their German friends to amass untouchable funds. But in February, as Allied troops swarmed across the Rhine, the Swiss agreed to meet an American Safehaven delegation headed by Laughlin Currie, an enthusiastic supporter of Roosevelt's New Deal program. The agenda was to negotiate the recovery not only of Germany's loot but also Germany's legal assets and the estimated $500 million deposited by Jews who had since perished in the gas chambers — a total of $1.5 billion. Currie, with Klaus at his side, arrived in Bern in a belligerent mood. First, they insisted, the Swiss government should conduct a methodical census of Swiss banks and industry in order to identify German assets and then, regardless of Switzerland's secrecy laws, present the Americans with a full account. Second, all German assets should be frozen for eventual payment to the Allies as reparations for war damage.

To Currie and Klaus's surprise the Swiss negotiators, while on the surface charming and anxious to please, displayed granite stubbornness and chilling insensitivity — the very qualities that had preserved and augmented the country's vast fortunes. Private property rights, the Swiss negotiators steadfastly maintained, were inviolable, and Switzerland's secrecy laws sacrosanct. Unabashed, the Americans threatened to enforce another crippling food and fuel blockade. Poker-faced, the Swiss told Currie that Washington had considerably exaggerated the German assets; but, after further prevarication, they bowed to his demands and signed an agreement. The American mission left Bern convinced that a country as tiny as Switzerland could not resist the just and moral demands of the most powerful nation in the world.

Allied unity, as Klaus had realized at the outset, was the key to success, but on the eve of peace it seemed elusive. The Foreign Office, he discovered on arriving in London, had become openly skeptical about the feasibility of removing German influence from the Western Hemisphere. Klaus's policy, wrote one British official, "is grossly exaggerated and it might even be in our interests to have some irritants of this kind in the western hemisphere affecting American relations with Europe."[16] Ignoring British lack of enthusiasm, Klaus returned to Washington, as firm as ever in his resolve. After all, his government had frozen Switzerland's assets in America. The Swiss might call it blackmail, but he was certain it was justice. His anger would have been uncontrollable had he known that, just ten days after he had left Bern, the Swiss had arranged with Emil Puhl, the reptilian vice president of the Reichsbank, for the transfer of more stolen gold to the safety of Swiss banks. Ecstatically, Puhl wrote to Berlin that the agreement had evaded the American blockade and showed "how strong the cultural ties are that connect our two countries."[17] Yet Klaus's determination to wave the big stick appalled the British: "The difficulty is that the Americans are itching for a fight with the neutrals on this issue."[18] Negotiations to overcome British hesitation were entrusted to Seymour Rubin.

In London during July and August, Rubin sought support for a public announcement that the Allies planned to pressure the neutrals to unconditionally hand over German assets. The British were unimpressed by the Americans' evangelical mission, even to deprive gangsters of their loot. Foreign Office officials told Rubin that there were simply no legal grounds for claiming German assets in neutral countries, since even in peacetime one government could not compel another to hand over property. The British quoted with approval Swiss diplomats who complained that the Americans wanted greater power over Switzerland than even Hitler had wielded; indeed, during the war Switzerland had refused to allow the Nazi government access to private funds held on behalf of German and French citizens. The British sympathized with Switzerland's legalistic assertions and were afraid that Klaus and Rubin were intent on establishing an unfortunate precedent that other governments could use against Britain and America in the future. "The Americans have a habit," commented one British official, "of assuming the propriety and legality of something they do which, if done by anyone else, they would regard as highly illegal and unethical."[19] Moreover, Britain had more to gain by persuading the neutrals to supply food and raw materials on favorable terms. Under the weight of argument Rubin's resolution began to buckle. An acceptable compromise, he suggested, might be for the Allies to use the moral argument. The Allies had suffered terrible losses to destroy Nazism that had also benefited the neutrals; in fairness and in the interests of the future, the neutrals should now contribute something toward the Allies' rehabilitation. Although Rubin seemed to the British to favor "the mailed fist in one case and the velvet glove in another," his proposal was grudgingly accepted by British officials, who meekly confessed: "Our hands were really forced."[20] But to his surprise, having secured admittedly reluctant backing in London, Rubin discovered that opinions had hardened and his moral appeal had no support in Washington. Since Sweden, Spain, and Portugal had already accepted the Bretton Woods declaration, Swiss resistance, his colleagues believed, would soon begin to crumble.

In Rubin's absence, Puhl's gloating letter boasting about Swiss duplicity had been discovered in the Reichsbank archives. The publication of the letter in Washington coincided with the arrival of detailed American intelligence reports from Bern revealing that the Swiss were guilty of systematically evading the agreement they had signed after the visit by Klaus and Currie. The Swiss had made no attempt to list German assets, nor were they trying to restore looted property to its rightful owners.[21] Instead, Germans in Switzerland were discreetly selling their assets to Swiss friends at ludicrously low prices in order to avoid confiscation, while the new Swiss laws supposedly passed to enforce seizure seemed to be deliberately riddled with loopholes. The documentary evidence of German-Swiss cunning, daily exposed by investigators burrowing in the captured archives, was overwhelming. While German corporations had successfully concealed their activities under the protection of Swiss secrecy laws, Swiss corporations had concealed their own illegal operations in America, using other ruses. Household names like Hoffman La Roche, Ciba-Geigy, the Zurich Insurance Company, and Credit Suisse were suspected by Britain's Ministry of Economic Warfare and by the U.S. Treasury Department of having been illegally swilling millions upon millions of dollars around the financial system. For dedicated young officials like Klaus and Rubin, a crusade against such blatantly amoral entrepreneurs seemed amply justified in view of the callous treatment accorded surviving victims of the Nazi era by the Swiss.

Europeans emerging from exile, hiding, or concentration camps to reclaim their property in Switzerland were confronted by cruelly expensive legal procedures and an insurmountable five-year statute of limitations. Swiss officials coldly replied to American and British protests that the victims of Nazism could not expect privileged treatment. Accordingly, German Jews who had been deprived of their citizenship by Nazi racial laws discovered on arrival from the concentration camps that under Swiss law they were still deemed to be German citizens and their property was therefore frozen. The Swiss had also unquestioningly assumed that they could keep the assets of the Nazis' victims who died without heirs. Non-Jewish Germans, Allied agents reported, did not suffer similar discrimination. Swiss bankers and businessmen were effortlessly crossing the border into Germany to meet old and new clients to arrange for their wealth to be securely hidden from confiscation.[22] In the meantime, the Swiss government played a "delaying game" vis-à-vis the Safehaven negotiators, provoking Klaus to demand the reimposition of a food and fuel blockade and renewed pressure on the British to support Washington's tough policy. Despite these "acute" disagreements with Washington,[23] by November the British, under pressure from France and Russia as well as America, had been dragooned into line. Self-pityingly, Foreign Office officials grumbled, "We leave the solar plexus unguarded"[24] and reluctantly agreed to the publication of a four-power ultimatum to the Swiss.

Just four weeks later, fearing a blockade, the Swiss handed the American embassy its census of German assets. The total value was just $250 million. Uncoincidentally, it was exactly the amount Switzerland was claiming from Germany. The list of assets was clearly far from complete. For those in Washington committed to extracting Germany's loot, the census did not augur well. To isolate the Swiss, Washington insisted that negotiations be held in America. Dr. Walter Stucki, Switzerland's obdurate wartime ambassador in Vichy France and later chief of the foreign ministry's political division, arrived in the American capital with a simple brief — to prevaricate and to concede absolutely nothing. Stucki denied the Allies' right to German assets, called on them to prove in detail every allegedly stolen bar of gold, and insisted on a restricted definition of German assets. The American negotiators were incensed but recognized that the lukewarm support of the British substantially weakened their case.

One year after the war, the efficacy of the blockade had dissolved, but Washington had another, more powerful weapon in its armory: Switzerland's own huge assets still frozen by the American government. The threat of maintaining the freeze produced immediate results. Displaying signs of pained submission and insisting that Switzerland could not recognize the legal basis of the Allied claim, Stucki effected a "compromise" by offering $250 million Swiss francs as compensation for the stolen gold, plus a more honest and complete census. The American negotiators hailed the offer as satisfactory and immediately released their commercial strangleholds. In fact, the Washington accord, as Stucki proudly realized, left Switzerland with everything in her favor. The compensation for the stolen gold underestimated Switzerland's illegal profits; Germany's assets were still safe, because their identification remained a matter of Swiss discretion; and most of the German property in Switzerland was already excluded from the deal, because ownership had, for the time being, been fraudulently assigned to non-Germans.

It was a full year before Washington realized how it had been outsmarted by the fat Swiss negotiator, and even then the full implications were not apparent. As American diplomats inquired about progress, Herr Stucki unleashed a series of bombshells upon the unsuspecting Allies: first, the question of the Swiss-German exchange rate, then conflicts about ownership, then details about compensating the Germans for the expropriation of their property, and finally the news that the newly created state of West Germany refused to recognize the accord. Naively, American diplomats had believed that Stucki accepted Rubin's argument regarding Switzerland's moral responsibility. At first, Stucki's prevarication was explained as an untenable but reasonably understandable defense of Swiss honor. Months later, Allied diplomats condemned him as "a notoriously obstinate man"[25] who was also "tricky, pompous and difficult"[26] to deal with. But their outrage and vows to avenge Swiss perfidy were hot air, and the British, predictably, refused outright to put pressure on Bern. Klaus, Rubin, and the other moral knights witnessed what they had always suspected, that a banker looks after his clients' interests in peace and in war, regardless of their misdeeds. Switzerland's future credibility as a safe haven depended upon its protection of its German deposits.

By 1948, when the emergence of a new sovereign German state was expected within months, Stucki boldly refused to liquidate any German property, explaining that he was not satisfied that the German owners would receive the 100 percent compensation he felt was their due. Washington countered that 5 percent was the maximum that could be justified; Bern protested that the Allies were making "unwarranted attempts to force the Swiss to adopt the Allied point of view"; and London accepted the unpleasant reality — that "the Swiss made an agreement and are now laughing in our face."[27]

Three years after the war, the Safehaven Program had become a farce. While Swiss banks, in defiance of all Allied laws, secretly negotiated with German industry, the Swiss National Bank adamantly refused to return the stolen Dutch gold lying in its vaults although Reichsbank documents discovered by Dutch investigators proved that the Swiss had always been aware of the gold's origin and true ownership. Moral arguments about Holland's plight were of no avail and were unashamedly ignored by Bern.[28] Worse still, other neutral countries like Portugal studied and copied the rewards of Swiss stubbornness faithfully. Among the forty-five tons of stolen gold deposited in Lisbon lay some of the Dutch gold still stored in its original wrappings. Mischievously, the Portuguese government insisted that the Allies would have to identify each of nearly two thousand bars of gold individually to prove it was looted. Although investigators painstakingly identified thirty-two tons — "as much loot as if the Bank held the Mona Lisa itself without even retouching it,"[29] reported one tired British diplomat — the Portuguese, emulating Swiss methods, refused to hand over more than three tons, and even then only in exchange for German assets in Portugal. Washington wearily acquiesced. The Swedish government also followed Switzerland's example. Having handed over seven tons of stolen gold, it retained another nine tons, dishonestly claiming that the gold had been acquired legally. When, in rapid succession, experts from France, Belgium, and Holland arrived to prove their ownership, the Swedish government produced spurious legal arguments to establish Sweden's title. Its stubbornness was richly rewarded.[30] No less enterprising were the Spanish, who found that forgery could be a lucrative variation on the methods so profitably pioneered by the Swiss. At the end of the Safehaven negotiations with Spain, practically nothing had been accomplished. With commendable success, the Spaniards and Germans conspired to fake pre–German surrender deals which "proved" that the German assets had been "sold."[31] Appealing for guidance, the British embassy asked London: "Is it worthwhile to continue?" The finger of blame pointed at Bern. The Foreign Office used decidedly undiplomatic language: The Swiss, they said, had "behaved abominably."[32]

In August 1949 the new government of Germany took office, and the presence of a resurgent power in Bonn cast the Safehaven Program into terminal paralysis. German government officials openly approached all the neutral governments, intimidating them into agreeing that the Safehaven negotiations were unlawful and that the Germans would expect compensation for the "theft" of their property. The reawakening belligerence of Germany indicated that it didn't have even the slightest notion of returning Nazi loot or of offering adequate compensation to the victims of the Third Reich. Encouraged by Bonn, Stucki told the Allies that Switzerland was regretfully unable to release any money without the explicit approval of the new German federal government. The Swiss, commented the Foreign Office, were "torn between two conflicting interests: on the one hand, political fear of Germany; on the other, native financial greed. . . . The Swiss are . . . sufficiently hypocritical to believe that they will emerge with flying moral (and financial) colours." Indeed, that was the outcome. In the final settlement Switzerland agreed to pay 121 million Swiss francs to the Allies minus 20 million Swiss francs toward a refugee fund. After Swiss administrative costs had been deducted, the Safehaven kitty amounted to just 52.4 million Swiss francs. Out of this pool Britain took a mere 2.5 million pounds, while the more determined America, ignoring the agreement, eventually seized $34 million in German assets in America.[33]

Anticipating the failure of Safehaven, Klaus's "targets" in Germany had clandestinely and diligently planned for the inevitable removal of every obstacle to German expansion. No one in Washington suspected that, from beneath the endless moonscape of rubble, a dispirited nation could so suddenly rise and be transformed into a series of booming megalopolises. Yet within months of statehood, every British fear was confirmed. Casting aside the ignominy of defeat, German industry and banks brazenly emerged to challenge, then rapidly overtake their conquerors. The banner headline in the *London Daily Mail* on January 21, 1949, registered the shock: "GERMAN REVIVAL — BRITISH INDUSTRY ALARMED." The newspaper's report explained how Britain's exports were endangered: "The resurrection of German industry since the currency reform last June has staggered British industrialists. Bomb-shattered factories have been re-equipped and day and night shifts are keeping the assembly lines moving. Output is now back to 75 per cent of prewar."

Many believe that West Germany's meteoric rise to riches was entirely due to the introduction of the Deutschmark, the new currency. But that myth was born of ignorance of what had occurred beyond the view of the public. The truth is substantially more sinister. In Washington a number of officials expected the resurgence of German industry, but only Samuel Klaus and a few sympathizers had wanted to prevent it, and they had failed for a series of reasons. Within Germany, the early schemes of the American military government to destroy the masonic industrial cartels had been curbed as a result of unrelenting political, commercial, and diplomatic pressure from Congress, New York bankers, and the British government. Plans to reequip American and British industry with German machinery, promised to the Allies by way of reparations, had foundered because of mass protests by German workers and the sabotage by German dismantlers who skillfully omitted to pack and dispatch vital parts. Also in Germany, powerful industrialists convicted of war crimes at Nuremberg — the directors of Krupp, I. G. Farben, Flick, and the Dresdener Bank — were promised early release and were able to plan new ventures from Landsberg Prison. The Allied policy and plans to remove the Nazis and their supporters from the civil service, the judiciary, the educational system, the professions, and the police had lamentably failed. Germany was not denazified. Four years after the war, those responsible for the day-to-day management of postwar Germany were remarkably similar to the management during the days of Hitler. Triggered by the evident failure of Safehaven, the bankers and industrialists who had conspired after June 1944 to lay the foundations of their postwar prosperity began to draw on their massive hidden funds. The looted money and machinery that had lain dormant in the neutral countries were used to finance and feed Germany's famed economic miracle — the *Witschaftswunder*. Throughout war-stricken Europe, survivors and victors alike were baffled by the pace and strength of Germany's revival. Surely all Germany's industrial and scientific secrets had been seized by the Allies for their own benefit, and the Germans would suffer crippling disadvantages for years to come?

The answers to this question were harsh and simple. To people outside Germany, Allied air raids appeared to inflict widespread damage, but the most devastating bombing struck the residential areas at the heart of the cities. Since the majority of factories were on the outskirts, they survived comparatively unscathed. Moreover, since Germany's wartime capacity was many times greater than her peacetime needs, the machinery and materials snatched as plunder or reparations were of little consequence to German industrialists. Much of the booty seized by the Allies was obsolescent or redundant and was replaced by improved and more modern developments, which were more valuable than their predecessors.

The Allies' great triumph was the recruitment of German scientists — or so they thought. But most of the scientists brought to the United States under the aegis of Project Paperclip were primarily of military interest. Knowing they would be virtually unemployable in postwar Germany, they made themselves freely available to the highest bidder. For the Allied military, the scientists were the intended booty of war, but in fact, with notable exceptions, the military was buying cast-offs of the German armaments industry and intentionally excluding civil interests from booty hunting.

Paperclip and the use of German scientists by the other Allies was profitable because it gave an invaluable boost to their scientific and technical expertise. Without it, the American space program would have been greatly delayed. But the question remains, At what price? Should the military be condemned for ruthlessly excluding the interests of industry and commerce, or of civilian science and medicine? Should it be praised or criticized for its single-mindedness? And can there be any justification for its determination to employ men who had committed crimes against humanity and for the web of conspiracy and deception that Paperclip inspired? In the ultimate reckoning, could it be that Klaus was right? Most would argue that West Germany's solid democracy and the West's enviable prosperity prove that the plunder of Germany caused no casualties. Others will say that the moral cost was too high. It was a final irony that only those who directly profited or lost would understand.

Aftermath

IN MID-OCTOBER 1984, the Paperclip conspiracy was publicly exposed. In a terse statement, the Department of Justice in Washington announced that Arthur Rudolph, the director of production at Nordhausen and later the director of the Saturn V rocket project at the George C. Marshall Spaceflight Center in Huntsville, Alabama, had on March 27 returned to Germany. The statement also announced that on May 25 Rudolph had voluntarily renounced his American citizenship at the American consulate in Hamburg. The department's explanation was simple. At Nordhausen Rudolph had "participated in the persecution of forced laborers, including concentration camp inmates, who were employed there under inhumane conditions." According to the Justice Department's press briefings, at least twenty thousand people had died in the camp. Justice Department officials, it transpired, had offered Rudolph a simple deal. He could either quietly return to Germany and keep the substantial pension that he had been awarded by the National Aeronautics and Space Administration or the department would initiate and vigorously prosecute the long legal battle to prove that the German scientist had obtained American citizenship under false pretenses. The seventy-seven-year-old rocket expert, who had been awarded NASA's highest civilian honors, had opted to avoid the anguish and embarrassment that would automatically accompany the courtroom debate.

The cause of Rudolph's sudden and silent departure had been an investigation launched by the Justice Department's Office of Special Investigation. The OSI had been established in 1979 to look into cases of suspected Nazi war criminals who had improperly obtained American citizenship, having arrived as apparently genuine refugees from Europe after World War II. The OSI's activities were followed by a succession of highly publicized exposures of former Nazi mass murderers who were leading ostensibly respectable lives in American communities. It was during the course of those investigations that Eli Rosenbaum, an OSI lawyer, happened to read the book *Dora*, a grim account of life in the underground Nordhausen factory written by one of its few survivors, Jean Michel. Comparing it with the account of the V2's development in *The Rocket Team*, a comprehensive and flattering history written with the full cooperation of Werner von Braun and his associates, Rosenbaum had been amazed by the German scientists' apparent callousness toward the Nordhausen workers. In particular, Rosenbaum was struck by a quotation from Rudolph about the inconvenience of leaving a convivial New Year's Eve party in 1943 and going into the freezing cold to attend to a production problem. Rudolph, it seemed, had harbored little compassion for the inmates. Stirred by this seeming immorality, Rosenbaum dug deeper and discovered in the U.S. Army's own archives Rudolph's voluminous and long-forgotten personal file, classified "secret," which JIOA had compiled on his entry to America, and his application for citizenship. Almost at a glance, Rosenbaum, then barely thirty years old, understood the conspiracy and manipulations of the revised security reports organized by a previous generation. On the open shelves at the National Archives in Washington, Rosenbaum found the microfilm reels that contained the record of the American army's Dora-Nordhausen war-crimes trial. Within the records were Rudolph's own 1947 interrogation and the incriminating testimony of eyewitnesses at the trial. The criminality of Rudolph and the rocket team, which originally had been successfully concealed, had by now been simply forgotten.

Over the previous thirty years the Germans had become highly respected for realizing John F. Kennedy's dream of putting a man on the moon and had then faded back into semi-obscurity, so that Rudolph reacted with neither suspicions nor unease when he received a sudden summons from the OSI in autumn 1982 to attend an interview at the Hyatt Regency Hotel in San Jose, California. Arriving without a lawyer on October 13, Rudolph was suddenly confronted with his past. Frostily, without any pretense of respect, Rosenbaum and the OSI's director, Neal Sher, questioned the former German about his responsibility for the Nordhausen inmates' conditions. For the most part, Rudolph was equivocal but occasionally damningly self-incriminatory. Four months later, at a second interview, Rudolph again reluctantly admitted some responsibility for demanding extra labor to build rockets in the factory while being aware of the conditions under which such work was performed. Rudolph shortly afterward heard from Sher that his citizenship would be contested. As a result of the ensuing plea bargaining, Rudolph left America forever.

For the OSI it was an undoubted although isolated victory. Within the previous decade von Braun, Kurt Debus, and Walter Dornberger had died, and the existing evidence against other surviving German scientists was at best circumstantial. In Huntsville and elsewhere, the Paperclip Germans were outraged that, during the evening of their lives, their services to America should be so swiftly ignored by the exposure of their conspiracy with the victors of World War II. It was blatant ingratitude. "I helped put the first man — an American — on the moon and then I was treated like this," complained Rudolph in Hamburg in 1986. "The Americans are very ungrateful and I am very bitter." Rosenbaum is equally hostile, albeit from another point of view: "We should have squeezed them like lemons and then sent them back to Germany, preferably for prosecution." Beneath these irreconcilable emotions lies the truth that, despite any dubious morality or circumventing of justice, the Pentagon's Paperclip conspiracy was, within its limitations, unquestionably successful.

Notes

IN THE INTEREST of brevity, certain commonly occurring references have been abbreviated.

Where there are quotes in the text and no reference to the Notes, the source was a personal interview by the author.

British documents from the Public Records Office in London come under the following categories:

ADM	Admiralty
AIR	Ministry of Air
AVIA	Ministry of Supply
BT	Board of Trade
CAB	Cabinet meetings and papers
FO	Foreign Office
T	Treasury
WO	War Office

American documents denoted by abbreviations fall under the following categories:

JIOA	Joint Intelligence Objectives Agency ("Gen. Cor." means the General Correspondence File)
RG	Record Group (National Archives, Modern Military Section)
OMGUS	Office of Military Government, U.S. (National Records Center, Suitland, Maryland)

For brevity, most references to the JIOA security reports on individual German scientists are omitted except where the source might not be clear. The files are all under RG 319 or RG 330 at the National Archives, and from Fort Meade, Maryland, available upon written application.

Other sources were the Maxwell Air Force Base, Alabama, and the Old Navy Yard, Washington, D.C.

1. IMPERIAL DELUSION

1. K. Macksey, *The Tank Pioneers*, p. 140.
2. FO 371/20731.
3. FO 371/17693.
4. M. M. Postan, *Design and Development of Weapons*, p. 240.
5. FO 371/17695/C4583.
6. FO 371/19945/C4999 7/9/36.
7. K. Strong, *Intelligence at the Top*, p. 46.
8. L. Mayo et al., *U.S. Army in World War II — Ordnance Department: Planning Munitions for War*, p. 190.
9. RG 165 MID 2016-1090 1/7/33.
10. Mayo, *U.S. Army in World War II*, p. 209.
11. Ibid., p. 214.
12. Institution of Naval Architects, 62nd session, March 1921.
13. C. Andrew, *Secret Service*, p. 350.
14. A. Price, *Instruments of Darkness*, p. 17.
15. F. H. Hinsley, *British Intelligence in the Second World War*, vol. 1, p. 15.
16. House of Commons, 3/20/39.
17. S. W. Roskill, *The War at Sea*, vol. 1, p. 136.
18. S. W. Roskill, *Naval Policy Between the Wars*, p. 227.
19. Ibid., p. 333.
20. CAB 16/179.
21. Andrew, *Secret Service*, p. 350.
22. FO 371/18840/C3891.
23. J. Terraine, *The Right of the Line*, p. 81.
24. Ibid., p. 90.
25. W. Gunston, *By Jupiter*, p. 91.
26. Hinsley, *British Intelligence*, vol. 1, p. 61.
27. Andrew, *Secret Service*, p. 389.
28. Postan, *Design and Development of Weapons*, p. 6.
29. Ibid., p. 192.
30. R. V. Jones, *Most Secret War*, p. 40.
31. Terraine, *The Right of the Line*, p. 21.
32. Roskill, *Naval Policy*, p. 459.

2. HARSH LESSONS

1. CAB 21/1421.
2. Ibid.
3. Ibid.
4. Ibid.
5. S. J. Peskett, *Strange Intelligence*, p. 88.

6. A. Price, *Instruments of Darkness*, p. 74.
7. R. V. Jones, *Most Secret War*, p. 82 ff.
8. J. Terraine, *The Right of the Line*, p. 268.
9. M. Hastings, *Bomber Command*, p. 108.
10. R. W. Clark, *Tizard*, p. 142.
11. Hastings, *Bomber Command*, p. 126.
12. Jones, *Most Secret War*, p. 302.
13. F. H. Hinsley, *British Intelligence in the Second World War*, vol. 3, pt. 1, p. 330.
14. Ibid., vol. 3, pt. 1, p. 329.
15. WO 208/3580 *Official History*, 1943.
16. Hinsley, *British Intelligence*, vol. 1, p. 393.
17. Tank Board, 11th meeting, 2/14/41.
18. Tank Board No. 47 (1941).
19. Tank Board No. 61 (1941).
20. WO 208/3580.
21. WO 106/2259 and WO 106/2286.
22. W. Churchill, *The Second World War*, vol. 4, p. 33.

3. UNPLEASANT REALITIES

1. V. Bush, *Pieces of Action*, p. 104.
2. Tank Board 2/3/42. (Most relevant quotations, unless stated otherwise in this chapter, are from the Tank Board records, available at Bovington, Dorset.)
3. Tank Board 6/30/42.
4. RTB 61 (42) 7/1/42.
5. RTB No. 59 (1942).
6. L. Mayo et al., *U.S. Army in World War II — Ordnance Department: Planning Munitions for War*, p. 280.
7. Ibid., p. 212.
8. F. H. Hinsley, *British Intelligence in the Second World War*, vol. 1, p. 234.
9. Ibid., vol. 2, p. 356.
10. J. P. Baxter, *Scientists Against Time*, p. 120.
11. Hinsley, *British Intelligence*, vol. 2, p. 312.
12. Bush, *Pieces of Action*, p. 88.
13. Ibid., p. 89.
14. S. Morison, *History of United States Naval Operations in World War II*, vol. 1, p. 244.
15. Hinsley, *British Intelligence*, vol. 2, p. 33.
16. Ibid., vol. 3, pt. 1, p. 517.
17. S. W. Roskill, *Naval Policy Between the Wars*, p. 33.
18. M. Hastings, *Bomber Command*, p. 227.
19. C. Webster and N. Frankland, *Strategic Air Offensive Against Germany*, vol. 2, p. 39.
20. W. Churchill, *The Second World War*, vol. 5, p. 579.

21. C. Barnett, *The Audit of War*, p. 154.
22. G. Constant, *The Origins of the Turbojet Revolution*, p. 222.
23. Webster and Frankland, *Strategic Air Offensive*; Hinsley, *British Intelligence*, vol. 3, pt. 1, p. 336.
24. AIR 8/784.
25. Ibid.
26. Hinsley, *British Intelligence*, vol. 3, pt. 1, p. 337.
27. AIR 8/784.
28. Barnett, *The Audit of War*, p. 150.
29. Hinsley, *British Intelligence*, vol. 2, p. 141.
30. Ibid., vol. 2, p. 145.
31. Ibid., vol. 3, pt. 1, p. 62.
32. Ibid., vol. 2, p. 159.
33. Ibid., vol. 3, pt. 1, p. 56.
34. A. Speer, *Inside the Third Reich*, p. 496.
35. D. Irving, *The Mare's Nest*. (The basic material for this episode is from Irving's revised and unpublished version of *The Mare's Nest* and Hinsley, *British Intelligence*.)
36. Hinsley, *British Intelligence*, vol. 3, pt. 1, p. 400.
37. Ibid., vol. 3, pt. 1, p. 449.
38. Ibid., vol. 3, pt. 1, p. 455.
39. Ibid., vol. 3, pt. 1, p. 446.

4. PLANNING PLUNDER

1. FO 942/27 March 1944.
2. Ibid.
3. FO 942/36.
4. WO 219/82.
5. WO 219/1984 8/23/44.
6. CAB 81/24 4/25/44 Joint Technical Warfare Committee.
7. FO 935/1.
8. FO 942/27.
9. FO 942/79 5/19/44.
10. RG 227 Liaison Office Item 194 Box 128A 4/15/46.
11. RG 165 Records of the War Department, General and Special Staffs 175.CSGID 210.68 Record Copies Scientific Intelligence Mission. Entry 187–Box 137 Alsos Mission File 1944–45. 3/14/44.
12. D. Irving, *The Mare's Nest*, p. 62.
13. A. Speer, *Inside the Third Reich*, p. 317.
14. Irving, *The Mare's Nest*, p. 202.
15. FO 942/79.
16. RG 165 Records of the War Department, General and Special Staffs Box 137 Alsos Mission File 1944–45.
17. Ibid.
18. FO 935/25 9/14/44.
19. WO 219/1984 8/4/44.

20. L. Mayo et al., *U.S. Army in World War Two — Ordnance Department*, p. 322.
21. CAB 81/47.
22. RG 165 Records of the War Department, General and Special Staffs New Development Div. WDSS Decimal File 1943–44; 300 Air and Ground Support. 6/22/44.
23. RG 165 Records of the War Department, General and Special Staffs ABC 471.6.; V. Bush, *Pieces of Action*, p. 99.
24. RG 165 Records of the War Department, General and Special Staffs New Development Div. WDSS Decimal File 1943–44; 300 Air and Ground Support. 7/3/44.
25. RG 107 Records of the Office of Sec. of War, Entry 42–Box 147; Office of Asst. Sec. of War for Air Plans, Policies and Agreements, 1943–47.
26. AIR 8/784 7/13/44.
27. G. Constant, *The Origins of the Turbojet Revolution*, p. 236.
28. AIR 8/784 8/30/44.
29. ADM 223/214 is the official history of 30 Assault Unit. There is also a top-secret section.
30. A. C. Hampshire, *The Secret Navies*, p. 179.
31. J. Pearson, *Ian Fleming*, p. 130.
32. WO 219/551 SHAEF Intelligence Directive 17 7/27/44.
33. WO 219/1195A 1/27/45.
34. CAB 81/47.
35. WO 219/1630A and FO 1031/49, history of T-force activities in 21 Army Group.
36. FO 935/25.
37. WO 219/1984 9/11/44.
38. WO 219/1986.
39. WO 219/1669.
40. WO 219/725 8/28/45.
41. FO 935/4.
42. WO 219/1987 12/21/44.
43. RG 227 Liaison Office Box 129.
44. WO 219/1986 12/26/44.
45. FO 935/7.
46. CIOS had sent 197 investigators to 115 blacklist targets. Eleven reports were published. AVIA 12/191 2/15/45.
47. FO 371/45750.
48. Ibid.
49. FO 942/81.
50. WO 219/1987 11/23/44.
51. RG 165 Records of the War Department, General and Special Staffs ABC.387 (Sect. 19).
52. V. Bush, *Pieces of Action*, p. 109.
53. T 160/1260.
54. Ibid.

55. FO 942/52.
56. AVIA 15/2084 1/8/45.
57. FO 942/52.
58. Ibid.
59. AVIA 15/2077.
60. BT 64/2832.
61. FO 942/53 6/20/44.
62. BT 64/2832 3/23/45. Ministerial committee on U.K. Civil Requirements from Germany.
63. BT 64/2832.
64. FO 942/53 6/27/44.
65. WO 219/1630A 8/10/44.
66. FO 1031/49 and WO 219/1986 March 1945.
67. FO 935/25.
68. WO 219/1986 3/7/45.
69. WO 219/1669.
70. AIR 8/784.
71. AIR 8/786 1/26/45.
72. AIR 40/2161.
73. AIR 40/1656.
74. AIR 8/784 1/24/45.
75. Ibid.

5.   THE HUNT

1. C. Lasby, *Project Paperclip*, p. 36.
2. Ibid., p. 69.
3. RG 165 Records of the War Department, General and Special Staffs New Development Div. WDSS Decimal File 1943–44; 300 Air and Ground Support.
4. RG 18 Records of the Army Air Forces (Organization of Research) Air Adjutant Gen. Classified Records Sect. 1946–47 Decimal File.
5. RG 165 H3 5/15/45.
6. DON 808 6/5/45.
7. FO 935/12.
8. FO 935/12 3/18/45.
9. WO 193/723 10/8/41.
10. WO 219/1986 4/9/45.
11. WO 195/9678.
12. WO 208/2182.
13. BT 211/25.
14. FO 1031/96 8/26/45.
15. WO 195/9678.
16. FO 1031/49.
17. I. G. Aylen, *Naval Review*, October 1977 and January 1978.
18. ADM 1/19148 May 1945.
19. ADM 228/10 9/15/45.

20. ADM 1/18378 8/29/45.
21. RG 165 ABC 387 Germany (Dec. 18, 1948) (Sect. 18) 5/17/45.
22. FO 942/79 6/20/44.
23. AVIA 10/113.
24. AVIA 9/85.
25. "Report on a Visit to Germany," July 1945, George Edwards, Vickers Armstrong Library, London.
26. AVIA 9/83.
27. M. M. Postan, *Design and Development of Weapons*, p. 152.
28. AVIA 9/88 10/31/45.

6. COMPROMISES

1. RG 165 JWPC 331 3/27/45.
2. RG 153 and RG 338 U.S. Army Investigation and Trial Records of War Criminals, U.S. v. Kurt Andrae et al.
3. Arthur Rudolph interview with John Hubner, *West* magazine, October 1985.
4. Office of Special Investigation (Department of Justice) 1982.
5. RG 338 Dora trial transcript.
6. RG 165, Alsos Mission 1944–45 Entry 187–Box 138.
7. F. Ordway and M. Sharpe, *The Rocket Team*, p. 274.
8. RG 260 OMGUS FIAT Box 5 17/2-30.
9. CAB 81/47.
10. CAB 81/47.
11. Tech. Memo G. W. 102 "History of the Development of the RTV 1" (Science Museum, London).
12. Office of Special Investigation (Department of Justice) 1982, p. 166.
13. Ordway and Sharpe, *The Rocket Team*, p. 283.
14. State Department Decimal File 840.414/3-3145.
15. State Department Decimal File 1945–49 862.542 4/27/45.
16. RG 319 Army Intelligence 1941–48 (Box 989 400.112).
17. State Department Decimal File 1945–49 862.542 5/22/45.
18. RG 319 Army Intelligence File Box 991 400.112 (Gen. Policy) 5/26/45.
19. RG 319 Army Intelligence Decimal File Box 991 400.112 (Gen. Policy).
20. RG 319 Army Intelligence Decimal File 1941–48 Box 989.
21. RG 319 Army Intelligence Decimal File Box 991 400.112 (Gen. Policy) 6/29/45.
22. State Department Decimal File 1945–49 862.542 6/15/45.
23. RG 319 Army Intelligence Decimal File Box 991 400.112 (Gen. Policy).
24. RG 319 Army Intelligence Decimal File Box 991 400.112 (Gen. Policy) 9/10/45.
25. RG 260 HQ 370.2 AG 1945/6 JCS 1067/8.
26. RG 260 OMGUS FIAT Box 5 17/2-30.
27. Ordway and Sharpe, *The Rocket Team*, p. 291.
28. CAB 82/7 9/24/45.
29. AVIA 22/753.
30. RG 319 JIOA Personal File — Dornberger.

7. COMPETITION AND CONFUSION

1. RG 218 JCS CCS 471.9 (1/5/45) Sect. 2 JCS 1363/3 8/27/45.
2. RG 319 Army Intelligence Decimal File Box 991 400.112 (Gen. Policy) 5/26/45.
3. RG 319 Army Intelligence Decimal File Box 991 400.112 (Gen. Policy) 9/10/45.
4. RG 319 400.112 Research Box 990 10/9/45.
5. CAB 82/6.
6. FO 935/12.
7. CAB 82/6 SCAF 394.
8. CAB 82/6 7/22/45.
9. FO 371/45695 CCS 864/2 7/14/45.
10. CAB 82/6 7/7/45.
11. CAB 82/6.
12. CAB 82/6 DCOS (45) 52 (Final) 8/17/45.
13. RG 260 OMGUS FIAT Box 17/3–14 9/19/45.
14. CAB 82/6 9/3/45.
15. CAB 82/6 DCOS (45) 61 (Final) 8/27/45.
16. Chiefs of Staff DO (45) 7.
17. C. Lasby, *Project Paperclip*, p. 90.
18. RG 260 OMGUS FIAT Box 1 17/1–15 Exec. Order 9568 and 9604 6/8/45.
19. RG 218 JCS CCS 471.9 1/5/45 Sect. 2 JIS 317/3; JIS 199/1 9/28/45.
20. RG 218 JCS CCS 471.9 1/5/45 Sect. 2 JIS 199/1 9/28/45.
21. RG 319 Army Intelligence Decimal File Box 991 400.112 (Gen. Policy) 5/26/45.
22. RG 218 JCS CCS 471.9 1/5/45 Sect. 2 JIS 199/5 10/11/45.
23. RG 330 Office of Sec. of Defense, 383.7b Exploitation JIOA Gen. Cor. 10/22/45.
24. Executive Order 9568 6/8/45.
25. RG 330 Office of Sec. of Defense, 383.7b Exploitation JIOA Gen. Cor. 10/17/45.
26. State Department Decimal File 1945–49 862.542 10/31/45.
27. State Department Decimal File 1945–49 862.542/11-1645.
28. RG 319 Army Intelligence File 1941–48 Box 989 400.112 10/17/45.
29. RG 332 USFET SGS Box 50 383.64 (Classified Gen. Cor. 1944–45) 11/13/45.
30. RG 260 OMGUS FIAT Box 2 17/1–33 10/25/45.
31. FO 935/9 1/1/45.
32. RG 218 JCS CCS 471.9 (1/5/45) Sect. 1.
33. RG 218 JCS CCS 471.9 (1/5/45) Sect. 1 5/18/45. Endorsed by CCS 5/26/45.
34. RG 260 OMGUS FIAT Box 7 17/3–18.
35. CAB 82/6 6/22/45.
36. CAB 82/6 7/15/45.
37. RG 218 JCS CCS 471-9 (1/5/45) Sect. 3.

38. AVIA 9/83 July 1945.
39. C. Lasby, *Project Paperclip*, p. 47.
40. FO 1031/20 9/12/45.
41. RG 260 OMGUS FIAT Box 41 17/19–5 9/8/45.
42. RG 260 OMGUS FIAT Box 41 17/19–5 10/17/45.
43. FO 1031/65 3/1/46.
44. BT 211/33 9/6/46.
45. RG 330 JIOA Gen. Cor. 10/26/45.
46. Paragraph 31c of JCS 1067/6.
47. RG 260 OMGUS FIAT Box 5 17/2–25 9/28/45.
48. ADM 116/5571.
49. FO 1010/60.
50. DON 24 10/10/45.
51. RG 260 OMGUS FIAT Box 4 17/2–8 2/28/45.
52. RG 260 OMGUS FIAT Box 7 17/3–8 5/29/45.
53. RG 260 OMGUS FIAT Box 7 17/3–18 8/4/45.
54. RG 260 OMGUS FIAT Box 7 17/3–18 10/24/45.
55. Engel SS File, U.S. Berlin Document Center.
56. AIR 40/1178 10/12/45.
57. CAB 82/7 10/29/45.
58. CAB 82/7 11/24/45.
59. CAB 82/7 12/23/45.
60. RG 330 383.7 U.S. British (Misc.) Folder 1 Period to January 1947 JIOA Gen. Cor. 1946–52 11/26/45.
61. C. Lasby, *Project Paperclip*, p. 92.
62. State Department Decimal File 1945–49 862.542 11/30/45.
63. RG 330 383.7 Policy 1946 JIOA Gen. Cor. 1946–52 12/4/45.
64. RG 330 383.7 Policy 1946 JIOA Gen. Cor. 1946–52 2/1/46.
65. RG 319 Army Intelligence Decimal File Box 991 400.112 (Gen. Policy) 12/13/45.
66. RG 218 JCS CCS 471-9 (1/5/45) Sect. 3 JIOA 1/1/M 12/17/45.
67. RG 330 383.7 Policy 1946 JIOA Gen. Cor. 1946–52 12/20/45.

8. The Irreconcilables: Diplomats and Soldiers

1. RG 319 JIOA case files, Patin.
2. RG 319 Army Intelligence Decimal File Box 991 400.112 (Gen. Policy) 10/17/45.
3. RG 330 383.7 Policy 1946 JIOA Gen. Cor. 1946–52 1/24/46.
4. RG 319 Army Intelligence Decimal File Box 991 400.112 (Gen. Policy) 1/17/46.
5. RG 18 Records of the Army Air Forces 091–4 People 1946–47 vol. 1 3/20/46.
6. RG 319 Army Intelligence Decimal File 1941–48 6–2 400.112 1/25/46.
7. RG 18 Records of the Army Air Forces Entry 1-Box Air Adjutant Gen. Classified 4/24/46.
8. RG 18 Records of the Army Air Forces Entry 1-Box Air Adjutant Gen. Classified 3/29/46.

9. JIC 317/10 RG 218 JCS CCS 471-9 (1/5/45) Sect. 3 1/5/45.
10. State Department Decimal File 1945–49 862.542 1/17/46.
11. Ibid.
12. State Department Decimal File 1945–49 862.542 1/24/45.
13. RG 218 JCS CCS 471–9 (1/5/45) Sect. 4 JIS 230 1/26/46.
14. State Department Decimal File 1945–49 862.542 1/9/46.
15. State Department Decimal File 1945–49 862.542 2/13/46.
16. RG 218 JCS CCS 471–9 (1/5/45) Sect. 4 3/6/46.
17. RG 330 383.7 Policy 1946 JIOA Gen. Cor. 1946–52 3/14/46.
18. BT 211/47 3/31/46.
19. RG 319 Army Intelligence Decimal File 1941–48 400.112 4/9/46.
20. RG 319 Army Intelligence Decimal File Box 991 400.112 (Gen. Policy) 4/18/46.
21. RG 330 Office of Sec. of Defense List U.S. (Misc.) JIOA Gen. Cor. 1946–52 3/13/46.
22. RG 319 Army Intelligence Decimal File Box 990 (Research) 400.112.
23. RG 319 Army Intelligence Decimal File Box 993 400.112 (014.32) 5/3/46.
24. RG 330 Office of Sec. of Defense, 383.7b Exploitation German Specialists JIOA Gen. Cor. 1946–52 5/15/46.
25. RG 319 Box 993 400.112 (014.32) 5/29/46.
26. State Department Decimal File 1945–49 862.542 5/17/46.
27. SWNCC 257/15 5/24/46.
28. RG 319 400.112 File Box 990 (Research) 5/20/46.
29. RG 18 Records of the Army Air Forces, 091.4 People 1946–47 vol. 2; Entry 1–Box 565 Air Adjutant Gen. Classified Records Sect. 1946–47 Decimal File 6/13/46.
30. RG 319 400.112 File Box 990 (Research) 6/5/46.
31. RG 18 Records of the Army Air Forces, 091.4 People 1946–47 vol. 2; Entry 1-Box 565 Air Adjutant Gen. Classified Records Sect. 1946–47 Decimal File 6/14/46.
32. RG 330 Office of Sec. of Defense, 383.7a Misc. Long Range JIOA Gen. Cor. 1946–52 6/10/46.
33. RG 218 JCS CCS 471-9 (1/5/45) Sect. 7 JIC 317/29 6/19/46.
34. RG 330 Office of Sec. of Defense, 383.7b Exploitation German Specialists/U.S. JIOA Gen. Cor. 1946–52 JIOA 1/9/M 7/3/46.
35. Cummings interview with author.
36. RG 218 JCS CCS 471.9 (1/5/45) Sect. 7 JIC 317/29 7/13/46.
37. RG 319 Army Intelligence Decimal File Box 991 400.112 (Gen. Policy) 7/15/46.
38. RG 218 JCS CCS 471.9 (1/5/45) Sect. 7 S-7556 JIC 317/31/D 7/17/46.
39. RG 330 Office of Sec. of Defense, 383.7a Immigration 46 JIOA Gen. Cor. 1946–52 7/17/46.
40. State Department Decimal File 1945–49 862.542 6/29/46.
41. RG 107 Office of Sec. of War, 211 Scientists Entry 76–Box 7 Asst. Sec. of War Cor. of Howard Petersen 7/24/46.
42. RG 218 JCS CCS 471.9 (1/5/45) Sect. 8 8/1/46.
43. RG 218 JCS CCS 471.9 (1/5/45) (Sect. 8) JCS 1363/29 SWNCC 257/22.

44. RG 319 Army Intelligence Decimal File Box 991 400.112 (Gen. Policy) RGN 319 9/20/46.
45. RG 330 Office of Sec. of Defense, 383.7b USFET VISIT JIOA Gen. Cor. 1946–52 8/19/46.
46. RG 319 Army Intelligence Decimal File Box 991 400.112 (Gen. Policy) 7/31/46.
47. RG 319 Army Intelligence Decimal File Box 991 400.112 (Gen. Policy) 10/14/46.
48. State Department Decimal File 1945–49 862.542 10/8/46.
49. RG 330 Office of Sec. of Defense, 383.7a Immigration 1946 JIOA Gen. Cor. 1946–52 10/16/46.
50. RG 330 Office of Sec. of Defense, JIOA Gen. Cor. Misc. 1946–52 10/14/46.
51. State Department Decimal File 1945–49 862.542 11/27/46.
52. RG 165 H2 JCS 1363/31 12/10/46.
53. RG 165 ABC 471.6 (Sect. 1-B) JCS 1363/21 and CCS 870/15 4/23/46.
54. RG 218 JCS CCS 471-9 (1/5/45) Sect. 7 7/11/46.
55. RG 330 Office of Sec. of Defense, JIOA Gen. Cor. Misc. 1946–52 9/15/46.
56. RG 260 AG Decimal File 1945–46 Box 41 231.2 7/27/46.
57. S. Tokaev, *Stalin Means War*, p. 149.
58. RG 260 OMGUS Dir. of Intelligence 27-2/7 (Box 65) 10/25/46.
59. RG 319 Army Intelligence Decimal File 1941–48 400.112 1/10/47.
60. RG 319 400.112 Research "Mail Regulations" Box 990 11/19/46.
61. RG 319 6-2 400.112 Research 12/3/46.
62. RG 319 Army Intelligence Box 989 12/5/46.
63. RG 330 Office of Sec. of Defense, G2 (Misc.) 1945–46 JIOA Gen. Cor. 1946–52 10/23/46.
64. RG 18 Records of the Army Air Forces 091.4 People 1946–7 vol. 3 Box 556 Air Adjutant Gen. Classified Records Sect. 1946–47 Decimal File 11/22/46.
65. RG 319 Army Intelligence (Box 989) 400.112 12/12/46.

9. The Conspiracy

1. RG 319 6-2 Army Intelligence Decimal File 1941–48 400.112 (014.32) 3/13/47.
2. *New York Herald Tribune*, Feb. 11, 1947.
3. RG 330 Office of Sec. of Defense, JIOA Gen. Cor. AAF Misc. 1946–52 3/2/48.
4. *PM* magazine 12/31/46.
5. *Dayton (Ohio) News*, Feb. 22, 1947.
6. RG 18 Records of the Army Air Force 091.4 People 1946–47 vol. 4 Box 556 Air Adjutant Gen. Classified Records Sect. 1946–47 Decimal File 3/11/47.
7. RG 18 Records of the Army Air Forces 091.4 People 1946–47 vol. 4 Box 556 Air Adjutant Gen. Classified Records Sect. 1946–47 Decimal File E. 3/7/47.
8. RG 330 Office of Sec. of Defense, JIOA Gen. Cor. Navy Misc. 1946–52 2/26/47.

9. RG 319 Army Intelligence Box 989 3/3/47.
10. RG 319 6-2 400.112 Research 2/18/47.
11. Legislation numbers: S 213, HR 1117 and HR 2763.
12. RG 330 Office of Sec. of Defense, Immigration Jan.-Dec. 1947 JIOA Gen. Cor. 1946–52 1/1/47.
13. State Department Decimal File 1945–49 862.542 1/16/47.
14. RG 319 400.112 Box 991 Army Intelligence Decimal File 1/21/47.
15. RG 330 Office of Sec. of Defense, Immigration Diary from Oct. 1, 1946, JIOA Gen. Cor. 1/29/47.
16. RG 330 Office of Sec. of Defense, 383.7 Cables JIOA Gen. Cor. 3/3/47.
17. RG 319 Army Intelligence Decimal File 1941–48 6–2 400.112 3/5/47.
18. RG 107 Office of Sec. of War 211 Scientists Entry 76–Box 7 Cor. of Howard Petersen 3/1/47.
19. RG 319 Army Intelligence Decimal File 1941–48 6–2 400.112 (1443/62) 3/11/47.
20. State Department Decimal File 1945–49 862.542 2/25/47.
21. RG 330 Office of Sec. of Defense, Immigration Diary from Oct. 1, 1946, JIOA Gen. Cor. 1946–52 5/26/47.
22. RG 330 Office of Sec. of Defense, State Department (Misc.) JIOA Gen. Cor. 1946–52 4/4/47.
23. SWNCC 257/25.
24. RG 330 Sec. of Defense, Immigration Diary from Oct. 1, 1946, JIOA Gen. Cor. 1946–52 4/9/47.
25. RG 312 400.112 Research 014.32 6/6/47.
26. RG 319 Army Intelligence Decimal File 1941-48 6-2 400.112 (014.32) 7/2/47.
27. RG 319 400.112 (448) 5/5/48.
28. RG 319 Army Intelligence Decimal File 1941–48 6–2 400.112 (014.32) 7/25/47.
29. *Washington Post*, Feb. 24, 1947.
30. JCS 1363/36 4/23/47.
31. RG 165 Records of the War Department, General and Special Staffs ABC 471.6 (Oct. 7, 1943) Sect. 1-D 3/13/47.
32. RG 218 JCS CCS 471–9 (1/5/45) Sect. 12 JIOA 1/25 7/30/47.
33. RG 319 Army Intelligence Decimal File 1941–48 6–2 400.112 (014.32) 11/17/47.
34. RG 330 Office of Sec. of Defense, 383.7 Cables Misc. JIOA Gen. Cor. 1946–52 10/17/47.
35. RG 330 Office of Sec. of Defense, 383.7 Navy (Misc.) JIOA Gen. Cor. 1946–52 3/21/47.
36. Aalmans, "History of Nordhausen Trial," private records of Aalmans.
37. RG 153 and RG 338 U.S. Army Investigation and Trial Records of War Criminals, U.S. v. Kurt Andrae et al.
38. RG 319 Army Intelligence File 1941–48 Box 989 400.112 4/14/47.
39. RG 319 Army Intelligence File 1941–48 Box 989 400.112 5/8/47.
40. RG 107 (Office of Sec. of War) Petersen papers Dec. 1945–August 1947.
41. RG 330 Office of Sec. of Defense, Axster, Herbert, 1/17/47.

42. RG 330 Office of Sec. of Defense, Axster, Herbert, 8/5/47.
43. RG 330 Office of Sec. of Defense, Axster, Herbert, 6/18/47.
44. RG 319 Army Intelligence Decimal File 1941-48 6-2 400.112 Research 5/21/47.
45. RG 330 Office of Sec. of Defense, Axster, Herbert, 9/8/47.
46. RG 330 Office of Sec. of Defense, 383.7 Cables Misc. July-Dec. 1947 JIOA Gen. Cor. 1946–52 9/19/47.
47. RG 319 Army Intelligence File 1941–48 Box 989 400.112 6/4/47.
48. RG 319 Army Intelligence Decimal File 1941–48 6–2 400.112 Research 7/19/47.
49. RG 319 Army Intelligence Decimal File Box 991 400.112 (Gen. Policy) 1/21/47.
50. RG 330 Office of Sec. of Defense, G2 Misc. Jan.-July 1947 JIOA Gen. Cor. 1946–52 3/7/47.
51. RG 218 JCS CCS 471.9 (1/5/45) Sect. 11 5/6/47.
52. RG 319 Army Intelligence Decimal File Box 991 400.112 (Gen. Policy) 7/30/46.
53. RG 319 Army Intelligence Decimal File Box 991 400.112 (Gen. Policy) 9/14/45.
54. RG 330 Office of Sec. of Defense, State Department (Misc.) JIOA Gen. Cor. 1946–52 8/29/47 and 9/18/47.
55. Two hundred nine for air force, 177 army, 71 navy.
56. RG 319 Army Intelligence Decimal File 1941–48 400.112/Research 319.4 7/18/47.
57. RG 319 Army Intelligence (Box 989) 400.112 1/24/47 and State Department Decimal File 860.542 2/13/48.
58. RG 319 Army Intelligence Decimal File 1941–48 6–2 400.112 12/12/47 (448).
59. RG 319 Army Intelligence Decimal File 1941–48 400.112 Research (032) 10/21/48.
60. RG 165 Records of the War Department, General and Special Staffs ABC 471.6 (Oct. 7, 1943) Sect. 1-E October 1947.
61. RG 319 Army Intelligence Decimal File 1941–48 400.112 (448).
62. SWNCC 257/33.
63. RG 330 Office of Sec. of Defense, Immigration Diary from Oct. 1, 1946, JIOA Gen. Cor. 1946–52 8/12/47.
64. RG 165 Records of the War Department, General and Special Staffs ABC 471.6 (Oct. 7, 1943) Sect. 1-E JIC 349/9 8/20/47.
65. RG 218 JCS CCS 471-9 (1/5/45) Sect. 13 WAR 87915 10/8/47.

10.   The Doctors from Berlin

1. Armstrong oral history interview, Aerospace Medical Division, Brooks Air Force Base, Texas. All quotes are from this source.
2. RG 165 187–Box 137 Alsos Mission.
3. CIOS report No. 24 "Treatment of Shock from Prolonged Exposure to Cold, Especially in Water."
4. A. Mitscherlich and F. Mielke, *The Death Doctors*, p. 24. The facts in

this chapter are drawn from this book; the CIOS report; and the transcript and evidence of the "Medical trial" at the subsequent trials held at Nuremberg after 1946–48.

5. Lauschner interview with author.
6. T. Bower, *Pledge Betrayed*, p. 397.
7. P. Campbell, *Oral History*, p. 38.
8. RG 330 Sec. of Defense, R & D JIOA case files.

11.   REWRITING THE PAST

1. RG 18 Records of the Army Air Forces 091.4 People 1948 vol. 1 Box 783 Air Adjutant Gen. Classified Records Sect. Decimal File 3/22/48.
2. RG 330 Sec. of Defense Cables master file Jan.-May 1948 1/9/48.
3. RG 18 Records of the Army Air Forces 091.4 People 1948 vol. 1 Box 783 Air Adjutant Gen. Classified Records Sect. Decimal File 1/15/48.
4. RG 330 Sec. of Defense Cables master file JIOA Gen. Cor. 1946-52 4/6/48.
5. RG 338 EUCOM Intelligence Div. Classified Decimal File 384 6/21/48.
6. RG 330 Office of Sec. of Defense, Axster, Herbert, 11/28/47.
7. RG Office of Sec. of Defense Investigations German Scientists Jan.-Dec. 1947 JIOA Gen. Cor. 1946–52 12/4/47.
8. RG 260 OMGUS AG file 1949 370.2 5/12/48.
9. RG 330 Office of Sec. of Defense, Navy (Misc.) Jan.-Dec. 1947 JIOA Gen. Cor. 1946–52 11/28/47.
10. RG 319 400.112 Research Box 990 1/20/48.
11. RG 319 Army Intelligence Decimal File 1941–48 6–2 400.112 Research 3/29/48.
12. RG 319 Army Intelligence Decimal File 1941–48 6–2 400.112 Research 4/16/48.
13. RG 330 Office of Sec. of Defense, Immigration Diary from Oct. 1, 1946, JIOA Gen. Cor. 1946–52 12/12/47.
14. RG 312 400.112 Research 014.32 2/10/48.
15. RG 330 Office of Sec. of Defense, Immigration Diary from Oct. 1, 1946, JIOA Gen. Cor. 1946–52 3/17/48.
16. RG 319 400.112 Research Box 990 1/20/48.
17. RG 330 Office of Sec. of Defense Cables master file JIOA Gen. Cor. 1946–52 1/19/48.
18. RG 330 Office of Sec. of Defense, Immigration Diary from Oct. 1, 1946, JIOA Gen. Cor. 1946–52 4/6/48.
19. RG 330 Office of Sec. of Defense, G2 Misc. JIOA Gen. Cor. 1946–52 5/11/48.
20. RG 319 Army Intelligence Decimal File 1941–48 Box 1001 400.112 (230.312) 6/11/48.
21. RG 18 Records of the Army Air Forces 091.4 People 1948 vol. 1 Box 783 Air Adjutant Gen. Classified Records Sect. Decimal File 6/4/48.

22. RG 260 OMGUS Dir. of Intelligence 27-2/7 Folder 19 10/8/48.
23. RG 319 Army Intelligence Decimal File 1941–48 Research (032) 10/21/48.
24. RG 330 Office of Sec. of Defense, Navy (Misc.) 1949 JIOA Gen. Cor. 1946–52 9/7/49.
25. RG 330 Office of Sec. of Defense, 383.7 Escape Clause 1948 JIOA Gen. Cor. 1946–52 10/21/48.
26. RG 330 Office of Sec. of Defense, Wazelt 11/23/49.
27. State Department Decimal File 1945–49 862.542 2/25/49.
28. RG 330 Office of Sec. of Defense, 383.7 Escape Clause 1948 JIOA Gen. Cor. 1946–52 5/20/48.
29. RG 319 Army Intelligence Decimal File 1941–48 400.112 (Box 987) 9/20/49.
30. RG 330 Office of Sec. of Defense, Army project 63 JIOA Gen. Cor. 1946–52 6/5/51.
31. RG 330 Office of Sec. of Defense, Alberts 11/23/48.
32. RG 330 Office of Sec. of Defense, R & D JIOA case files.
33. T. Bower, *Pledge Betrayed,* p. 418.
34. RG 330 Office of Sec. of Defense Cables master file JIOA Gen. Cor. 1946–52 7/14/50.
35. JCS 1363/63.
36. RG 218 JCS CCS 471.9 (1/5/45) (Sect. 19) 12/8/50.
37. RG 330 Office of Sec. of Defense, State Department 1951 JIOA Gen. Cor. 1946–52 12/7/51.
38. RG 330 Office of Sec. of Defense Hicog Denial JIOA Gen. Cor. 1946–52 6/15/51.
39. RG 330 JIOA case file — Blome.
40. RG 330 JIOA case file — Schreiber 2/12/52.
41. RG 330 Office of Sec. of Defense RCD 200.2 10/31/52.

12. THE FINAL IRONY

1. FO 371/45812 1/15/45.
2. WO 219/1655 1/15/45.
3. RG 169, *Safehaven History,* FEA, p. 131.
4. FO 371/34877 11/18/43.
5. D. Gordon and R. Dangerfield, *The Hidden Weapon,* p. 10.
6. FO 371/34877 11/18/43.
7. N. Faith, *Safety in Numbers,* p. 93.
8. FO 371/39169 7/12/44.
9. FO 371/39169 7/7/44.
10. FO 371/40579 12/30/43.
11. FO 371/40579 5/12/44.
12. Ibid.
13. FO 371/40959 8/23/44.
14. FO 371/40959 7/22/44.
15. FO 837/1285 3/16/45.
16. FO 371/45812 5/18/45.

17. FO 371/46767 10/20/45.
18. FO 371/45813 9/13/45.
19. Ibid.
20. FO 371/45813 9/6/45.
21. RG 226 XL 24595.
22. FO 1031/10 1/25/46.
23. FO 371/48021 10/6/45.
24. FO 371/45814 11/5/45.
25. FO 837/1288 10/20/47.
26. FO 837/1293.
27. FO 837/1288.
28. FO 837/1159 1/25/47.
29. FO 837/1159.
30. FO 837/1287.
31. FO 837/1283.
32. FO 837/1293.
33. FO 371/105776.

Bibliography

THIS BOOK is based largely on the recently declassified files of the armies, air forces, and navies of America and Britain; the files of the Foreign Office, Treasury, Board of Trade, Ministry of Supply, Cabinet Office, and War Office; and the American files of the War Department, State Department, and Treasury, and of their subordinate agencies. In addition, I have read through many collections of personal papers, which are mentioned in the footnotes.

The literature on the development of weapons over the past fifty years, the Allied occupation of Germany, political events, and the tribulations of the military during and after the war is considerable. I have listed only those that were directly helpful.

Andrew, C. *Secret Service*. London: Heinemann, 1985.
Arnold, H. H. *Global Mission*. London: Hutchinson, 1951.
Aylen, I. G. *Naval Review*, October 1977, January 1978.
Bar-Zohar, M. *The Hunt for the German Scientists*. London: Barker, 1967.
Barnett, C. *The Audit of War*. London: Macmillan, 1986.
Baxter, J. P. *Scientists Against Time*. Boston: Little, Brown, 1946.
Beesly, P. *Very Special Intelligence*. London: Hamish Hamilton, 1977.
———. *Very Special Admiral*. London: Hamish Hamilton, 1980.
Beyerchen, A. D. *Scientists Under Hitler*. New Haven, Conn.: Yale University Press, 1977.
Bower, T. *Pledge Betrayed*. New York: Doubleday, 1982.
Burnet, C. *Three Centuries to Concorde*. London: MEP, 1979.
Bush, V. *Modern Arms and Free Men*. London: Heinemann, 1950.
———. *Pieces of Action*. London: Cassell, 1972.
Cairncross, A. *The Price of War*. London: Blackwell, 1986.
Campbell, P. *Oral History*. Washington, D.C.: Office of Air Force History, 1974, 1976.
Clark, R. W. *Tizard*. London: Methuen, 1965.

————. *The Rise of the Boffin*. London: Phoenix, 1962.

Collier, B. *The Defence of the United Kingdom*. London: HMSO, 1957.

Compton-Hall, R. *The Underwater War 1939–45*. Poole, England: Blandford, 1982.

Constant, E. *The Origins of the Turbojet Revolution*. Baltimore, Md.: Johns Hopkins University Press, 1980.

Dyson, F. *Disturbing the Universe*. New York: Harper & Row, 1979.

Engle, E., and A. Lott. *Man in Flight*. Washington, D.C.: Leeward, 1979.

Faith, N. *Safety in Numbers*. London: Hamish Hamilton, 1984.

Gimble, J. *The American Occupation of Germany*. Stanford, Calif.: Stanford University Press, 1968.

Gordon, D., and R. Dangerfield. *The Hidden Weapon*. New York: Harper & Bros., 1947.

Goudsmit, S. *Alsos*. Annapolis, Md.: Sigma, 1947.

Gunston, W. *By Jupiter — The Life of Sir Roy Fedden*. London: Royal Aeronautical Society, 1978.

Hallion, R. P. *Test Pilots*. New York: Doubleday, 1981.

Hampshire, A. C. *The Secret Navies*. London: William Kimber, 1978.

Harris, R., and J. Paxman. *A Higher Form of Killing*. London: Chatto & Windus, 1982.

Hastings, M. *Bomber Command*. London: Michael Joseph, 1979.

————. *Overlord*. London: Michael Joseph, 1984.

Hinsley, F. H. *British Intelligence in the Second World War*, vols. I–III. London: HMSO, 1981.

Hughill, J.A.C. *The Hazard Mesh*. London: Hurst and Blackett, 1962.

Hunt, L. "U.S. Coverup of Nazi Scientists." *Bulletin of Atomic Scientists*, April 1985.

Irving, D. *The Virus House*. London: William Kimber, 1967.

————. *The Mare's Nest*. London: William Kimber, 1964.

Jones, R. V. *Most Secret War*. London: Hamish Hamilton, 1978.

Kurowski, F. *Allierte Jagd auf deutsche Wissenschaftler*. Munich: Kristall, 1982.

Lasby, C. *Project Paperclip*. New York: Atheneum, 1971.

Lipscomb, F. W. *The British Submarine*. London: Conway, 1975.

McGovern, J. *Crossbow and Overcast*. New York: William Morrow, 1964.

Macksey, K. *The Tank Pioneers*. London: Jane's, 1981.

McLaughlin, C. et al. *U.S. Army in World War Two — Ordnance Department: Planning Munitions for War*. Washington, D.C.: U.S. Government Printing Office, 1955.

Mayo, L. et al. *U.S. Army in World War Two — Ordnance Department: On the Beachhead and Battlefront*. Washington, D.C.: U.S. Government Printing Office, 1955.

Michel, J. *Dora*. London: Weidenfeld and Nicolson, 1979.

Milward, A. *The German Economy at War*. London: London University, 1965.

Mitscherlich, A., and F. Mielke. *The Death Doctors*. London: Elek Books, 1962.

Morison, S. *History of United States Naval Operations in World War II*, vols. I–XV. Boston: Little, Brown, 1960.

Ordway, F., and M. Sharpe. *The Rocket Team*. New York: Crowell, 1979.

Pearson, J. *Ian Fleming*, rev. ed. London: Pan, 1976.

Peskett, S. J. *Strange Intelligence*. London: Hale, 1981.

Postan, M. M. *Design and Development of Weapons*. London: HMSO, 1964.

Price, A. *Instruments of Darkness*. London: William Kimber, 1967.

Roskill, S. W. *The War at Sea*, vols. I–III. London: HMSO, 1960.

——. *Naval Policy Between the Wars*. London: HMSO, 1968.

Ross, G. M. *The Business of Tanks*. Ilfracombe, England: Stockwell, 1976.

Speer, A. *Inside the Third Reich*. London: Weidenfeld & Nicolson, 1970.

——. *The Slave State*. London: Weidenfeld & Nicolson, 1981.

Strong, K. *Intelligence at the Top*. London: Cassell, 1968.

Terraine, J. *The Right of the Line*. London: Hodder & Stoughton, 1985.

Thiesmeyer, L., and J. Burchard. *Combat Scientists*. Boston: Little, Brown, 1947.

Tokaev, S. *Stalin Means War*. London: Weidenfeld and Nicolson, 1951.

Turner, I. "British Occupation Policy & Volkswagen." Ph.D. thesis, Manchester University, 1984.

Von Karman, T. *The Wind and Beyond*. Boston: Little, Brown, 1967.

Webster, C., and N. Frankland. *Strategic Air Offensive Against Germany*. London: HMSO, 1961.

Winterbotham, F. W. *The Nazi Connection*. London: Weidenfeld & Nicolson, 1979.

——. *The Ultra Secret*. London: Weidenfeld & Nicolson, 1974.

Index